MODERN  ING: THE 196

VOICES, DOCUMENTS, NEW INTERPRETATIONS

Steve Nicholson is Chair of Twentieth Century and Contemporary Theatre in the School of English at the University of Sheffield, UK. His research has centred primarily on British political theatre and playwrights in the twentieth century, and the interplay between politics, morality and aesthetics. His other books include *British Theatre and the Red Peril: The Portrayal of Communism 1917–1945* (University of Exeter Press, 1999), and a four-volume series entitled *The Censorship of British Drama, 1900–1968*: *Volume One, 1900–1932* (University of Exeter Press, 2003); *Volume Two, 1933–1952* (University of Exeter Press, 2005); *Volume Three: The Fifties* (University of Exeter Press, 2011); and the forthcoming *Volume Four: The Sixties* (University of Exeter Press, 2013).

MODERN BRITISH PLAYWRITING: THE 1960s

VOICES, DOCUMENTS, NEW INTERPRETATIONS

Steve Nicholson

Series Editors: Richard Boon and Philip Roberts

Methuen Drama

Methuen Drama

1 3 5 7 9 10 8 6 4 2

First published in Great Britain in 2012 by Methuen Drama

Methuen Drama, an imprint of Bloomsbury Publishing Plc

Methuen Drama
Bloomsbury Publishing Plc
50 Bedford Square
London WC1B 3DP
www.methuendrama.com

Copyright © 2012 by Steve Nicholson

General Preface copyright © 2012 Richard Boon and Philip Roberts
'John Arden' copyright © 2012 by Bill McDonnell
'Harold Pinter' copyright © 2012 by Jamie Andrews
'Alan Ayckbourn' copyright © 2012 by Frances Babbage

The rights of the authors to be identified as the editors of these works have been asserted
by them in accordance with the Copyright, Design and Patents Act, 1988

Paperback ISBN 978 1 408 12957 9
Hardback ISBN 978 1 408 18198 0

Available in the USA from Bloomsbury Academic & Professional,
175 Fifth Avenue / 3rd Floor, New York, NY 10010.

A CIP catalogue record for this book is available from the British Library

Typeset by Mark Heslington Ltd, Scarborough, North Yorkshire

CONTENTS

General Preface   ix
by series editors Richard Boon and Philip Roberts
Acknowledgements   xi

Introduction to the 1960s   **1**
  Domestic life   1
  Society   3
  Science, technology and industry   8
  Culture   9
  Media   15
  Political events   20

1 Theatre in the 1960s   **29**
  1960–64   31
    Performance and politics   31
    Cruelty and violence   34
    Shakespeare   36
    Staging reality   38
    The age of satire   41
    Theatres of war   43
    Beyond words   49
    Aunt Edna versus the RSC   54
  1965–69   58
    Documentary theatre   62
    Staging Vietnam   64
    Race   67
    The American avant-garde   72
    The golden age   74
    Waiting for paradise   79
    Conclusion   82

2 **Introducing the Playwrights**   **85**
   Introduction to John Arden *by Bill McDonnell*   85
   Introduction to Edward Bond   91
   Introduction to Harold Pinter   97
   Introduction to Alan Ayckbourn   102

3 **Playwrights and Plays**   **108**
   John Arden *by Bill McDonnell*   108
     Serjeant Musgrave's Dance   110
     The Workhouse Donkey   119
     Armstrong's Last Good Night   126
     Britain's Brecht   134
     Conclusion   134

   Edward Bond   136
     Saved   139
     Early Morning   147
     Lear   154
     Conclusion   160

   Harold Pinter *by Jamie Andrews*   161
     The Caretaker   163
     Early audience response; or, 'A bloody pain in the neck' 168
     The Homecoming   171
     Pinter beyond Britain; or looking for Beckett 175
     Censorship   178
     Landscape and *Silence*   181
     Afterword   187

   Alan Ayckbourn *by Frances Babbage*   190
     1960–64: taking (first) steps   192
     1965–70: comedies of sex and class   196
     Relatively Speaking   198
     How the Other Half Loves and *Family Circles* 205
     Afterword   214

4 Documents   **216**
   John Arden   216
   Edward Bond   224
   Harold Pinter   233

Afterword   **243**
   John Arden *by Bill McDonnell*   243
   Edward Bond   249
   Harold Pinter   254
   Alan Ayckbourn   260

   Notes   266
   Select Bibliography   288
   Index   295
   Notes on contributors   304

GENERAL PREFACE

This book is one of a series of six volumes which seek to characterise the nature of modern British playwriting from the 1950s to the end of the first decade of this new century. The work of these six decades is comparable in its range, experimentation and achievement only to the drama of the Elizabethan and Jacobean dramatists. The series chronicles its flowering and development.

Each volume addresses the work of four representative dramatists (five in the *2000–2009* volume) by focusing on key works and by placing that work in a detailed contextual account of the theatrical, social, political and cultural climate of the era.

The series revisits each decade from the perspective of the twenty-first century. We recognise that there is an inevitable danger of imposing a spurious neatness on its subject. So while each book focuses squarely on the particular decade and its representative authors, we have been careful to ensure that some account is given of relevant material from earlier years and, where relevant, of subsequent developments. And while the intentions and organisation of each volume are essentially the same, we have also allowed for flexibility, the better to allow both for the particular demands of the subject and the particular approach of our author/editors.

It is also the case, of course, that differences of historical perspective across the series influence the nature of the books. For student readers, the difference at its most extreme is between a present they daily inhabit and feel they know intimately and a decade (the 1950s) in which their parents or even grandparents might have been born; between a time of seemingly unlimited consumer choice and one which began with post-war food rationing still in place. Further, a playwright who began work in the late 1960s (David Hare, say) has a far bigger body of work and associated scholarship than one whose emergence has come within the last decade or so (debbie tucker green, for example). A glance at the bibliographies for the earliest and latest volumes quickly reveals huge differences in the range of secondary material available to our authors and to our readers. This inevitably means that the later volumes allow a greater space to their contributing essayists for original research and scholarship, but we have also actively encouraged revisionist perspectives – new looks – on the 'older guard' in earlier books.

So while each book can and does stand alone, the series as a whole offers as coherent and comprehensive a view of the whole era as possible.

Throughout, we have had in mind two chief objectives. We have made accessible information and ideas that will enable today's students of theatre to acquaint themselves with the nature of the world inhabited by the playwrights of the last sixty years; and we offer new, original and often surprising perspectives on both established and developing dramatists.

Richard Boon and Philip Roberts
Series Editors
April 2012

Richard Boon is Emeritus Professor of Drama at the University of Hull.

Philip Roberts is Emeritus Professor of Drama and Theatre Studies at the University of Leeds.

ACKNOWLEDGEMENTS

I would like to express my thanks to the University of Sheffield for supporting this project, and particularly to my colleagues Dr Frances Babbage and Dr Bill McDonnell whose contributions go well beyond the parts of this volume formally credited to them. I would also like to thank senior staff at the British Library – especially Jamie Andrews – for their considerable assistance and advice in helping me to access and make use of archive material. I am also grateful to the series editors, Professors Richard Boon and Philip Roberts, for their generous support and enthusiasm throughout the project. Finally, thanks, as always, to Heather, and to Katya and Vikka for letting me have a go on the laptop sometimes.

While this book was being prepared for press, one of the featured and most important playwrights of the decade – John Arden – passed away. The interview with him and his partner Margaretta D'Arcy, which is included here in Chapter 4, now stands as one of the last he gave. Sometimes compared to those of Brecht and Shakespeare, Arden's plays are a fit monument to a great theatre poet and an indefatigable political activist.

INTRODUCTION TO THE 1960s[1]

1. Domestic life

Things we bought

Hard toilet rolls, wooden tennis rackets, footballs with laces, polyar-moured cricket bats, roller skates, pink shrimps and raspberry chews at four an (old) penny, jamboree bags, chocolate cigarettes, Gibson Flying V guitars, Sindy ('the doll you love to dress'), duvets, formica tables, stainless-steel kitchens, stacking chairs, cardboard chairs, plastic chairs, inflatable chairs, paper furniture, electric fires with real-istic living flame coal effect, golliwogs, Minis and miniskirts, vinyl floor coverings and vinyl LPs, mono records, stereo records, a cartridge to play stereo records on mono record players, stereograms (so you don't need the cartridge), reel-to-reel tape recorders, cassette tape recorders, transistor radios, electric typewriters, denim skirts, parkas, braces, flared trousers, bell-bottomed trousers, beads, joss sticks, kimonos, Afghan coats, flowers for our hair, plastic pacamacs, camera films that take eight small black-and-white photographs, anything to do with the Beatles, Dalek soap, Dalek wallpaper, Dalek slippers, Dalek jelly babies, Dalek porridge bowls and crème de menthe.

Things we saw that we hadn't seen before

Multi-storey car parks, high-rise tower blocks, town-centre ring roads, Sunday newspaper colour supplements, parking meters, high-street travel agents, supermarkets, aubergines, Chinese takeaways, Indian curry houses, tea bags, hover mowers, men with long hair, skinheads, hippies meditating, football hooligans smashing up trains, Laura Ashley shops, Habitat, Mary Quant, Twiggy, yoga, Yogi Bear, the Maharishi Mahesh Yogi (guru to the Beatles), more pornography and sex shops in Soho, a decline in church attendance; at a Christmas Day service in 1965 a rector in York takes a model Dalek into the pulpit and threatens to exterminate his congregation. Credit cards and cash machines start to appear around 1967, but are not yet common.

Home life

Incomes rise throughout the decade, and spending on household appliances soars by 100 per cent – with many items bought through hire purchase. In the early 1960s only a third of households have a refrigerator and even in the early 1970s the figure is around two-thirds. Freezers come later. Washing machine ownership grows (mostly twin tubs rather than automatics) but many people still go to launderettes or have their washing collected. Only around half of houses have their own telephone line – red phone boxes are in common use; no mobiles, of course. Full central heating is unusual, but some people have large storage heaters. Hot-water bottles are more common than electric blankets. Other electric applicances marketed 'for Mrs Everyman of Acacia Avenue' include coffee makers ('a superb gift for any house-wife'), heated hair rollers ('with free record token') and a three-speed food mixer ('the extra pair of hands you've always wanted').

Britain has a high rate of marriages, with an average of around 2.5 children. It also has the highest divorce rate in Europe; in 1969, marriage breakdown becomes the sole grounds for divorce, removing the necessity to apportion blame.

Work life

Male unemployment is low for most of the decade, with average weekly earnings rising by 130 per cent between 1955 and 1969. However, faced with a growing trade deficit and economic difficulties the Labour government imposes a freeze on wages, which leads to austerity and bitter industrial confrontations. By the late 1960s, union power is strong, and strikes over pay and conditions are frequent and widespread. Between 1962 and 1968 the total number of working days lost to strikes is less than 3 million; in 1968 alone it is 4.7 million, in 1969 it is 7 million, and by the early 1970s an extraordinary 23.8 million.

There is an increase in the number of married women in paid employment (though many work part-time). From one in five in the early 1950s, by the 1960s it is one in three, and by the 1970s almost one in two. Women are often paid less than men for doing the same jobs, and in 1970 the government introduces the Equal Pay Act.

2. Society

Sex

A poem by Philip Larkin suggests that the very invention of sexual intercourse can be dated to 1963 – 'Between the end of the "Chatterley" ban and the Beatles' first LP'.[2] While this was not strictly accurate, the decade's reputation for sexual freedom, liberation and promiscuity is partly deserved. In 1967 a new law makes it possible for consenting same-sex adults over the age of twenty-one to have a private sexual relationship (except in Scotland) without liability to prosecution. Abortion also becomes legal, as Harold Wilson's Labour government pursues a programme of liberal reforms. Also crucial is the invention of 'the pill' which – at least in theory – allows women to take control of contraception and thus their own sexual behaviour. At first, the pill is only for married women, and it is only in the latter part of the decade that it becomes more readily available. In fact, a survey undertaken in 1970 suggests that only 10 per cent of women have ever used it. But in the second half of the 1960s we are told that all we need is love, and encouraged to see it as a way of opposing war. There is more provocative sexual imagery to be seen in the media and in fashion than ever before, while prurient stories about the dissolute antics of young people in general, and pop and film stars in particular, provide great newspaper copy.

Violence

Violent crimes had increased in the 1950s, and the trend continues. In 1955 some 6,000 are recorded; by 1960 the figure has doubled to nearly 12,000 and by 1970 it is 21,000. Violent south-coast clashes between tooled-up mods and rockers become a regular feature of bank-holiday weekends, and fighting around football grounds is equally disturbing and destructive of property as well as people. Some attribute this hooliganism to a loss of religious belief and of respect. Others blame violent films and American television imports; the woolly liberalism of parents and teachers; the ending of national service and military discipline; the softness of judicial sentencing and of prison life. The Left argues that the root cause is an unjust and unequal society, and even that the syphoning of aggression into fights between rival football or music fans is a useful safety valve which deflects protests against the real oppressors.

There are some shocking crimes of violence during the decade, and the arrest of the Kray twins in 1969 uncovers a history of organised crime based on brutality and intimidation. But most disturbing of all is the campaign of sadistic terror and murder carried out in Lancashire against innocent children by the 'Moors Murderers', Ian Brady and Myra Hindley.

Obscenity

In 1965, the theatre critic Kenneth Tynan makes history – and the front pages of the national press – when he becomes the first person to use the word 'fuck' on television. A couple of years earlier, Lenny Bruce – 'the farthest-out of all the American sick comedians'[3] – has been banned from entering Britain to perform 'because in the view of the Home Secretary it would not be in the public interest' to allow him to do so.[4] One of Bruce's provocative and satirical riffs mocks the insistence of the establishment on censoring images and language related to love, by comparison with its much greater tolerance of hatred and violence. He points out that the only context in which films can show a female breast is when it has been mutilated in a violent crime, and that 'unfuck you' would be a better term of abuse than the one we commonly use. Society moves slowly, but some shifts do take place through the 1960s. In 1959, the Obscene Publications Act had ruled that artistic quality and significance could be taken into account when making judgments, and in 1960 a prosecution against Penguin Books for publishing *Lady Chatterley's Lover* is defeated. The decision reverberates throughout the decade. For some, it marks a more grown-up attitude to sexuality; for others, the start of a decline into anti-Christian permissiveness and immorality, which must be challenged. In 1968, a new Theatres Act finally brings to an end an archaic and unique system of theatre censorship and control which has lasted for over 230 years, and has been presided over by the Lord Chamberlain in his role as a servant to the royal household.

Education

At the start of the decade, all children take an eleven-plus examination to decide whether they can go to grammar school. Between 75 and 80 per cent fail the exam and go to a secondary modern school, which they will probably leave at fifteen. Grammar schools are much better resourced, and around half their pupils continue into the sixth form, and go on to university. This division at the age of ten is increasingly recognised as unfair, and the Labour government rapidly expands the number of comprehensive schools – though not without considerable opposition and resistance from those who believe it will lead to a fall in standards.

Meanwhile, a government report recommends increasing higher education opportunities by 50 per cent. New universities are created, and polytechnics are also introduced to counter the universities' perceived bias towards the arts. Another alternative is art colleges, and some of these acquire a reputation for radical practices not just in art but in politics and in ways of living. One of Harold Wilson's greatest achievements and legacies is The Open University (or 'University of the Air'), which is conceived and created in the late 1960s.

Housing

The early 1960s is a time of severe housing shortages and homeless-ness in major cities, largely due to slum clearances, and a decline in the private renting sector. In 1966 the charity Shelter is launched, following a huge public response to *Cathy Come Home*, a powerful and shocking television play about homelessness. In some areas, housing conditions remain appalling. In the mid-1960s there are reportedly around three million urban homes without bathrooms or running hot water, and a report in Sunderland suggests that 90 per cent of houses there have no indoor toilets, 75 per cent no bath and 50 per cent no running water.

Architects and city councils start to embrace Le Corbusier's idea of cities in the sky, and vast blocks of high-rise concrete flats are erected. The disadvantages soon become apparent: lack of gardens and playing space for children and pets, a reliance on lifts which break down too often and a lack of social community. Also, many have been built on the cheap with sub-standard materials and inadequate provision for maintenance, so they quickly become run-down and unsafe. The collapse of Ronan Point in the East End of London some two years after it has been built undermines their reputation further, but many councils are already committed and building continues.

Drugs

In 1960, there are 235 cannabis convictions; in 1964, 544; in 1967, 2,393; and in 1970, 7,520. The number of teenagers registered as heroin, cocaine or opium addicts triples between 1964 and 1965, and by the late 1960s heroin addiction in Britain is growing at the fastest rate in the world. In the second half of the decade, some campaign for the legalisation of drugs, asserting their power to expand the mind and open new worlds. They argue that whereas alcohol encourages violence and hate, dope encourages peace and love. Drug taking becomes particularly associated with rock music, with hippies and with utopian visions of a better world, and a persuasive phrase invented by the maverick American psychiatrist Timothy Leary becomes a slogan: 'Tune in, turn on, and drop out.'[5] Indeed, 'dropping out' (from main-stream society and values) becomes an aspiration and the rebellion of choice for many educated young people from middle-class homes. Some drop back in again when their holiday is over, but others create alternative lifestyles and continue to live in communes.

Environment

In 1960 it is announced that all insurance policies covering property and personal injuries will now exclude damage 'arising out of ionising radiation or contamination by radioactivity emanating from nuclear fuel or nuclear waste'. Successive governments remain committed to nuclear power for cheap electricity, but the 1957 disaster at the Windscale nuclear power station in Cumbria (the full details of which are suppressed for thirty years) has caused some soul-searching, and although a new station opens in Gloucestershire in 1962, the programme to expand is temporarily slowed. In the mid-1960s, however, the government announces plans for a new generation of supposedly safer nuclear power stations based on gas-cooled reactors.

In 1962, the writer and naturalist Rachel Carson publishes *Silent Spring*, warning that current industrial practices are polluting the earth and threatening life forms. Her book effectively launches the environmental and ecology movement. In *Spaceship Earth* (published four years later) James Lovelock puts forward his Gaia Hypothesis, suggesting that the Earth is a single living organism with a self-regulating system which is now under threat from human behaviour. An environmental disaster in 1967 widens awareness of environmental issues when the *Torrey Canyon* runs aground off the Scilly Isles, spilling thousands of tons of crude oil into the sea and devastating sealife and coastline. Friends of the Earth is founded in 1969, and environmental campaigns start to put pressure on governments to change policies.

Women's liberation

The National Organisation for Women (NOW) is launched in America in 1966 to campaign for equal rights, and the world has three women prime ministers (in Ceylon, India and Israel) as well as the first female astronaut in space. In Britain, Barbara Castle becomes the first female Secretary of State (though men make up 95 per cent of all MPs), and it is the 1968 strike for equal pay by women machinists at Ford which paves the way to the Equal Pay Act. There are no overtly feminist magazines yet in the UK, though the *Guardian* launches a women's section which 'deals frankly with topics that otherwise get wrapped up in cosy euphemisms' and 'treats them as free and independent equals of men'.[6] Some of the political energy of the 1960s comes to fruition in 1970, which sees the first national meeting of the women's liberation movement, the passing of the Equal Pay Act, the publication of Germaine Greer's *The Female Eunuch*, and the disruption of the annual and televised Miss World Beauty Contest by protesters armed with flour, stink-bombs and water pistols.

Travel

The number of cars on British roads rises during the decade from 2.3 to 11.5 million. Yet even in 1969, less than half of households own one. In 1960 there are less than 100 miles of motorway across the whole of the UK; by 1970, the figure has gone up to over 600 (at time of writing it is well over 2,000). The number of deaths on the road is high – nearly 150 people are killed just in the four-day Christmas period of 1959. In 1960, the Ministry of Transport introduces the first annual MOT test, which becomes increasingly rigorous. A legal drink-drive limit is introduced for the first time in 1967, along with breathalyser tests; it is a restriction which draws remarkable levels of vitriol and venom from the Jeremy Clarksons of the day against Barbara Castle, the minister responsible. Seat belts are also introduced to the front seats of new cars, though it is not compulsory to wear them.

In 1961, Dr Beeching is appointed as Chairman of the British Railways Board; the annual government subsidy of the network is around £100 million, and to make the system economically viable, Beeching proposes massive cuts on unprofitable branch lines, involving the loss of 5,000 miles of track, more than 2,000 stations and thousands of jobs. Many rural communities lose access to their key form of transport, and more traffic takes to the roads.

Electrification of railway lines takes place, and before the end of the decade steam trains have disappeared. In 1968, the National Bus Company is created – the forerunner of National Express.

3. Science, technology and industry

At the start of the 1960s, Harold Wilson predicts 'a socialist-inspired scientific and technological revolution', and he comes to power in 1964 on the back of his vision of a new Britain 'forged in the white heat' of this technological revolution. Wilson quickly creates a Ministry of Technology, and acts to encourage a growth in the number of scientists. Among the developments to which they contribute in the next few years are carbon fibres, nuclear reactors, jet engines, satellite stations and polythene. In 1966 cross-Channel hovercraft ferries start running; in 1969, Concorde has its maiden flight and the Americans go to the moon. The first computers appear – enormous beasts and with no thought of home use; musicians – even Bob Dylan – throw away their acoustic guitars and go electric. Meanwhile, middle-class houses are filled with new labour-saving household equipment, as we start to brush our teeth, shave and dry our hair electronically.

Medical boundaries are crossed, with blood transfusions, kidney and liver operations, and x-rays becoming almost routine. The first open heart transplant is carried out, and it seems science will soon be able to replace any bits of us that go wrong. 'Do you know,' says Tony Hancock in amazement during one of his best-known comedy routines, 'there are some people walking about with hardly anything they started out with.'[7] Some anxiety about what science might do to us is evident in the most threatening enemies encountered by Doctor Who – the Daleks and cybermen who sacrifice individuality and imagination to their rational and mechanical effectiveness. Yet one early story presents two forms of alien inhabiting the same planet; the first is a race composed almost entirely of attractive young women who turn out to be evil; the second, some cheerful and well-meaning little robots who befriend the Doctor and friends.

4. Culture

Music

Even now, many of those who dismiss or trash the ideals of 1960s counterculture still pay homage to its music. For some, the decade is synonymous with a succession of mostly white and mostly male bands who invented rock music; they include the Beatles, the Rolling Stones, the Who and Cream, and these bands – and others – provide a collective and totemic soundtrack for a generation which rejected the values and world-view of its predecessors and dared to dream of a different way of living. In 1969, two legendary open-air pop festivals take place, one at Woodstock in New York State, the other on the Isle of Wight. For three days, Woodstock attracts up to half a million people. Much dope is smoked, there is naked dancing in the mud, and little sign of violence or threat – just lots of 'beautiful people' having a good time (or 'getting their rocks off' as they might have said). For many of the participants, it represents an alternative to the rat race of competition; a world of incense, magic mushrooms and chanting rather than one of money, rules and competition. In a much-remembered moment, the brilliant Black/Native American guitarist Jimi Hendrix performs a version of the US national anthem full of distortion and feedback, within which some hear the sounds of (American) bombs falling and victims wailing.

Such bands and singers represent only one side of the music scene. On the whole, it is not the one seen on *Top of the Pops* on television every Thursday evening – a show held in disdain for its rampant commercialism by the disciples of Woodstock. Motown music also has a big following with bands and artists including the Four Tops, Diana Ross and the Supremes, the Jackson 5, the Temptations, Stevie Wonder and Marvin Gaye. Others are still listening to Cliff Richard, to Tom Jones or to Engelbert Humperdinck; to Cilla Black, Petula Clark, Helen Shapiro, Sandy Shaw (who shocked a nation by dancing barefoot on television) or Shirley Bassey. And in fact the soundtracks of *South Pacific* and *The Sound of Music* dominate the top of the album charts for many years. The 1960s also sees a growing interest in contemporary folk music – Dylan and Donovan, Pete Seeger, Joan Baez, Peter, Paul and Mary, Tom Paxton and others. By the end of the decade reggae has arrived in the mainstream, and Desmond Dekker's 'The Israelites' reaches number one in the singles charts.

In contemporary 'classical' music, minimalism emerges as a major strand in North America, with Philip Glass one of the key proponents. In Steve Reich's groundbreaking 1964 piece 'Come Out', a recording of a single phrase spoken by a black youth after a confrontation with the police is played on a loop simultaneously on two channels which gradually go out of synch with each other. In Britain, Peter Maxwell Davies and Michael Tippett are among the most respected contemporary composers. One of the most powerful pieces of the decade is Benjamin Britten's *War Requiem*, which takes as its text a series of poems by the First World War poet Wilfred Owen. Although the ostensible setting for this oratorio is the 1914–18 war, the first performance is given to consecrate the new Coventry Cathedral, built after the destruction of the previous building in Nazi air raids. But in 1962, the performance speaks also to fears of a possible future and devastating Third World War between America and the Soviet Union.

Concerts of Indian classical concerts can be heard on the radio, and the sitar and tabla find their way into the progressive rock scene. The lead comes mainly from the Beatles and George Harrison, whose interest in meditation, yoga and Indian culture inspires an instant following. Ravi Shankar is one of the top names at the Woodstock Festival.

Books

The early 1960s sees the publication of several novels focused on contemporary working-class life – notably Stan Barstow's *A Kind of Loving* and David Storey's *This Sporting Life*. Other important writers who publish during the decade include Kingsley Amis, Anthony Burgess, John Fowles, William Golding, Graham Greene, Doris Lessing, Iris Murdoch, Anthony Powell, J. G. Ballard, A. S. Byatt and Margaret Drabble. Bestsellers include works by Ian Fleming, Alistair MacLean, Georgette Heyer, Agatha Christie and Barbara Cartland. John le Carré's Smiley novels start to appear from 1961 onwards. Other notable books of the decade include *Catch-22*, *One Day in the Life of Ivan Denisovich*, *Kes*, *The Bell Jar*, *Last Exit to Brooklyn*, *The Spire*, *One Flew Over the Cuckoo's Nest*, *The Crying of Lot 49*, *Herzog*, *The Magic Toyshop* and *The Third Policeman*. Tolkien's *The Lord of the Rings* makes it on to the W. H. Smith bestseller lists, and becomes a more or less compulsory text for literate drop-outs. One work of non-fiction which captures the spirit of the times (it is even serialised in the *Daily Mirror*) by challenging previous certainties is Desmond Morris's *The Naked Ape*, which analyses human society – not least our sexual behaviours – in terms which emphasise our closeness to the animal kingdom.

There is a big increase in the number of books being published, from 25,000 titles in 1961 to 33,000 by 1970. Spending on public libraries doubles through the 1960s; in 1959 libraries issue 397 million books, in 1970 more than 600 million. The huge expansion of paperback publishing is crucial here. In 1960 there are 6,000 Penguin paperbacks in print – by 1970 more than six times as many. Of the first eighteen books to sell a million copies in Britain, ten are James Bond titles. The biggest Penguin sellers include *Lady Chatterley's Lover*, *Animal Farm*, *Room at the Top* and *The Odyssey*.

Poetry

In June 1965 the Royal Albert Hall is the site for the so-called International Poetry Incarnation, an extraordinary evening of American and British Beat poetry which sells out the venue's 7,000 seats. For some it marks the arrival of a counterculture, and it is also a significant moment in the development of performance poetry. Readers at the Albert Hall include Allen Ginsberg, Christopher Logue, Michael Horovitz, Adrian Mitchell and George MacBeth. The second half of the decade also sees the rise of the Merseyside poets, Brian Patten, Roger McGough and Adrian Henri, though for many, the most important British (or British-based) poets of the decade would include John Betjeman, Philip Larkin, Ted Hughes and Sylvia Plath.

Sport

The highlight of the decade (in one part of Britain at least) is England winning the 1966 football World Cup, after staggering their way through to the semi-finals. We might have seen it coming three years earlier when they implausibly defeat a Rest of the World team including Yashin, Pelé, Di Stéfano, Puskás, Denis Law and Eusébio. In successive years, Celtic and then Manchester United win the European Cup to break the decade-long stranglehold of Spanish, Italian and Portuguese teams.

In tennis, the 1961 women's singles final at Wimbledon is an all-British affair (Angela Mortimer beating Christine Truman) and in 1969 Ann Jones wins the same event. The best showings by British men are in 1961 and 1967 when Mike Sangster and Roger Taylor (respectively) reach the semi-finals. Until 1968, when the 'open' era begins, tennis is divided between amateurs and professionals, who play in separate tournaments. The latter are rarely seen on British television since it is still considered vulgar to play sport for money. After 1968, Rod Laver dominates the men's game and Billie Jean King the women's.

Prior to 1962, cricketers in England are also divided between amateurs ('Gentlemen') and professionals ('Players') who have separate dressing rooms and are designated differently (a 'Mr' for the Gentlemen) on scorecards and in reports. One-day domestic cricket is introduced for the first time in the early 1960s, though the international version comes later. The West Indies are led by the exceptional all-rounder Gary Sobers – the first person to hit every ball in an over for 6 – and are the outstanding cricket team of the decade, along with Australia. When they play in England (especially in London) they gather enormous and passionate support from Caribbean immigrants. England are much better than the worst teams but not nearly as good as the best.

Sport, politics, power

Although some – usually on the political Right – try desperately to argue that sport can exist in its own bubble without reference to the world beyond, issues of politics – especially race – frequently burst in. Most often this involves South Africa, where apartheid policies extend fully into the sporting arena. Only white people have access to decent facilities there, only white people can represent the country and crowds are segregated by race. In the second half of the decade, a key member of the England cricket team is Basil D'Oliveira, born in South Africa as a so-called 'Cape Coloured', but escaping to England to further his career. In the winter of 1968, England are due to tour South Africa, whose prime minister makes it clear privately that D'Oliveira will not be welcome. Indeed, the South African government tries to bribe D'Oliveira to make himself unavailable. By chance, the President of the MCC – the organisation which governs cricket in the UK – is a former member of the British Union of Fascists and, to their eternal shame, the English selectors drop D'Oliveira for the tour, a week after he has scored a major century for the team against Australia. They claim the decision is made on grounds of ability, but the minutes of the meeting mysteriously disappear. 'Far more is known about the cabinet meetings of the Harold Wilson government, the activities of the secret service in Moscow, or the details of the

Poseidon nuclear missile programme, than what the England selectors said and did that night.[8] Following outraged protests, the selectors back down and announce that D'Oliveira will be part of the team after all, and the South African government promptly cancels the tour. This appalling act should be enough to ensure South Africa's sporting isolation, but many countries – including England – try to carry on with them as normal. In 1969, the Davis Cup tennis tie between Great Britain and South Africa is disrupted by protesters throwing flour bombs, and the South African rugby team's tour of England and Wales meets demonstrations and protests at every match. The 'Stop the Tour' campaign is led by the nineteen-year old Peter Hain – a future MP and Labour minister; police protection ensures the games go ahead, but they are played behind barbed-wire fences and with small crowds. Largely because of the disruption and the policing costs – not to mention a threatened boycott of the 1970 Commonwealth Games in Edinburgh by African and Asian countries – the 1970 cricket tour by South Africa to England is cancelled.

American society is also riddled with appalling racism. The heavy-weight boxing champion Cassius Clay changes his name to Muhammad Ali, and then creates a storm by refusing the compulsory call-up to join the army. Ali declares that he will not fight in Vietnam because he has 'no quarrel with them Vietcong' and that he is 'not going 10,000 miles to help murder, kill, and burn other people to simply help continue the domination of white slavemasters over dark people the world over'. In case the message is not clear enough, Ali adds that 'If I thought the war was going to bring freedom and equality to twenty-two million of my people, they wouldn't have to draft me, I'd join tomorrow.' Ali is denounced by the American press and politicians ('He is an instrument in the hands of the subversive forces seeking to undermine our nation'), has his boxing licence and title taken away, is prosecuted and found guilty in court, and is threatened with large fines and imprisonment.[9] Ultimately, though, he wins his case. Meanwhile, at the 1968 Mexico Olympics, two black American athletes (Tommie Smith and John Carlos) come first and third in the final of the 200 metres; standing on the podium to receive their gold and bronze medals, they generate huge publicity by raising their arms with clenched fists during the playing of the American national anthem, in salutes to black power and black unity. In a protest designed to draw maximum public attention to racial injustice in America, they wear no shoes to show their solidarity with 'black poverty in racist America' and beads 'for those individuals that were lynched, or killed . . . hung and tarred'.[10] Smith and Carlos are sent home and made to return their medals, accused of bringing politics into a non-political event. Like Ali and D'Oliveira, they should be remembered as not only sporting but also political heroes.

In rugby union, which remains an amateur sport, Wales dominate the domestic game. In Athletics, Britain wins four gold medals at the 1964 Tokyo Olympic Games, and five at Mexico in 1968. In world boxing, everyone falls to Cassius Clay.

5. Media

Television and radio

Until the launch of BBC2 in 1964, there are only two TV channels to choose between – BBC1 and ITV. Just under three-quarters of people have access to these, though in my house we are not allowed to watch ITV because of the advertisements. Pictures are in black-and-white and screens are small, while broadcasting generally begins in the early afternoon with children's programmes, and ends with an epilogue and the National Anthem before 11 p.m. There are no programmes about cookery, and only one about gardening. Most televisions are rented, and they break down frequently – often at crucial moments; pictures frequently roll – sometimes fast, sometimes slowly – and on occasions the screen is spilt by a horizontal bar, with the top of the picture showing on the lower half of the screen, and the bottom part at the top. Sometimes the back of the television exudes an unpleasant smell which resembles fish cooking, and it is not unknown for householders to take a large stick to their televisions. Colour broadcasts begin in 1967, but it is almost the end of the decade before all three channels are transmitting fully in colour. When *Match of the Day* begins broadcasting in 1964, it is often only by looking at the patterns on a player's socks that you can identify which side he is on. There are, of course, no video recorders, so you watch a programme when it is on or risk missing it altogether.

The BBC retains some of its original Reithian principles to educate and enlighten, though from 1967 the more serious and educative programmes become increasingly concentrated on BBC2. Nevertheless, series such as *The Wednesday Play* and *Play for Today* remain on BBC1, dramatising controversial subjects and often exciting considerable controversy. Other famous series of the decade include *Z Cars*, *The Forsyte Saga*, *Dr Finlay's Casebook*, *Coronation Street* and *Doctor*

Who. A children's show – *The Magic Roundabout* – also achieves cult status and is rumoured to contain hidden references to drugs (its characters include a guitar-playing hippy-like rabbit called Dylan and a dog addicted to sugar lumps, and it is set entirely in a garden).

Until Radio One is launched in 1967 there are three BBC radio stations – the Home Service (forerunner of Radio Four), the Third Programme (forerunner of Radio Three) and the Light Programme (forerunner of Radio Two). Pirate stations (notably including Radio Caroline, Radio London and Radio Luxembourg) broadcast from offshore and attract young audiences with non-stop pop music, and the BBC launches Radio One to meet the same market.

The box in 1960

In January, BBC television launches a series of adaptations of twentieth-century stage plays by writers including Shaw, Maugham, Coward, Anouilh and Bulgakov. Sunday broadcasting starts with a service at 11 a.m. and continues with 'The Weather Situation', then a farming programme, *Sergeant Bilko*, a film, Sooty ('Say bye bye, Sweep'), a quiz, a programme about zoos, a serial adaptation of *The Secret Garden*, a documentary about life on board an aircraft carrier, a magic show, a clergyman offering agony advice to people about which hymns they should sing, a long-running panel show (*What's My Line?*), an adaptation of John Galsworthy's *Justice*, a documentary about the Mexican artist Diego Rivera, a charity appeal and music with Max Jaffa, before closing down at 10.55 with an Epilogue from the Bishop of Portsmouth entitled 'It's Your Baby'. What more could anyone want from television? ITV mixes in table tennis, *Sunday Night at the London Palladium* and a dramatisation of a story by Oscar Wilde.

Radio highlights in the first week of 1960 include interviews with Carl Gustav Jung and King Hussein I of Jordan, a talk by the Director of the National Portrait Gallery on his 'Painting of the Month', poetry readings, a series on art and anti-art in the theatre, a debate on the rival merits of 'Rare and Common Birds', and 'Mourning for Kant' – the first in a series entitled *Germany Today*. There are regular classical concerts – including one of Indian music – and commentaries on cricket from Barbados, rugby from Scotland and horse racing from Sandown. In a presumably unremarked clash, an interview in French with the absurdist playwright Eugene Ionesco ('The Emptiness of the Real') begins on the Home Service at exactly the same time as the Light Programme offers *The Goon Show*. Other 'light entertainment' on offer includes three new 'pop shows'.[11]

Film

With no home videos or rentals, and television offering so few channels and not permitted to broadcast recent films, cinema visits are a
regular agenda item. Unlike almost everything else in Britain (shops,
theatres, sports stadia) cinemas are open on Sundays – indeed, it is
usually the day their programme changes. Most cinemas have only
one screen, but towns may have several venues. Films are licensed
with U, A or X certificates, the latter indicating adults only, the A
requiring adult supervision and the U open to all. A programme typically involves a double-bill of features, often with a travelogue or other
short film as well. Audiences can come in at any point and sit (or
doze) through as many showings as they want – though on quiet days
it is not unknown for reels to be shown in the wrong order, without
anyone appearing to notice. American films dominate, but there are
some notable British commercial successes as well, including several
James Bond films, the Carry On comedies and a couple of Beatles'
films. The early part of the decade sees a continuation of the gritty
depictions of working-class life which had begun in the 1950s, with
films such as *Saturday Night and Sunday Morning*, *This Sporting Life*,
The Loneliness of the Long Distance Runner and *Billy Liar*. Joseph
Losey makes two powerful films with screenplays by Harold Pinter,
while Edward Bond works on the screenplay for Antonioni's *Blow-Up*.
In 1968, comes Stanley Kubrick's masterpiece *2001: A Space Odyssey*,
and the following year Lindsay Anderson's extraordinary *If....*, in
which a group of schoolboys (led by Malcolm McDowell) destroy
their public school and all it represents by gunning down the staff and
parents attending a Founders' Day service. Many of us cheer them on.

Art

In 1960, London holds an exhibition of abstract art, defined as work
which is 'without explicit reference to events outside the painting'.[12]
'Pop Art' becomes another key term, as artists challenge not just forms
and conventions but principles and ideals. In America, Andy Warhol
bases much of his two-dimensional work on photographic reproduc-
tions of mass-media advertisements or labels from products – notably
including Campbell's soup tins and Coca-Cola bottles. His sculptures

include replicas of supermarket product boxes. In Britain, Peter Blake (who designs the acclaimed cover for the Beatles' *Sgt. Pepper* album) and David Hockney are part of a movement which incorporates images of consumerism and mass culture.

Leisure

The decade sees a massive growth of interest in DIY and gardening. Travel agents' shops start to appear on the high street, as more people take package holidays abroad; Spain is the most popular destination. Some fly, but coach also remains a popular option. Yet although the number of traditional British seaside holidays and trips to holiday camps declines, in the middle of the decade only 4 per cent of British holidays are foreign package trips, and even in 1971 the figure is less than 8.5 per cent. Caravanning becomes a popular form of British holiday.

There is no National Lottery, but a 1962 survey shows 75 per cent households taking part in weekly football pools. Many people have premium bonds (introduced in the late 1950s) with monthly winners chosen by Ernie (Electronic Random Number Indicator Equipment).

Architecture

In 1965, London's Post Office Tower is proudly opened by government ministers. It becomes the tallest building in London, changing the city's skyline for ever, and while the height and design serve its function, it is also an architectural statement. Yet the decade will be more associated with the concrete brutalism still visible in most towns and cities today, and typified in London's South Bank complex of the Hayward Gallery, the Queen Elizabeth Hall and the Purcell Room. It is also the decade of 'new towns' constructed and expanded to cope with rising populations at Redditch, Telford, Runcorn, Skelmersdale, Warrington, Peterborough and Milton Keynes. As well as the 'streets in the sky', it is a decade of shopping centres (Birmingham's Bull Ring is the first to open in 1964), flyovers, underpasses, subways and multi-storey car parks, as towns and cities are increasingly shaped around cars rather than pedestrians. In 1969, little red and green men appear on traffic lights to control our pace and movements further.

Newspapers

In 1960, more people in Britain read national newspapers than in any other European country except Sweden. The most popular daily paper is the *Daily Mirror*, which is selling around 5 million copies a day, followed by the *Express* (4.3 million), the *Mail* (2.6 million), the *Herald* (1.4 million) and the *Telegraph* (1.2 million). In 1964 the left-leaning *Daily Herald* disappears and is replaced by the *Sun*, a broadsheet which initially leans in the same direction. Sunday colour supplements start in the early 1960s, and in 1966 *The Times* puts news on its front page for the first time, replacing its traditional columns of notices and advertisements. The *Guardian* advertises itself as the *Avant-Guardian*, but becomes better known as the *Grauniad* on account of its frequent misprints. There is no *Independent* yet. In 1969 the *Sun* is sold to Rupert Murdoch and becomes a tabloid.

Comedy

At the start of the decade, the airwaves feature several 'service comedies', including *The Army Game* and *Tell It to the Marines*, which look back with some nostalgia to the Second World War. Tony Hancock is a household name for his radio shows in the 1950s, but his most remembered television episode – 'The Blood Donor' – is not made until 1961. Hard-hitting satire of a kind not previously seen on television appears with *That Was the Week That Was*, and some elements are maintained in *The Frost Report*. Meanwhile Hancock abandons his writers, Galton and Simpson, and they invent *Steptoe and Son*. Harry Worth is a television clown, and Peter Cook and Dudley Moore produce *Not Only . . . But Also*. By far the most controversial – and arguably the funniest – comedy of the second half of the decade is *Till Death Us Do Part*, with its central figure of Alf Garnett displaying his ignorant and reactionary political views yet somehow attracting our sympathies even while we condemn him. Right at the end of the decade, *Monty Python's Flying Circus* brilliantly reinvigorates the absurdist brand.

6. Political events

1960

A wave of anti-semitic attacks occur in Britain, Germany and elsewhere. The Nazi war criminal Adolf Eichmann is captured and sent for trial in Israel. An American reconnaissance plane is shot down over the Soviet Union. The Congo achieves independence from Belgium. In apartheid South Africa, the Sharpeville massacre occurs when white armed police fire on unarmed black protesters opposing the racist 'pass laws'.

The Conservative British prime minister, Harold Macmillan, makes a speech in South Africa about 'the winds of change' blowing through Africa; it is seen as heavily critical of that country's white minority regime, and he meets significant opposition both in South Africa and within his own party. This leads to the formation of the right-wing Monday Club. At home, National Service is abolished, and the Labour Party leader, Hugh Gaitskell, resists attempts by CND to make him adopt a policy opposing nuclear weapons.

1961

J. F. Kennedy becomes president of the USA, succeeding Eisenhower. East Germany closes its border with the West and begins constructing the Berlin Wall. American forces invade Cuba in a failed attempt to overthrow President Castro (the Bay of Pigs). The USSR detonates an enormous H-bomb in the Arctic, and there are meetings between American and Soviet officials to discuss disarmament; meanwhile, the Soviet astronaut Yuri Gargarin becomes the first man in space – a defeat for the USA in the race to the stars. Gargarin visits Britain – his reception in London is low-key but in Manchester he is fêted and the Soviet flag flies over the town hall. The USA sends military aid to assist South Vietnam in its civil war against Communist North Vietnam. Cyprus achieves independence. South Africa leaves the Commonwealth. Eichmann is found guilty at his trial in Jerusalem.

The Campaign for Nuclear Disarmament (CND) holds a mass rally in Trafalgar Square. Trials begin in London of members of a spy ring accused of passing military secrets to the Soviet Union. Britain begins negotiations for entry to the European Common Market. The Tory government tries to gain control over the erratic British economy by imposing a 'pay pause' to hold down public-sector earnings; it proves an unpopular and ineffective measure. A ban on thalidomide is introduced, too late to prevent hundreds of children being born with disabilities. Amnesty International is founded. The contraceptive pill is introduced. *Private Eye* is launched.

1962

The USA and USSR come desperately close to nuclear (world) war over Cuba. The former establishes military command in South Vietnam. In Israel, Eichmann is hanged. In America, the first black man enrols at the University of Mississipi, having been banned by the state governor; he is attacked and riots ensue, which are ended only when President Kennedy sends in 5,000 troops to restore order.

Harold Macmillan agrees to allow American Polaris missiles to be sited on British submarines – effectively abandoning the idea of Britain continuing as an independent nuclear power. Uganda and Tanganyika become independent of Britain. The government passes the Commonwealth Immigration Act to limit the numbers of people entering the country from its former colonies. With his government increasingly unpopular and his economic policies in disarray, Harold Macmillan sacks his chancellor and a third of his cabinet in what becomes known as 'the night of the long knives'.[13] The move fails to restore his popularity.

1963

Increasingly violent racial conflicts take place in America, with serious riots in Birmingham, Alabama. Martin Luther King is arrested, and also makes his famous 'I have a dream . . .' speech.[14] The USA, USSR and Britain agree to ban nuclear tests, and a direct 'hot line' is established between the White House and the Kremlin to diffuse future nuclear confrontations. In November, President Kennedy is assassinated in Texas. His killer is subsequently murdered on live TV. The Organisation of African Unity is established in Addis Ababa with thirty-two African countries joining.

In Britain, confidence in the government is further damaged when a junior minister at the War Office, John Profumo, is revealed to have had an extra-marital affair with a young dancer, Christine Keeler, who has also been sleeping with a Soviet naval attaché. Worse, Profumo has lied about it to the House of Commons. He resigns, and Macmillan soon follows him on health grounds. An aristocrat, Sir Alec Douglas-Home, becomes prime minister. Meanwhile, the leader of the Labour Party, Hugh Gaitskell, dies, and is succeeded by Harold Wilson.

The government publishes the Beeching Report on the railways. The French President, General de Gaulle, rejects a British application to join the European Economic Community (EEC). Kim Philby, a former head of MI6's anti-Soviet section, is identified as a long-time Soviet agent, and defects to the USSR. Kenya becomes independent.

1964

Lyndon Johnson is elected as president of the USA and more American troops are sent to fight in Vietnam. In the Soviet Union, Nikita Khrushchev is deposed by a peaceful coup and replaced by Leonid Brezhnev. In Africa, Kenya becomes a republic under Jomo Kenyatta, while Tanzania and Zambia are created with Julius Nyerere and Kenneth Kaunda as presidents. Ian Smith is elected as leader of the remaining part of Rhodesia which remains under British authority. Arafat becomes leader of an Arab guerrilla force, Al Fatah. There are race riots in New York and other American cities. President Johnson signs the Civil Rights Act, outlawing racial discrimination and segregation; but in Mississippi, three civil rights workers are murdered by the Ku Klux Klan. In South Africa, Nelson Mandela is sentenced to life imprisonment.

In Britain, new anti-drug laws are passed. There are violent clashes between mods and rockers at seaside resorts on bank holidays. Mary Whitehouse launches a Christian 'Clean Up TV' campaign. The Labour Party under Harold Wilson narrowly wins the general election, ending thirteen years of Tory government.

1965

The USSR admits supplying arms to North Vietnam. There is heavy bombing of North Vietnam by the Americans, and some US planes are shot down. In America itself, there are significant demonstrations against the war. There are more bitter clashes over race and civil rights, and Malcolm X (the American black Muslim leader) is shot dead in New York.

In Africa there is a revolution in Algeria, and Gambia becomes independent. Humberto Delgado, who had founded a National Liberation Movement in Portugal and stood for the presidency against the country's right-wing dictator, is murdered by Portuguese secret police. The murder takes place shortly after Delgado has been refused a visa for entry to the UK. In Rhodesia, Ian Smith declares unilateral

---

Empire

In 1962, a former US Secretary of State declares in a widely reported speech that 'Britain has lost an empire and not yet found a role'. The process of break-up and independence for former colonies had started before the 1960s, and it is inevitable that the remaining countries will soon follow. Nations which achieve freedom from Britain during this decade include British Somaliland, Nigeria, Sierra Leone, Tanganyika, British Cameroons, Jamaica, Trinidad and Tobago, Uganda, Western Samoa, Kenya, Zambia, Zanzibar, Malta, Botswana, Lesotho, Malawi, Gambia, Mauritius, Swaziland, Aden, Fiji and Tonga.

The case of Rhodesia (now Zimbabwe) is very different. In the mid-1960s it is ruled over by a white minority government headed by Ian Smith, which has no intention of sharing power or wealth with a black population which outnumbers whites by more than twenty to one. Britain will grant independence to former subject nations only on condition that majority rule is guaranteed, but in 1965 Smith unilaterally declares independence (UDI), confident Britain can do nothing about it. Harold Wilson employs a mixture of trade sanctions and negotiations with Smith to try to resolve the situation. None of these is successful. The United Nations endorses the sanctions, but a small number of countries (including South Africa) break the embargo, and it will be the end of the 1970s, following a long and bloody civil war, before the white minority finally cedes power and Zimbabwe is formed. It is a legacy which continues to be deadly today.

independence from Britain following the breakdown of talks with Wilson; Britain imposes an oil embargo.

Sir Winston Churchill dies at the age of ninety and is given a full state funeral. His passing is widely seen as symbolising the end of an era – one in which Britain had been a dominant world power. Meanwhile, the Labour government abolishes capital punishment for a trial period – against majority public opinion. Ted Heath becomes leader of the Conservative Party. The government passes the Race Relations Act, and establishes the Race Relations Board.

1966

In China, the ruling Communist Party declares a Cultural Revolution and imposes repressive and hard-line policies. Indira Gandhi becomes prime minister in India. The South African prime minister, Hendrik Verwoerd, is assassinated, but is succeeded by the equally right-wing John Vorster. There is fighting between Israel and Jordan, and a military coup takes place in Ghana. Albert Speer (Hitler's architect) is released after twenty years in Spandau prison. American Gemini missions begin to prepare for a Moon landing, and the USSR lands an unmanned probe on the Moon.

In Britain, Wilson shrewdly calls an early general election and increases Labour's majority from 4 to 97. He admits his government has been 'blown off course' by the worsening economic situation and announces a 'standstill' in wages and prices. In Dublin, an IRA bomb destroys Nelson's Pillar, and there are sectarian killings in Northern Ireland, following the fiftieth anniversary of the Easter Uprising.

1967

Following growing tensions, Israel launches a military attack against Egypt and the Six-Day War occurs. The Arab powers are defeated, and Israel takes control of significant new territories. Heavy American bombing of Hanoi in North Vietnam leads to big anti-war protests in Washington. Martin Luther King leads an anti-war march, and some people refuse their draft papers. Race riots continue in America, and there is a Black Power conference. During a visit to Canada, General de Gaulle calls for the freeing of Quebec. Che Guevara is killed in

Bolivia. There is a bloodless coup in Greece. The eastern part of Nigeria secedes and declares its independence as Biafra, leading to a bloody civil war which lasts until 1970.

In Britain, the National Health (Family Planning) Act gives local authorities the right to provide family planning services and the contraceptive pill. The Sexual Offences Act is passed, legalising homosexual acts between consenting adults over twenty-one. The Abortion Act is passed allowing women to terminate pregnancies on medical or psychological grounds; Wilson devalues the pound as a way to deal with the economic crisis and the trade gap. Jeremy Thorpe succeeds Jo Grimond as leader of the Liberal Party. De Gaulle rejects a second UK application to join the EEC. Britain withdraws its occupying force from Aden.

1968

America is shaken by two more political assassinations – those of the black civil rights and religious leader Martin Luther King (a former winner of the Nobel Peace Prize), and Robert J. Kennedy, a senator standing for the Democratic presidential nomination, and brother of J. F. Kennedy. Richard Nixon becomes president, promising to end the war in Vietnam. There are student uprisings across Europe, but especially in France ('*les événements*') where demonstrators occupy the Sorbonne and take control of other important public buildings. The protests are partly about Vietnam, but more broadly embody an attack from the Left on the injustices inherent within a capitalist system. There is extensive fighting in Parisian streets between the authorities and the protesters, who include students and workers. The army is called in, and De Gaulle returns early from a foreign trip to deal with the crisis. Meanwhile, Russian tanks invade Czechoslovakia, one of its satellite Communist states which had begun to institute a programme of liberalising reforms. Alexander Dubček is removed from office, and the so-called Prague Spring is forcibly ended.

In Britain, there are riots in Grosvenor Square at the American Embassy following large-scale protests against the Vietnam War. The government makes a £716 million cut in public spending in an effort to address the trade gap, and increases taxation by £923 million.

Enoch Powell, a right-wing Conservative MP, makes his infamous and confrontational 'Rivers of Blood' speech, warning about the supposed dangers of black immigration and anti-racist legislation. He predicts that violent, race-based conflicts are inevitable.

Wars of the 1960s

In international politics, the decade is dominated above all by the Cold War between America and the Soviet Union, and the threat that this might easily become the hottest of nuclear wars with devastating consequences for Britain. The divide between the Communist regimes based in Eastern Europe and the democratic West is symbolised by the Berlin Wall, constructed by East Germany in 1961 to prevent its dissatisfied citizens emigrating to the attractions of the 'free' West. In the autumn of 1962, the world comes desperately close to the edge when America discovers that in response to its own attempts to overthrow the anti-American Cuban regime on its doorstep, the Soviet Union is installing nuclear bases and weapons on the island. Britain is allied with the United States, with formal agreements to share equipment and knowledge. Indeed, from 1961 onwards, American nuclear missile submarines are sited on Scotland's Holy Loch – one of several American military installations within the United Kingdom.

The manifestation of the US–Communist conflict which dominates much of the decade is the Vietnam War. America had entered the civil war between North (Communist) and South (anti-Communist) Vietnam in the mid-1950s, and direct involvement increases through the 1960s, notably under Lyndon Johnson. In 1965, the strategy of 'saturation bombing' is introduced, with the American air force chief of staff famously promising to 'bomb them back into the Stone Age'. A ground invasion of Vietnam by American troops soon follows, and the United Kingdom is one of several countries which declines American requests to contribute troops. Public opinion within America divides as the number of 'home' deaths grows, and increasing numbers of young people seek to evade the compulsory draft. Revelations and television images of acts of violence committed by American troops on Vietnamese civilians inspire the growing anti-war movement inside and outside America, and by the end of the decade an American withdrawal is finally under way.

1969

American astronauts are the first to walk on the Moon. De Gaulle resigns as president of France and Georges Pompidou succeeds him. Two American military officers stand trial for their part in the My Lai massacre – an atrocity committed by US soldiers against a village of unarmed women and children, and an event so shocking that it helps turn public opinion against the war. The American withdrawal from Vietnam begins.

Race

Race – and prejudice – is a key area of social conflict in Britain in the 1960s, with sections of the white population fearful of the changes that immigration may bring, and unwilling to question racial stereotypes. In 1962, the Conservative government introduces a Commonwealth Immigration Act which limits the rights of entry for Commonwealth passport holders to those able to obtain a work voucher. Labour opposes the Act, but once in office, reduces the number of available vouchers, and in 1968 introduces a second Act which requires that successful applicants must have a parent or grandparent who was born in (or is a citizen of) the UK. In 1968, the Conservative MP Enoch Powell makes an infamous speech warning of the threat to Britain posed by (black) immigration, and predicting a racial war and rivers 'foaming with much blood' unless the government not only cuts immigration but puts pressure on those already here to return 'home'. Powell also attacks the Labour government's Race Relations Acts of 1965 and 1968, which have made it illegal to discriminate 'on the grounds of colour, race, or ethnic or national origins'. Although his party leader, Ted Heath, expels him, Powell earns disconcertingly large amounts of media and public support, with thousands of workers marching and striking to demonstrate their agreement. The Labour government decides to introduces a Commonwealth Immigrants Act to restrict the number of Asians able to enter Britain from Kenya and Uganda.

Racial abuse and discrimination are widespread – visible not least in the humour. One of the most controversial television comedies of the period is *Till Death Us Do Part*, written by the left-wing playwright Johnny Speight, but featuring the deeply racist and offensive character of Alf Garnett. While Speight and Warren Mitchell – who plays the role – detest everything Garnett stands for, this is self-evidently not the case for all audiences, and a character who is supposedly being ridiculed becomes hard to hate.

In Britain, Enoch Powell proposes that the government should finance repatriation of black and Asian people. The voting age is lowered from twenty-one to eighteen. After years of trade deficit, British exports increase and the trade balance moves into the black. There are Red Cross airlifts to Biafra. British troops are sent to patrol the streets of Belfast and Londonderry after violent clashes and shootings between Catholics and Protestants which mark the beginning of 'the Troubles' which will ruin so many lives.

The 1960s is sometimes remembered fondly as a decade of peace and love; it was equally a time of war and hate. In terms of theatre, it was also a decade – perhaps the last one – when people believed it not only reflected the times but helped to shape them.

CHAPTER 1
THEATRE IN THE 1960s

In the second half of the 1950s, British theatre had undergone a radical transformation. The infiltration of the 'angry young men' and the working class at the Royal Court; the anti-realistic absurdism of Beckett, Ionesco and (arguably) Pinter; the innovative creative approaches pioneered by Joan Littlewood and the Theatre Workshop at Stratford East. All these developments had shaken – though hardly destroyed – some of the complacent conventions on which post-war theatre had previously been built. At the start of the 1960s there were other significant events on the horizon. The plans for a National Theatre in London seemed – finally – to be close to materialising, and the appointment of Peter Hall, a young director with a reputation for theatrical innovation, to run the Shakespearean shrine at Stratford would further change the face of British theatre.

So why was it that in the autumn of 1961, the radical and widely read theatre critic and future literary manager at the National Theatre, Kenneth Tynan, could write his weekly *Observer* column under the headline 'The breakthrough that broke down'? Revolution, he asked? What revolution? 'So little, in ten years, seems to have changed.' Tynan acknowledged the Royal Court as 'a beach-head for our splashing new wave', but he found little else to celebrate, and little sense that the wave had penetrated inland: 'A decade ago, roughly two out of three London theatres were inhabited by detective stories, Pineroesque melodramas, quarter-witted farces, debutante comedies, overweight musicals and unreviewable revues,' wrote Tynan; 'the same is true today.'[1] An editorial in the magazine *Encore* ('the voice of vital theatre') made an equally cautious assessment of what was on offer:

> In John Arden, Harold Pinter and Arnold Wesker we have a trio of playwrights from whom we can expect major work in the next few years . . . We have actors, directors and designers

to match. We never had it so good. Theatre Workshop is doing fine. The English Stage Company is doing fine. And . . . er . . . well. Yes. There's the rub . . .[2]

For the actor Ian Bannen, who had recently played the title role in John Arden's *Serjeant Musgrave's Dance* at the Royal Court, the problem was clear: 'In England there is really so little following for the drama that sometimes you feel you are barking up the wrong tree if you believe that, as an actor, you have some social function. I mean, everybody raves about *Serjeant Musgrave's Dance* now, but hardly a soul came to see it.' The theatre, said Bannen, was doing its best to initiate change, but audiences – 'still so often composed of old ladies' – lagged behind: 'You hear the most insane remarks from the stalls, and you wonder what the hell we are all doing. In some beautiful scene, where everything is going right and the meaning is quite clear, you hear remarks like, "I wish she'd stop dragging her leg!"'[3]

Bannen's perspective is a reminder that in assessing and understanding the theatre of any period it is not enough to look only at what was occurring on the stage; we need also to pay attention to what was happening in the auditorium (and beyond) and in the press. If you were watching from the right place, the 1960s would prove to be a hugely exciting and groundbreaking decade for new writing and performance; but from other angles the view might seem altogether more restricted. When the decade dawned, *My Fair Lady* had already been running for two years in Drury Lane, and it would keep going for well over 2,000 performances. *Oliver!*, which premiered in the West End in June 1960, would enjoy an even longer run, as would *The Sound of Music*, which opened in May 1961. Meanwhile, *The Mousetrap* spanned the decade – as it has every one since. 'How big *is* the audience which is prepared to assist in the growth of the theatre by supporting the dissenters, the off-beat and the experimental?' worried *Encore*.[4] It was not alone in its concern. 'The young dramatists are full of energy, are fresh, are often very amusing,' wrote the theatre critic of the *Manchester Guardian*, 'but they don't in fact write many plays which give great pleasure.' On the contrary, 'older regulars are alienated' and younger audiences 'come away feeling very often that their evening out has been a disappointment'.⁵ The revolution, then, had barely begun.

In 1960, most theatre performances – even at the Royal Court – began with audiences standing for the National Anthem, and the raising of the stage curtain; they ended with applause and a curtain call. By 1970, such conventions could not be counted on. In seeking to offer some insights into a decade which is really several different decades, this chapter will combine a broadly chronological with a thematic approach, as it charts some of the key challenges and shifts, the performances and the arguments, as they occurred through the 1960s.

1960–64

Performance and politics

The most revolutionary director of the late 1950s and early 1960s – probably both aesthetically and politically – was Joan Littlewood. Based at the Theatre Royal in the East End of London, Littlewood had established Theatre Workshop as a creative ensemble which brought innovative approaches to its work on both classical and new plays, and to the training of actors. In 1961, however, Littlewood announced that she was abandoning the British theatre (albeit briefly, as it turned out), frustrated by its economic structures and their impact on the company's work. Theatre Workshop's problem was not lack of an audience but the opposite; several of their recent productions had transferred successfully into the West End, but this had inevitably prioritised commercial gain over creative development. Explaining her reasons for leaving, Littlewood accused the West End of having 'plundered our talent and diluted our ideas', and expressed her distaste for a culture where financial profit rather than art was the driving and irresistible imperative, and where theatre 'belongs to the managers or the landlords'.⁶ *Encore* published a paean of praise for what she had achieved:

> To Joan Littlewood we owe many things . . . she created the
> one true permanent company which has existed in London for
> many years . . . she showed that it was still possible to make a
> cast act as an ensemble rather than as individual entities. She
> fostered a style of acting which did much to help break down
> the barrier of polite restraint between actor and audience. She
> showed that classical plays could be produced as if they had
> only just been written, and that new plays with serious intent
> need not necessarily be addressed only to a minority audience.
> She has done much to break down the conception of the
> theatre as a preserve of the upper and middle classes dealing
> exclusively with their interests for their benefit. She has, in fact,
> brought to life the puny body of the post-war British theatre.

The article concluded: 'We apologise for Britain.'[7]

There were many differences between the approach and methods
of the Royal Court and those of Theatre Workshop; one believed in
placing the playwright at the heart of creation, while the other saw the
written script as a starting point for actors and director to use to
develop their performance. One thing they shared was a commitment
to giving a stage voice to the working class. For some, this raised
ethical questions about authenticity and integrity, and above all about
the practice of exposing that voice to potentially voyeuristic
middle-class audiences. Part of Littlewood's annoyance was that her
most successful work, intended for the Stratford East community
among whom it was made and where it was first presented, was being
annexed by well-heeled audiences in the West End. Similarly, when
Wesker's *Roots* – a Royal Court play set in the East Anglian rural
setting from which the playwright himself had escaped – was broadcast on national radio in 1960, the local press was reportedly 'full of
letters complaining about the "absolute libel on Norfolk people"' and
the 'travesty of Norfolk village life' it presented. 'If we must be written
about, let the play be clean and uplifting.'[8] Yet Wesker himself was
at the centre of a movement the very aim of which was to open up
a broader culture to working-class audiences. In September 1960,
the Trades Union Congress passed a resolution – number 42

– 'recognising the importance of the arts in the life of the community', and acknowledging that historically the trade union movement had contributed little to encouraging it. As the unions were now meeting with success in their campaigns for shorter working hours, the increase in leisure time for workers placed this issue firmly on the agenda, and Centre 42 was established, with Arnold Wesker as its champion. The original intention was to create a 'gymnasium of the arts' in London, funded partly by the TUC, which would provide opportunities for working people to experience culture in ways which would 'destroy the mystique and snobbery associated with the arts'. It was to be based in a converted theatre and offer activities such as a youth club, jazz groups, exhibitions, concerts, films, plays, revues and lunchtime concerts. The repertoire would be 'flexible, experimental, non-commercial', and the aspiration was that similar centres would quickly establish themselves across the country.[9]

When Centre 42 was launched in 1961, it immediately encountered cynicism – even from those who might have sympathised with its aims: 'At least it is trying to do *something*,' acknowledged the *Guardian*, but the intentions seemed misguided and naive. By coincidence, Centre 42 revealed its plans on the very day that Littlewood announced her departure on television. Wesker was seen as 'taking over the attempt to wake up the slumberer where Miss Littlewood has left off', and both were accused of condescension: 'Littlewood . . . often talked as if the working people were a pack of noble savages just waiting for an artistic saviour; much of the Centre 42 talk had the same ring.'[10] By 1962, the emphasis of Centre 42 had shifted slightly, as Wesker spoke of plans to establish it more as an umbrella organisation – 'a kind of communities Arts Council to which groups can come and ask not only for money but also for practical assistance in the staging of festivals'.[11] Some such events did follow, but these never matched up to the rhetoric or the goals set, and by the middle of the decade Centre 42 had drifted off the radar, with some of its own supporters criticising the quality of the things it had supported:

> Centre 42 is in a mess . . . it's terrible compared to what we want . . . the work done was, in the main, dreadful, and didn't

even measure up to the standards we are seeking to abolish. The play turned out as a travesty, far from being genuinely aimed at these audiences, it came to be looked upon as a pre-West End run. The fact that the audiences loved it is only evidence of the conditioning that we must overcome . . . unless we have a play we are burning to do then conventional theatre is not the best method of attracting any mass audience.[12]

Wesker came to feel he had been betrayed by the Labour government which should have supported him, and that the offer of an MBE was an attempt to buy him off and avoid backing the movement. The Labour government's newly created minister for the arts, Jennie Lee, had initially championed Centre 42 and even served on its management council; but she focused instead on creating a new charter for the Arts Council, with a key commitment 'to increase the accessibility of the arts to the public throughout Great Britain'.[13] Centre 42 may have inspired some of the ideas behind this, but the organisation itself was sidelined.

Cruelty and violence

Some theatre makers were asking even broader questions about the place and role of theatre in a modern society. What was its function and its value? What could it contribute? And would it really matter if live theatre disappeared? 'If you are honest with yourself, you know in your heart of hearts that what you do is totally unnecessary,' wrote Peter Brook in 1961.

The terrible truth is that if in this country you closed all the theatres the only loss would be that of a well-bred community feeling that a certain civilised amenity – like buses or tapwater – was lacking . . . There would be one less subject to talk about, maybe. But would there be a real sustained crying-out, a feeling of lack?[14]

Brook – already established as one of the most challenging and exciting directors of his generation for his approach to classical texts – believed that theatre in Britain was stagnant and required a complete change of focus. In 1963 he took charge of an experimental arm within the RSC, where his work on texts by writers including Jean Genet, Peter Weiss, Antonin Artaud and even Shakespeare drew heavily on Artaud's own manifesto for a Theatre of Cruelty. *Theatre and Its Double* had been written before the Second World War, but published in English only at the end of the 1950s. Some hailed it for seeking an alternative to a realistic, text-based and moribund art form; others were appalled by what it proposed putting in its place. For although Artaud's manifesto was about much more than the representation of physical cruelty and the release of extreme and discomforting emotions, to many, this was where his ideas seemed to lead. As the *Sunday Times* critic put it when reviewing the RSC production of David Rudkin's *Afore Night Come*: 'It is the policy of the current avant-garde theatre to unsettle us – not to stimulate us through laughter, or make us think through argument, or offer an emotional catharsis, but simply to make us feel bruised and uncertain.' Prefiguring critical responses to what in the 1990s would become known as 'in-yer-face' theatre, the entire movement was dismissed as a self-indulgence: 'The so-called Theatre of Cruelty is in fact no more than Theatre for Kicks.'[15] A more considered approach was offered by Martin Esslin, who in 1964 gave a talk at the ICA tracing the connections between violence and drama, and defending those who used theatre 'to wake people up rather than to put them to sleep'. Esslin argued that 'the most aggressive and the most immoral theatre is the ordinary entertainment theatre of the West End and television', which 'covers up and prettifies the human situation' and 'pours a chocolate sauce of contentment and complacency over people's lives'.[16]

Concern about stage violence dated back to the very start of the decade. As early as January 1960, in an article called 'The Hidden Face of Violence', Tom Milne identified it as the 'common theme' of three recent and controversial plays – Arden's *Musgrave*, Pinter's *The Birthday Party* and John Whiting's *Saint's Day*. He argued that it reflected contemporary concerns: 'We are . . . living in an age of violence,' he pointed out, and he linked the everyday violence which he believed was increasingly visible in society with the extreme but very real threat of nuclear attack and conflagration which was hanging over almost the whole of humanity. In a world 'waiting . . . for the big bang', wrote Milne, 'the chain reaction of release is one of violence'.[17] In 1961, in an article entitled 'The Theatre of Cruelty', *The Times* also noted the use of violence by contemporary playwrights, including Wesker (in *The Kitchen*) and Pinter (in *The Room*). 'As for directors, they fit into the scheme by taking full advantage of our barbaric Shakespearean heritage.' While acknowledging that it might be difficult to pin down 'the borderline between tragic inhumanity and sadism confected for the kicks', the article questioned whether Artaud was an appropriate model to be invoked by contemporary artists. Writing a fortnight after an Israeli court had passed the death sentence on Adolf Eichmann for his role in the murder of millions of Jews by the Nazis, *The Times* went on to propose a possible link between Artaud and the rise of Fascism: 'Artaud's letters on cruelty date from the early 1930s, when the regime which has led to Eichmann was finding its feet. Are they symptoms of the disease about to infest Europe at that time?'[18] Similarly, the writer and academic Laurence Kitchin attacked Artaud's writings and theories as 'the bible of sick theatre'. For Kitchin, too, Artaud's arguments for cruelty in the theatre 'resemble the equivocations of the Nazi exterminators'; and 'his wish to replace articulate speech by primitive chanting . . . reveals a personality . . . qualified for the Theatre of Cruelty, the real one, which began with the Nuremberg rallies and ended in Belsen.'[19]

Shakespeare

Inevitably, Shakespeare was drawn into the argument about violence. In 1961, the avant-garde theatre writer and director Charles Marowitz provocatively defined the Bard in his 'Cynic's Glossary of Theatre Terms' as 'a popular tourist attraction'. Stratford-upon-Avon was his 'main factory' and Waterloo Road (the Old Vic) his 'London distributor'.[20] But Shakespeare was changing. In the autumn of 1960, the

Italian director Franco Zeffirelli had been 'invited to put new life into *Romeo and Juliet*' at the Old Vic.[21] According to reviews, the production downplayed the lyrical evocation of young love and instead 'concentrated on the themes of youth and violence', and 'the lack of understanding between one generation and the next'. Juliet – played by a young Judi Dench – was given 'a beatnik heart', and the production was praised above all for the 'authenticity' of the world it evoked – a world in which 'children scuffle in the alleys and vendors bawl their wares'. This was 'Romeo with the gloves off', with characters who 'seem to have stepped out of a painting by some Italian Breughel'.[22] Five years later, the Polish theatre writer and critic Jan Kott published a book which was to prove hugely influential, entitled *Shakespeare Our Contemporary*.[23] Kott cited Shakespeare in relation to current political and philosophical arguments, and to absurdist playwrights such as Beckett and Ionesco. Peter Brook made a similar connection in an article called '*Endgame* as *King Lear* or How to Stop Worrying and Love Beckett'.[24] Meanwhile, the Royal Court director Lindsay Anderson rewrote parts of *Julius Caesar* in order to 'improve' it, declaring that 'There is no more exciting and contemporary writer now represented on the London stage than William Shakespeare.'[25]

Kott's analysis caught a mood of the times, and suddenly Shakespeare was found to fit comfortably within a Theatre of Cruelty. Brook's landmark production of *King Lear*, for example, excised a passage in which two servants express their disapproval of the vicious blinding of Gloucester they have just witnessed (here carried out by Cornwall using the spur of his boot). Instead, Gloucester is 'pushed from side to side by a group of servants as he tries to stagger away'.[26] But Kitchin, whose book was published in the same year as Kott's, took a very different view. He was contemptuous of such 'distortions of Shakespeare', which he saw as misguided attempts to bring the Bard 'into line with popular taste' and make him 'conform to the trends of pulp literature and mass-media drama'. For Kitchin, this was 'Pop Shakespeare', 'Shakespeare packaged and marketed in such a way as to reach people living at our tempo, in our world, inhabiting our environment of supermarkets, advertisements and television'. He attacked recent productions of *Henry V* which had adopted a less adulatory attitude to the King than Olivier's famous war-time version. Where Olivier had linked Henry's triumphant war on the French to the contemporary fight against Hitler, recent productions had made the young king 'an anti-hero', 'astute and cowardly', 'a creep', 'cunning', or even a rather ridiculous 'Ivor Novello hero in cricket flannels'.[27] Such re-interpretation marked a generational shift and a new cynicism – about war, heroes and authority.

Staging reality

A very different challenge to British expectations was offered by an American import, *The Connection*. Written by Jack Gelber and staged by New York's Living Theatre, this play centred on a group of heroin addicts waiting for their next fix – a sort of *Waiting for Godot* in which Godot is both the dealer and the drug. But where the style and setting of Beckett's play had abstracted it from everyday reality, *The Connection* sought to confuse the boundaries between reality and fiction and to make the action as lifelike as possible – to an extent where audiences would become uncertain which it was they were watching. The press warned theatregoers in advance that during the off-Broadway production trained nurses had always been present because 'at each performance men and women faint, or stagger out stunned'. In particular, there was an 'agonisingly real' scene of injections which 'really knocks the audience'.[28] What took the performance to another level was the deliberate scrambling of the boundaries between reality and fiction. The *Daily Mail* ran a story describing the dress rehearsal and featuring a photograph of a man apparently in agony as he injected himself:

> It was a day of some confusion. On stage, the members of the cast – some American, some English – were lounging about in attitudes of dejection, waiting for the 'pusher' named Cowboy to arrive with the drugs.
>
> Were they actors or real junkies? The point about *The Connection* is that one can never be sure . . .[29]

The actual text of the play consisted largely of apparently inconse-
quential and disjointed dialogue, interspersed with jazz music. As
with *Godot*, the focus is on the waiting itself. Reviews agreed that 'The
actors are utterly convincing', as they 'laze about and chat . . . pick
their noses, exchange languid or hysterical confidences, squeeze their
boils, are sick, and are injected with heroin'. In America, audiences
were reportedly uncertain whether genuine addicts had been put on
stage – especially as the text exploits the Pirandellian notion of a play
within a play, informing an audience that the addicts have been
brought to the theatre to act out a play in return for their next fix. 'No
trick is unused in an effort to make it "real"', reported the press:

> No curtain goes up. As the audience trickle in the cast is already
> on stage, pacing up and down. They are unshaven, dirty. They
> wear old sweaters and jeans and bite their finger-nails . . .
> Actors get to the stage via the auditorium . . . They explain that
> they have brought these addicts along and don't really know
> what will happen . . .

Certainly, there was no scope for a curtain or National Anthem here,
and the *Daily Mail* described *The Connection* as 'the most controversial piece of theatre in years', which had 'landed like a bomb in the
precincts of St Martin-in-the-Fields last night'.[30] Peter Brook was
among those who hailed it for opening a new door:

> The actors who are portraying these characters have sunk
> themselves into a total, beyond Method, degree of saturated
> naturalism, so that they aren't acting, they are being . . . it is the
> ultimate development of the utterly naturalistic theatre and yet
> we are completely 'distanced' all through the evening . . . I
> think it shows that there is a super-naturalistic theatre ahead of
> us in which pure behaviour can exist in its own right.[31]

But few of the regular theatre critics shared his enthusiasm. 'The
subject of decadence seems to have produced a play form which is
itself decadent – and boring into the bargain', wrote one; 'an evening

of relentless squalor, unrelieved by any plot or grace', wrote another. 'It is no play – but it is quite an experience.'[32]

There is another aspect to the history of the London production of *The Connection* which gives a particular insight into theatregoing in the early 1960s. There still existed a group of people known as 'the first nighters' who took it upon themselves to occupy the gallery during opening performances of West End productions and to make their views loudly known, in the hope that they could influence a show's success or failure. According to Robert Muller in the *Daily Mail, The Connection* 'met with the bitterest hostility I have ever had the misfortune to observe in a London theatre'. His review appeared under the banner headline 'THEY CACKLED A WORK OF ART TO DEATH', and he reported that 'The whole second half was drowned in catcalls, derisive laughter, and slow handclapping.' Muller realised that while what was said and done on stage might appear random and unplanned, everything had, of course, been carefully crafted. The production's effect could 'only be achieved by a meticulous precision in the performance, and this the galleryites brutally prevented'. As a result of their antics, wrote Muller, 'the cast lost heart, the carefully balanced rhythm of the play was upset. The entire evening was destroyed.'[33] Nor did the sabotage end when the performance did. Rather 'a near-riot' occurred in the streets outside the theatre as the 'galleryites' demanded their money back and confronted the actors and producer in an argument which continued for ninety minutes and was stopped only when the police intervened. The following day, the play's American producer threatened to put 'hidden persuaders' in the gallery 'to deal with the trouble-makers' and prevent them from disrupting another performance. 'Misbegotten creeps', he called them. 'Filthy scavengers, thick-skinned and all wrapped up in their smug little selves' whose 'lives are so bleak and barren that the only attention they get is when they cause a disturbance'.[34] Even reviewers who had not necessarily appreciated the play were shocked by the 'callous display' of 'the first-night yahoos'. Some saw it in a broader context:

> Under our Ealing-film cosiness, an appalling vein of crude brutality runs in the English character; it has often appeared in

our colonial policy, often in the way our police treat an under-sized enemy, and daily in our uniquely savage yellow Press. The mood that once drew us to Tyburn and Bedlam was shamefully revived at *The Connection*, and the cast, nearly all American and therefore unused to such barbarism, looked as if it had been hit between the eyes.[35]

The age of satire

April 1960 saw the opening of Harold Pinter's *The Caretaker* at the Arts Theatre and Ionesco's *Rhinoceros* at the Royal Court. N. F. Simpson's *One Way Pendulum* had already transferred from the Court to the Criterion Theatre, and all of these plays found themselves labelled within the category now invented by Martin Esslin under the term 'Theatre of the Absurd'.[36] Comedy was a significant element of most plays within this genre, but a more popular form of humour which also surfaced at this time focused less on the strangeness of the human condition and more on the strangeness of contemporary society. *Beyond the Fringe* was a revue created and performed by four young Oxbridge graduates – Peter Cook, Dudley Moore, Alan Bennett and Jonathan Miller – and it took the Edinburgh Festival of 1960 by storm with its daring and satirical attack. *The Times*, under the headline 'Revue that is Really Funny', was full of praise – though there was a slight hint of uneasiness about the choice of target: 'It is decidedly hard on the Conservative Party that Mr Miller should so much enjoy reproducing the Prime Minister's vocal and literary style and should reproduce it so devastatingly well.' It was unfair, thought *The Times*, that Macmillan should be 'made to bear the whole weight of the ridicule that might otherwise be fairly distributed among politicians in general'.[37] Politics and politicians were by no means the only butts; Shakespeare, the clergy and the philosopher A. J. Ayer were among the others, and physical clowning was central to the show's appeal. But several sketches mocked attitudes which had not previously been mocked. In one of the most quoted gags, a commanding and very British army officer invites his junior to volunteer for a mission:

Peter   War is a psychological thing, Perkins, rather like a game of football. You know how in a game of football ten men often play better than eleven – ?

Jon   Yes, sir.

Peter   Perkins, we are asking you to be that one man. I want you to lay down your life, Perkins. We need a futile gesture at this stage. It will raise the whole tone of the war. Get up in a crate, Perkins, pop over to Bremen, take a shufti, don't come back.[38]

Arguably, the satire here looks backwards to the past, but in a more contemporary sketch, a government representative reassures a women's institute meeting – in essentially the same voice as that of the army officer above – that there is no need to worry about nuclear attack:

Peter   Now, we shall receive four minutes' warning of any impending nuclear attack. Some people have said, 'Oh my goodness me – four minutes? – that is not a very long time!' Well I would remind those doubters that some people in this great country of ours can run a mile in four minutes.[39]

Beyond the Fringe was comedy for the middle and intellectual classes. When it opened in London in 1961, *The Times* noted that it 'smacks a little of the Third Programme'.[40] But the new tone and irreverent attitude towards the establishment and the powerful reflected shifts in British society; according to one review, the show had 'pulled the contemporary world to shreds'.[41] Indeed, much of the satire was directed against the very people it attracted. 'We audiences have tasted our own blood and liked it.' Where British revue had previously seemed safe and comfortable, this felt very different. 'One by one they hold up by the tail our dead prejudices, our diseased snobberies, our wounded bigotries like so many skinned rats.'[42] Some critics found the show took a definite political stance which targeted 'right-wing Tories, VC's, transcendentalists, Empire Loyalists, Lord Beaverbrook, and Civil Defence workers'.[43] Others thought it lacked any principles and cared only about one thing: 'Laughter is what they are after, and they get it.'[44] Either way, *Beyond the Fringe* ran in

London for over five years and two thousand performances, and reports speak of audiences being helpless with laughter. Why was it so popular? In a perceptive analysis written at the time, Michael Frayn suggested that the show seemed almost to be responding to an unspoken and previously unrecognised need:

> Conceivably the demand arose because after ten years of stable Conservative government, with no prospect in 1961 of its ever ending, the middle classes felt some vague guilt accumulating for the discrepancy between their prosperous security and the continuing misery of those who persisted in failing to conform, by being black, or queer, or mad, or old. Conceivably they felt the need to disclaim with laughter any responsibility for this situation, and so relieve their consciences without actually voting for anything which might have reduced their privileges . . .[45]

The success of *Beyond the Fringe* spawned a new wave of satire, not least the magazine *Private Eye* and the revolutionary television series *That Was the Week That Was*. As Frayn observed, not all of it was good, and satire quickly lost its ability to surprise:

> The 'Fringe' made its audience laugh at the unthinking attitudes of respect which up till then they themselves had shared. Unfortunately, once the 'Fringe' had annihilated the convention, to go on mocking the so-called Establishment has more and more meant making the audience laugh not at themselves at all, but at a standard target which is rapidly becoming as well-established as mothers-in-law. To do this is not to undermine but to confirm the audience's prejudices, and has less in common with satire than with community hymn-singing.

Theatres of war

Despite this, even a production such as Theatre Workshop's 1963 masterpiece *Oh, What a Lovely War!* was built on the willingness and success of *Beyond the Fringe* in daring to attack cows which had once been sacred. Joan Littlewood's most celebrated production opened at Stratford East in March, transferring to Wyndham's Theatre in June. Some accused *Oh, What a Lovely War!* of political naivety and selling out to commercial values; they claimed that audiences went home cheerfully singing escapist songs which made light of the horrors of the First World War. Others thought it brilliantly combined political punch with popular entertainment. The immediate inspiration had been a radio programme of First World War songs, superficially cheery but often deeply layered with irony. 'We're here because we're here because we're here because we're here' to the tune of 'Auld Acquaintance'; 'Gassed last night and gassed the night before' to 'Drunk Last Night'. We witness naive young men seduced into signing up by a female music hall performer who promises 'to make a man of any one of you'; the lies of media propaganda which persuades English and German women back home to make identical assumptions and accusations ('You know what they're doing now? . . . Melting corpses for glycerine' . . . '*Weisst du, was sie jetzt tun? . . . Sie schmelzen Körper für Glyzerin*'). The war itself is presented as a kind of seaside entertainment, performed by a pierrot troupe on the promenade. Most unsettling were the juxtapositions of generals celebrating a 'success', or insisting on the cheerfulness of wounded and dying soldiers, with authentic photographs and unadorned facts projected on to a Newspanel ('SOMME BATTLE ENDS . . . TOTAL LOSS 1,332,000 MEN . . . GAIN NIL' . . . 'AVERAGE LIFE OF A MACHINE GUNNER UNDER ATTACK . . . FOUR MINUTES').[46]

Oh, What a Lovely War! was seen by some people as 'anti-British propaganda' – and it certainly was an attack on aspects of Britishness. Yet, with few exceptions, the critics enthused. The *Daily Mail* called it 'a devastating musical satire', and endorsed its portrayal of General Haig as 'the villain of the piece' – a man who 'in any decently ordered society, would have been employed, under the supervision of an intelligent half-wit, to run the very simplest sort of public lavatory. Instead, he ran a war.'[47] Most critics treated *Oh, What a Lovely War!* as a play about the past – safely remote. However, others recognised that its implications went beyond the events of 1914–18: 'It attacks everything that is sacred and decent'; 'It is an all-out attack upon our Christian faith.' Therein lay its danger: 'What a picture of our country to give to those who come to our theatre from abroad at this time of year, and what a misbegotten philosophy to feed to the hundreds of younger people of our own country who appear to flock to this kind of thing.'[48]

From a contrasting political perspective, A. J. P. Taylor – a leading and well-known historian – adopted the play's title for his own valedictory lecture at Oxford University, and praised the production for 'doing what the historians have failed to do' in providing a valid analysis of what the war was about. 'Stage Says It Better than Historians', as the headline in *The Times* put it, in reporting his lecture. But Taylor's main point pulled the politics out of the past and firmly into the present of the nuclear age and contemporary debate. The key principle in the argument for developing nuclear weapons – the justification for spending millions of pounds on weaponry and missiles which everyone hoped would never be used – was that their very existence would act as a 'deterrent', preventing an enemy from attacking because they would know that you would respond in kind. In discussing Theatre Workshop's production, it was this principle which Taylor sought to expose:

> The cause of the First World War was the deterrent: the belief that if you are strongly enough armed you can prevent a war ... When you say if you have the deterrent you can prevent a war you have the example of the First World War to show you that you are wrong. Those who are so bitterly preparing against the third world war have it there. They are merely speeding the pressing of the button, the explosion of the world.

Littlewood was more than happy to accept Taylor's reading of the play: 'His material on the deterrent is so important, and I was so glad he agreed', she said; 'That is the point we try to make in our production.'[49]

With Britain – and the world – living under the threat of a confrontation between two superpowers, and with a strategy built on

'Mutually Assured Destruction' (MAD) being presented as both sensible and sane, it is hardly surprising that plays about wars found their way on to a number of stages. In 1963, the RSC mounted a widely celebrated production of a sequence of Shakespeare's history plays under the collective title of *The Wars of the Roses*. 'The plays were about war and warring politics, as well as endless and increasingly vicious, senseless battles, and the steel-floored staging presented the very image of Armageddon. Both sets and costumes had a curiously timeless quality, suggestive not just of these wars but also of more recent combats.'[50] The cycle was sufficiently powerful and compelling to be filmed and broadcast on BBC1 in weekly fifty-minute episodes.

A different take on war and military life was offered by the Living Theatre, who returned to London in 1964 with *The Brig*. Based on the personal experiences of its author, Kenneth H. Brown, this was a pounding and hypnotic performance depicting shocking images of the casual and sadistic brutalities of life inside a United States Marine prison, where any hint of a challenge to authority is viciously punished. The audience viewed the entire action through a barbed-wire mesh, and the acting area – the prison – was marked out with white lines which prisoners were forbidden to cross without authority. As in *The Connection*, *The Brig* depended on a kind of super-naturalism in which audiences appeared to be watching real life rather than a play, and again it was partly the blurring of fiction and reality which unsettled those who disliked it. That and the violence: 'From curtain-up to curtain-down the ten prisoners are continually thumped in the guts and made to perform at the double by their sadistic guards.'[51] There was no real plot, no development, and not much sense of characters. Action was deliberately and monumentally repetitive, with the request 'Sir! Permission to cross the white line, Sir?' recurring endlessly. For *The Times* it was 'An Ugly Spectacle of Licensed Cruelty'; the *Daily Mail* called it 'horrifying, inescapable and brilliant'. Others found it 'A Bit of a Bore', or objected to the lack of development. Some critics argued that the world and the system depicted by *The Brig* were so peculiarly and specifically American that the performance was of no relevance to a British audience. Not everyone agreed. 'Belsen – or Aldershot?', asked one headline. For some, it was an allegory with broader implications of the life we inflict on each other, and our willingness to submit to authority and to rules.[52]

An equally powerful war play to emerge at the end of 1964 – though it was only licensed for performance three years later – was Charles Wood's *Dingo*, 'a bitter, pungent attack on war and heroism'.[53] Set among the soldiers and battles of the Second World War, it directly asks us to consider 'What were we fighting for?' In one early scene, a British soldier burns to death in a tank, screaming, while his colleague, Tanky, tries to persuade two uninterested soldiers to help rescue him:

Tanky It's Chalky . . . He's in there.

Dingo Yes – he is isn't he? . . .

Tanky I tried to open his hatch. He couldn't open his hatch you see – it was glowing red hot all round his hatch – can you imagine his skin against that?

Mogg I put my hand on a stove once . . .

Dingo Couldn't you put a bullet in him? . . .

Tanky Shut up Chalk – belt up you bastard.

Dingo That's it. Get it out of your system – you'll feel better.

Mogg Burn – you bastard.

Tanky I've got to get him out.

Dingo He owe you money?

Mogg He'll be alright when his brain goes . . .

Tanky I can't listen – I can't listen.

Mogg He wouldn't want you to.

Tanky later returns talking and dancing with the charred corpse, though the others claim it can't be a British soldier because it doesn't look like one, and because it screamed too much ('No British squaddie goes on like that'). The script was also laced with a dark humour and sexuality (two soldiers compare 'mirages' and masturbate to the music of a belly-dance tune, while the loading and firing of a gun is narrated in terms of a sexual encounter with a woman's body). Even Winston Churchill – the ultimate icon of Britain's glory and military success – is mauled by the play. In one scene, a touring comedian sits on the lavatory with puppets of Churchill and Eisenhower on either hand, conversing together: Churchill is clearly spoiling for a battle and expresses himself 'determined to get as much fun and personal satis-faction as I possibly can out of this war and bring my rich and rousing personality to bear upon the men and women engaged in the day-to-day jobs of battle'.[54]

Wood's play was proposed for production at the National Theatre. But it was one thing to question the conduct, and perhaps even the values of the 1914 war; the Second World War was more recent and clearly constructed as 'Britain's finest hour'. Moreover, there was a risk that the tone and message of the play might promote opposition to current and future wars:

> it falls into the pattern of the 'avant-garde' of this country which now secures such disproportionate publicity for its efforts to undermine in every way the nation's will to resist. The ghastly effects of propaganda of this sort were seen in the abject surrender of France to the Germans, and the effects could be just as serious here.[55]

By chance, Churchill himself died just when Laurence Olivier, the director of the newly opened National Theatre, was discussing Wood's play with the Lord Chamberlain, and plans for a production were abandoned. Coincidentally, it was Olivier who voiced Churchill's words during the solemn commentary for the ITV live broadcast of Churchill's funeral in January 1965.

Beyond words

In May 1964, *The Times* published an editorial headed 'Wanted, New Plays'. While acknowledging the importance of the new theatre buildings planned, the achievements of the first five years at Nottingham Playhouse, and the RSC's history cycle at Stratford, the writer bemoaned the dearth of new plays to recommend to a 'serious foreign theatregoer' visiting the country. 'There would have been no difficulty, five years ago, in helping him. He would have been confronted with an array of new talent the like of which has appeared in no other European country since the war. If he returned this summer . . . there would be little new English drama to recommend.'[56]

In some respects, this is a surprising judgement. A key plank in Peter Hall's strategy at the RSC was his commitment to staging contemporary work alongside Shakespeare – a policy he inaugurated in February 1961 by producing John Whiting's *The Devils*, a play based on Aldous Huxley's account of witchcraft, diabolism and sexual hysteria in a seventeenth-century French convent. The following year, the company premiered David Rudkin's *Afore Night Come*, a disturbing contemporary drama set among fruit pickers in the Midlands. Rudkin's is a hard play to pin down. It combines everyday realism with a sense of ancient sacrificial ritual and mythology, and culminates in the violent murder and on-stage beheading of an Irish tramp known as Shakespeare. Predictably, the playwright was accused of revelling in violence for its own sake, but the play also carries clear resonances of Pinter (it was famously nicknamed *The Peartaker*), not least when – in an echo of the attack on Stanley in *The Birthday Party* – the persecution of the tramp is instigated by the deliberate smashing of his glasses. *Afore Night Come* remains a distinctive and compelling drama which carries powerful metaphorical overtones; at the climax, a mist drifts across the stage as the decapitation of the tramp coincides with the deafening roar of a helicopter spraying the fruit – and the people – with a chemical poisonous to humans.[57]

Back at the Royal Court, Ann Jellicoe's *The Knack* – 'an outrageous comedy about sex and young people'[58] – had provoked plenty of passion and discussion: 'Red Meat Returns to the Royal Court', said the *Daily Mail*,[59] while for Kenneth Tynan it was 'a feminist docu-ment' and 'an attack on the dominant male and the submissive female who puts up with him'.[60] Or, as the *Evening Standard* headline put it (in what was unlikely to have been intended as a compliment): 'only a woman could write about sex like this'.[61] The Royal Court also staged John Osborne's two satirical *Plays for England*, one attacking royalty and the other press corruption, though his attack on English society was not generally well reviewed: 'his hatred has the effect of blinding his eyes, choking his throat, and clogging his pen' and 'Osborne Misses with Both Barrels' were not untypical judgements.[62]

Alongside Arden's *Workhouse Donkey* and Theatre Workshop's *Oh, What a Lovely War!*, 1963 brought Spike Milligan's irreverent and occasionally political comedy *The Bed-Sitting Room*, as well as *Skyvers*, a study of a disaffected generation of young people in their final days at a comprehensive school, written by the Jamaican-born playwright Barry Reckord. The RSC– after long arguments and extensive negoti-ation with the Lord Chamberlain's Office – gave the first British performances of Rolf Hochhuth's *The Representative*, a highly contro-versial German play and 'a violent indictment of Pope Pius XII, and tacitly, of Christianity itself, that the former made no overt gesture to prevent the wholesale massacre of Jews by Hitler'.[63] Performances of *The Representative* were approved only after the theatre agreed to insert material in the programme contesting these claims and telling a different version of history. Other highlights of 1964 included John Osborne's *Inadmissible Evidence*, Joe Orton's provocative first play *Entertaining Mr Sloane* and Peter Shaffer's *The Royal Hunt of the Sun*, with its notorious mime sequence in which Spanish conquistadors scale the Andes to invade a kingdom ruled over by Robert Stephens as Atahuallpa, the Sun God of the Incas. In a play which invites us to contrast European rationalism with the creative innocence of the pre-civilised, we witness a mimed massacre in which 'wave upon wave of Indians are slaughtered' by Spanish soldiers, until 'a vast blood-stained cloth' billows over the stage as 'howling Indians . . . rush off; their screams fill the theatre'.[64] Even here, perhaps, we can catch an echo of Artaud. Altogether more physically restrained was the National Theatre's production of Beckett's *Play* – in which a man and two women buried to their necks in urns recount through three separate and intercutting monologues the mundane story of an affair – speaking without pause or expression, and as if under interrogation by a spotlight which provokes their speech.

Such examples make the complaints about the lack of new plays somewhat surprising. However, there was also a growing challenge to the prevailing assumption that all theatre has at its heart the playwright and the word. In January 1963, the experimental director and writer Charles Marowitz suggested that 'the theatre is moving towards movement and silence'. Following Artaud, he declared that a new art form was developing in which 'imagery will be paramount, words relegated to the level of sound-objects, and gesture given a new and vital pertinence'.[65] Of course, such calls and predictions had been made before, but they had had relatively little effect on theatre in Britain. A few months later, Marowitz launched a more vehement attack: 'In fleeting moments of clarity, I suddenly see the contemporary theatre as a mouldy, gnarled and arthritic old man decked out in the latest Savile Row fashions', he taunted; 'No matter what shape it assumes, its stilted gait and tired old accent give it away. It thinks in old frames, moves in beaten paths.' The problem was not simply a matter of 'crusty old playwrights', but 'the entire diction of that theatre which no longer holds up; which begs to be annihilated'.[66]

In the same month, Marowitz was part of a performance event which was arguably the first example of 'Action Theatre' or 'a happening' to occur in Britain, and which reached the front pages of the newspapers. In September 1963, everyone who was anyone in the world of contemporary theatre attended an International Drama Conference in Edinburgh, timed to coincide with the Festival. The many contributors included Brook, Wesker, Tynan, Albee, Arden, Littlewood, Pinter and Priestley, and one speaker, the playwright John Mortimer, confidently told the conference 'that writers should be grateful that at present they were in a writer's theatre'.[67] Marowitz was unimpressed by the level of discussion and ideas on display:

The week had been filled with intellectual belching and critical one-upmanship . . . each delegate had his own definition of words like 'reality', 'style', 'commitment', 'aesthetics', etc. Ionesco, the long-awaited star attraction, arrived on the final afternoon, spoke about 50 words and then fell into an impenetrable silence. After twenty minutes of bored attendance, he left the platform for a smoke and never returned . . .[68]

On the final afternoon, the event was interrupted by a carefully planned and orchestrated intervention. Depending on your perspective, it was either a brilliant piece of provocative Dadaism or a childish stunt. Marowitz's role was to begin the event by giving a spurious but apparently serious lecture proposing the adoption of an official and definitive interpretation of *Waiting for Godot*, which was to be published in all future editions of the play. This was the starting point for a seven-minute event, the outline script of which reads as follows:

An audience member (Charles Lewsen) attacking the speaker for being unclear and not heroic enough.
From outside a tape of cable-pullers at work.
Low and barely audible organ sounds.
The silhouette of a large head at the top of the dome of the hall.
A second tape made from fragments of speeches at the conference.
A man walking the tiny ledge high up at the base of the dome.
Figures appearing at other windows high above the hall and occasionally staring down at the people.
An actress on the platform (Carrol Baker) beginning to stare at someone at the back of the hall (Allan Kaprow), eventually taking off a large fur coat and moving towards him across the tops of the audience seats.
A nude model (Anna Kesselaar) being whisked across the organ loft on a spotlight stand.
The men at the high windows . . . shouting 'Me! Can you hear? Me!'
Carrol Baker reaching Allan Kaprow and both running out of the hall together . . .
A bagpiper . . . crossing the top balcony.

A sheep skeleton hung on the giant flat with Cocteau's symbol of the conference.

The piper reaching the other end of the hall as all other sounds stopped, and a blue curtain behind the platform being dropped to reveal shelves containing about fifty white plaster death masks . . .

A woman with a baby, and a boy with a radio entering the hall, mounting the platform, looking at everything as if in a museum, and leaving.

The piper tapering off in the distance.[69]

Unfortunately, the event was accidentally announced to the audience in advance, but it still caused a furore in the hall and beyond.

The majority, led by an incensed Ken Tynan . . . deplored the interruption . . . Celebrated producers from Yugoslavia, India, Ireland and Germany called it 'nonsense' and 'child's play'. Joan Littlewood immediately came to its defence . . . Alexander Trocchi spat the word 'Dada' back into Tynan's face and exclaimed that critics could not simply explain away new forces in art by bundling them into ready-made classifications. Martin Esslin pointed out that the Happening had forced the conference to distinguish between what was real and what was contrived . . . Jack Gelber looked pained. Alan Schneider tried to change the subject. Edward Albee was non-commital.[70]

Inevitably, it was the 'Nude Girl Incident' that attracted the press.[71] The City Provost for Edinburgh described the disruption as the 'irresponsible actions of a few people sick in mind and heart', while Kesselaar, who had been paid four guineas for her role, was duly charged with having acted 'in a shameless and indecent manner' and John Calder, as conference organiser, with failing to prevent the incident.[72] But performance art, or performance as intervention, had arrived.

Aunt Edna versus the RSC

According to *Plays and Players*, 1964 was the year when 'Theatre of Cruelty replaced Theatre of the Absurd as the number one talking point'.[73] In January and February, Peter Brook and Charles Marowitz staged an experimental season at the LAMDA theatre club, a rotating series of short plays, including Artaud's own extraordinary *Spurt of Blood*. Later in the year, the project fed directly into the company's mainhouse season at the Aldwych, and it was this which stirred up bitter opposition. In June, the RSC revived *Afore Night Come*, which was licensed by the Lord Chamberlain only on condition that 'the severing of the murdered man's head ... takes place not only "upstage" of a tree but also with a screen of large boxes hiding it from the audience'.[74] In August they gave the premiere of Peter Weiss's *The Persecution and Assassination of Jean-Paul Marat as Performed by the Inmates of the Asylum of Charenton Under the Direction of the Marquis de Sade* (or *Marat/Sade*), a text influenced both by Brecht and Artaud, in which the actors play the inmates of an asylum, who are themselves performing a play about the French Revolution, in which Marat is stabbed to death in his bath by Charlotte Corday. Taking lessons from the Living Theatre, Brook aimed for an immersive performance with no clear start or finish, and the audience both enter and leave the auditorium with the inhabitants of the asylum on stage.

Marat/Sade carries an intellectual debate between its two principal characters, but it was above all the visual imagery which gave the performance its impact: a mass guillotining with buckets of blue and red blood to represent aristocracy and commoners, for example, and the whipping of a half-naked de Sade by Corday, carried out with her hair. Reviewers called it 'two hours of agony'; 'an assault on the senses, emotions and intellect that never stops'; 'a bloodbath violently attacking the emotions and sensibilities of any audience'.[75] *The Times* said it was an 'Ambitious Example of Theatre of Cruelty'; the *Guardian* that it would 'send Aunt Edna round the bend' but was 'the best theatre to be seen in London at the moment'; Bernard Levin in the *Daily Mail* described it as 'one of the most amazing plays I've ever seen', which came 'as close as this imperfect world is ever likely to get to the *Gesamtkunstwerk* of which Richard Wagner dreamed, in which every element, every force, that the theatre could provide would fuse in one overwhelming experience'.[76]

Others were less ready to endorse the direction the RSC seemed to be taking, and a campaign which targeted not just this production but the whole ethos which it seemed to typify quickly built up. Murmurings of discontent had already been expressed when the RSC staged *Victor*, a French satire on the bourgeoisie by Roger Vitrac. *Victor* had attracted considerable advance publicity, following some judicious leaking to the press of correspondence between the RSC and the Lord Chamberlain. He had particularly objected to a scene involving a woman who is unable to stop farting. ('Cut "Who goes pop, pop, pop all the time" . . . "I'd like you to fart for me" . . . "She went phut, phut, phut" . . . "You can have a belly ache without needing to do biggies".') The RSC eventually substituted the opening bars of Beethoven's Fifth Symphony played on a tuba for the actual sounds, but this was not enough to appease everybody: 'There is little more now short of the actual sexual act left to be done on the English Stage and the London Theatre is suffering badly from a number of plays which have offended public taste, and driven away audiences in thousands.'[77] The *Daily Telegraph* critic attacked 'the intelligentsia cordon' guarding London theatres and supposedly dictating their repertoires.[78] The theatre correspondent of the *Evening News* joined in the debate with an article entitled 'Dare you take your daughter to the theatre?' Bill Boorne said he was 'all for the theatre attracting new audiences', but warned managements they should 'take care not to drive away those they have had for years'. He mocked the focus in the RSC season ('There is, of course, so little cruelty in the world that we need to be reminded of it in the playhouse') but his attacks extended over a wider field, lumping together some pretty disparate examples, including Orton's *Entertaining Mr Sloane*: 'This sort of play and those by Brecht and Samuel Beckett leave audiences baffled and bewildered,' he insisted; 'They have done as much damage to the theatre as anyone.' Such works, he declared, could never be commercially successful, because their appeal was inherently narrow: 'So many of the weirdies – authors and plays – do not appeal to families at all,' he complained; 'Mum and Dad hate 'em. They would never dream of taking the children.' Why, he asked, were theatres abandoning what people really wanted?

> *The Mousetrap* is now in its 12th year. *Boeing-Boeing* is in its third. *Half a Sixpence* has had more than 500 performances. *Oliver!* is in its fourth year. Harry Secombe and *Pickwick!* is packing them in every night at the Saville. *A Funny Thing Happened on the Way to the Forum* is a money-spinner at the Strand. Brian Rix is a permanent magnet at the Whitehall. And *The Black and White Minstrels* lure people from all over the country.
> FAMILY FAVOURITES, ALL OF THEM.[79]

In August, Peter Cadbury, the influential chairman of Keith Prowse and Company Ltd, used his annual address to shareholders to launch an attack on plays that were 'unsuitable and unacceptable to a large part of the public', and which depended on language and events that 'reflect the lowest forms of human life'. He was supported by Peter Saunders, a former president of the Society of West End Managers (and the producer of Agatha Christie's *Mousetrap*) who proposed awarding an 'F for filth' label to such plays. Cadbury told *The Times* that he objected 'to plays that rely for their appeal solely on the uninhibited use of a gamekeeper's vernacular' and called for 'a stricter control to discourage profanity and to spare embarrassment to those who go to the theatre to be entertained'.[80] He also claimed he had theatre's long-term interests at heart, since it was important not to alienate the majority:

> Our box-office returns show how small is the potential audience for plays that are written only to shock, as compared with the universal appeal of a show like *My Fair Lady*; and the short time they run proves only that the public will not support them. The goose in this case is the theatre-going public, which will merely be turned away if dramatic art is to be sacrificed at the altar of profanity.[81]

Next to weigh in and express his support for a restoration of tradi-tional values was the impresario Emile Littler. Littler was actually on the governing board of the RSC, but he now publicly attacked the company for producing 'a programme of dirt plays' which were 'entirely out of keeping with our public image and with having the Queen as our Patron'.[82] Val Gielgud – a playwright and BBC producer/director – also agreed that it was 'time that self-consciously intellectual critics, and devotees of those Theatres so accurately labelled as 'Of Cruelty' and 'The Absurd', were reminded that Entertainment is not a dirty word, and that the Theatre exists for the benefit of audiences rather than for the amusement of certain producers, writers and actors'.[83]

The RSC held an open discussion on the issue. In the press, Peter Brook – 'the MAN IN THE MIDDLE of the "dirty" theatre row' – was quoted as saying that 'Violence is the natural artistic language of the times', and that 'disturbance . . . was the proper function of the Royal Shakespeare Company'.[84] With resignations being both threat-ened and demanded, Peter Hall, the overall director of the RSC, took up the gauntlet, accusing Littler and Cadbury of being 'anti-art'.[85] And – to its credit – *The Times* ultimately came down against Cadbury, suggesting his 'remedy . . . would be worse than the disease he purports to have diagnosed'.[86] Perhaps surprisingly, that old-fashioned playwright who pre-dated the Royal Court revolution, Terence Rattigan, also rallied wittily to the defence of the new. Rattigan had once insisted that he wrote for the prim and decorous Aunt Ednas of the world, and his well-made dramas had become an object of contempt for many in the post-1956 generation of play-wrights and directors. However, Rattigan was now an enthusiastic (and financial) supporter of Joe Orton's early work. He mocked the 'mildly fatuous . . . vapourings' of Cadbury and Littler, and made his point through satire by suggesting that the Home Secretary 'gives up fussing about all those harmless strip-tease joints and makes a raid on the Aldwych Theatre, to arrest all those dirty-minded people in the lobby'. 'Finally, I suggest he goes on to Chichester and collects his biggest haul yet, tier upon tier of breathlessly excited, brutish, inhuman, un-British pigs who are unashamedly revelling nightly in a theatre of "violence, lust and cruelty", with a "ritual killing" thrown in, by the notorious W. Shakespeare.'[87]

1965–69

By the mid-point in the decade, Aunt Ednas everywhere would presumably have deleted the RSC as well as the Royal Court from the list of places and companies offering a good night out, but there were still plenty of other theatres which could be trusted. In 1965, *Encore* offered a depressed overview of a largely moribund mainstream theatre: 'Of the thirty-six commercial theatres in London's West End, twenty are presenting musicals; eight are showing comedies or farces; there are two thrillers and a few miscellaneous items like one-man shows and period pieces.'[88] They might also have mentioned the Daleks, now turning up in pantomimes (including, terrifyingly, in *Babes in the Wood*) and with their own Christmas show – *The Curse of the Daleks* – at Wyndham's Theatre. (*The Times* noted that they 'possess a magnetism lacking in the flesh-and-blood characters', but that the dialogue was 'strangely reminiscent of British war films'.[89]) *Encore* acknowledged that the RSC, the National and perhaps the Royal Court provided alternatives but this was not enough to challenge the domination of a tradition which, it now seemed, had not, after all, been seriously damaged:

> Nothing that the two major companies are doing eradicates the fact that the London theatre is in a dismal state. Managements are more cautious and conservative than ever before ... holding their crumbling fort with thrillers and the threat of old Coward stand-bys ... looking more and more towards the family comedy and the 'happy' musical. One has nothing against either form; what is distressing is the monstrous imbalance.[90]

With the exception of Bond's *Saved* and Pinter's *The Homecoming*, 1965 was a fairly quiet year for new texts. Harold Hobson 'noticed no new plays of particular promise', and found even *The Homecoming* to be 'a diseased and in some ways a deplorable play'. One or two critics drew attention to *The Investigation* by the German playwright Peter Weiss, and *Road* by the Nigerian playwright Wole Soyinka, but they agreed about the 'hollowness of writing talent' and the 'paucity of new names' emerging from within Britain: 'Osborne marched backwards . . . Pinter marked time', only 'Arden crept stealthily forwards'. It was also a year of 'excessively bad' new musicals and 'swank revivals', as the 'commercial theatre made a come-back'.[91] The annual award of the London Theatre Critics for the best new play went to Frank Marcus's West End success *The Killing of Sister George* – a work entirely conventional in form and carefully crafted for West End success. The central character of Marcus's play is an actress whose character is killed off from a radio soap opera to improve the ratings. But what made this old-fashioned comedy distinctive was that she – and all the other principal characters – were clearly lesbians. The play attracted little – if any – protest, perhaps because its treatment of the theme was innocuous; there is no direct discussion of sexuality at all. But perhaps this also reflected changing social attitudes. By contrast, one home-grown play which did have the Aunt (and Uncle) Ednas reaching for their smelling salts was Joe Orton's *Loot*. What was striking about *Loot* was its mixture of outrageous and extreme comedy (farce) with the subject of death – in particular the use of a corpse, shoved first into a cupboard, and then into a coffin where the dead person's son is hiding the proceeds of a bank robbery. For many, such a display of 'shocking bad taste' was more than enough.[92] But equally offensive was the depiction of an incompetent and casually corrupt police detective ('waste your time on the truth and you'll be pounding the beat till the day you die'[93]), and a nurse who is responsible for the deaths of seven (and counting) husbands. 'I do not think I have ever witnessed such an unpleasant and wickedly-worded play in my life', wrote one complainant who left before the end of the first Act; 'I can only say I was thankful that our women-folk and young people were not present.'[94] Several reviewers questioned whether *Loot* had any real point behind it, but *The Times* saw this as precisely what was innovative about Orton: 'Audiences at present seem disposed to accept the theatre's new range of permissible subject-matter only if some "serious" purpose is involved. Mr Orton's plays ventilate the atmosphere by claiming this material as equally legitimate for farce.'[95]

One minor breakthrough in 1965 was the first public performance in Britain of Frank Wedekind's *Spring Awakening* at the Royal Court. Written in the 1890s, and long considered a seminal text of German Expressionism, this exploration of adolescent sexuality had been refused a licence on many occasions, and was permitted now only with extensive cuts. The Lord Chamberlain's reader described it as 'one of the most loathsome and depraved plays I have ever read', 'a sick, diseased unhealthy play with no redeeming features whatsoever'.[96] But it was a much more recent German playwright who took centre stage, for 1965 was also the year when the reputation and significance of Bertolt Brecht impinged on a wider British audience, following the Berliner Ensemble's visit from Communist East Germany to the Old Vic with *The Threepenny Opera, The Resistible Rise of Arturo Ui, The Days of the Commune* and *Coriolanus*. The company also ran a three-day symposium on Brecht which, according to *The Times*, was 'one of the most persuasive advertisements for life on the other side yet to have appeared in this country'.[97] Critics hailed the productions for showing us 'the way Brecht wanted the theatre to be: skimming, speculative, beautiful, fun'.[98] Harold Hobson – no great admirer of Brecht's politics – wrote an article headlined 'Brecht for grown-ups' in which he insisted on 'the superiority of these four productions to anything that has been offered us of Brecht in English'.[99] Although there were dissenting voices – particularly in relation to the 'travesty' of *Coriolanus* ('The Man Who Made the Bard a Bore') and *The Days of the Commune* ('this ponderous and shoddy piece of propaganda') the widespread critical enthusiasm signalled that a reappraisal of Brecht was overdue.[100] As the *Daily Mail* put it after watching *Arturo Ui*: 'The anti-Brecht chorus that has been gaining in volume in recent years (thanks largely to some inept productions badly acted in translation) has, after last night, only one decent course open to it! To go jump in the lake.'[101] So successful was the visit in raising Brecht's reputation that even the Queen was taken to see a production of *Galileo* in Edinburgh – some kind of measure of status, surely.

The year 1965 also brought two significant cultural innovations which would have considerable implications for theatre. One was the decision by Harold Wilson's Labour government to appoint a Minister of the Arts, and to choose for this role the veteran MP and widow of Aneurin Bevan, Jennie Lee. Lee would prove herself an inspirational and dedicated minister who did much to ensure the expansion of funding through the Arts Council, and who helped to establish more firmly its independence from government: 'Political control is a shortcut to boring, stagnant art', she declared, and she also insisted on the right – the duty – of the arts to tread new paths, even when the destinations could not be predicted: 'there must be freedom to experiment, to make mistakes, to fail, to shock – or there can be no new beginnings'. But as Lee herself acknowledged: 'It is hard for any government to accept this.'[102]

The other new arrival in 1965 was the modern Theatre-in-Education movement (TIE), which was born in Coventry. When Gordon Vallins arrived at the Belgrade Theatre as assistant to the director he came with a background in teaching; dissatisfied with the theatre's educational policy, which consisted of little more than bringing largely uninterested school parties to an annual Shakespeare production, his first initiative was to develop a youth theatre group which devised a show about life in post-war Coventry. In an extraordinary review, Albert Hunt, sometime collaborator with Peter Brook and the RSC, described *Out of the Ashes* as 'by far the most exciting thing I've seen in British theatre this year'. The performance, he said, had the 'freshness, immediacy and invention' which was lacking in most professional theatre:

> Dressed in black sweaters and dark jeans, and using a popular idiom which was part of their own experience, the group gave us Coventry, Dresden, Hiroshima, the Berlin Wall, all the major events that have helped to shape our lives, and they presented these events in terms of children's games, pop songs, radio programmes.[103]

Vallins then proposed that the Belgrade should establish a permanent company of people trained both as actors and teachers who would offer a free service to schools. Supported by the local education authority, three interactive shows were created for infants, juniors and secondary pupils, and in 1966 Belgrade TIE was established as a permanent and funded company – a model which a number of other theatres quickly followed or adapted.[104]

Documentary theatre

'It was overdue. It was inevitable that it should come. And sure enough it has arrived.' So declared *Plays and Players* at the end of 1966.[105] The 'it' was 'Theatre of Fact', for documentary theatre was 'now fashionably in'.[106] Although there was no shared understanding of what the term meant – both Arnold Wesker's *The Kitchen* and Peter Shaffer's *Royal Hunt* were described as 'documentary' by some critics[107] – the form had a history in Britain that went back at least thirty years to Unity Theatre and its Living Newspapers. But if its definition and boundaries remained necessarily vague, it was a genre which was indeed beginning to take centre stage. At Stoke's Victoria Theatre, Peter Cheeseman had already presented a series of musical documentaries about local history, researched and authored by the company. Moreover, Cheeseman was adamant that staging the past was anything but a retreat from the present: 'I find that by using historical subjects one can comment with greater freedom on contemporary situations,' he insisted. Following *The Jolly Potters* and *The Staffordshire Rebels*, his most successful and acclaimed production was *The Knotty*, staged in 1966, which focused on the history of railways in the region, but has as 'its real subject . . . the impact of science on a community'.[108]

Cheeseman was far from alone in the field. *Oh, What a Lovely War!* was one of several productions by Theatre Workshop to which the slippery 'documentary' label could be applied. In 1964, Oxford University's Experimental Theatre Club presented *Hang Down Your Head and Die*, an attack on capital punishment which presented a range of materials in the form of a circus 'where the clowns are macabre figures who build gallows, shift scenery, or become judge and jury as occasion demands'.[109] The performance had seemed likely to be banned until its case was taken up by MPs and members of the House of Lords. In 1965, the RSC planned to produce a documentary drama about the 1926 General Strike, closely based on historical documents, and incorporating well-known historical figures, including George V. The production fell through, but in the same year they presented *The Investigation*, Peter Weiss's edited adaptation of the Nazi war crimes trials in Frankfurt. The RSC had already staged *The Representative*, and in 1966, after long-drawn-out arguments and negotiations, they were finally able to produce an equally controversial text *In the Matter of J. Robert Oppenheimer*. Written by the German playwright Heinar Kipphardt, the drama focused on the 1954 American security investigation of the senior nuclear physicist and 'father of the atomic bomb', Robert Oppenheimer, in which he was humiliated and discredited for his Communist affiliations. It was sometimes suggested that Oppenheimer's real 'crime' in American eyes was a reluctance to allow his experiments to be channelled to the creation of a hydrogen bomb, so the underlying theme and implications of this play were anything but remote.

Kipphardt's text drew heavily on the 3,000-page transcript of the month-long Atomic Energy Commission hearing. 'Every effort has been made to give a faithful interpretation of what happened without altered emphasis', the RSC insisted, but it set a series of alarm bells ringing for the censorship. 'All those impersonated are living and the event is very recent', warned one of the Lord Chamberlain's advisers. Especially concerning was the question of setting a precedent: 'this would be a dramatic representation of an actual trial of recent date', wrote the adviser, which 'might open the flood gates' and lead to 'a mass of plays depicting trial scenes involving living people – e.g. the Ward/Profumo case'.[110] Another problem in the equation was how the Americans might respond, and after consultations with Washington via their ambassador in London, the RSC production was delayed by a requirement that the company check the absolute accuracy of the playtext against the transcript of the actual proceedings. The production eventually opened in a private performance at the Hampstead Theatre, while the RSC and the Lord Chamberlain quibbled over the authenticity of the script, and the juxtaposition of fictional monologues with verbatim material. Eventually a licence was issued, and in the late autumn the production transferred from Hampstead to the West End. It divided the critics. For some, Kipphardt's play had 'all the excitement of a court room thriller with the extra thrill of being a true story'; it was 'the most successful example so far of the Theatre of Fact'.[111] Others continued to dismiss the form: 'this is not *theatre* in any artistic sense of the word', wrote one reviewer; 'I cannot see the course of drama advancing very far along this road.'[112]

Staging Vietnam

There was even more friction around another RSC documentary involving the Americans and war which opened at the RSC's main London base at almost the same time. *US* was devised and created under the direction of Peter Brook, and although it too was based on fact, and in some cases documents, it was far less tied to these and far more speculative and imaginative in approach. The title itself carried two meanings. On the one hand it names the United States, but the 'us' is also Britain or, more specifically, the mainly young and leftish movement which opposed the war and was seeking the most effective way to try to stop it. The performance documented aspects of the war and the history of Vietnam, as well as the experiences and views of the company devising the production. It was not for nothing that the actors retained their own names. Punctuated by the powerful and direct poetry of Adrian Mitchell set to music by Richard Peaslee ('I'm really rocking the delta/from coast to coast/Got em crawling for shelter/Got em burning like toast./And the President told me/That it wouldn't take long/But I know I'm in heaven/When I'm zapping the cong') and sometimes stylised action (the above verse is performed while the chorus mime a torture sequence and the killing of a group of Vietcong) the performance slips between styles, settings and issues. Sometimes it is a history of Vietnam, sometimes it evokes the American invasion and the bombing and napalming of innocent civilians, and sometimes it focuses on the impotence and desperation of those who oppose and want desperately to end the war. Often it quotes directly from the words of politicians and other public figures, or presents the audience with simple facts. At other times it juxtaposes childish verse patterns with the horrors of what is going on ('You put your bombers in, you put your conscience out/You take the human being and you twist it all about'). In the final scene, Glenda Jackson delivers a devastating speech directly to the audience, wishing on us the reality of war as the only thing which will finally break through our comfort and complacency:

> I want it to come HERE! I want to see it in an English house, among the floral chintzes and the school blazers and the dog leads hanging in the hall. I would like us to be tested. I would like a fugitive to run to our doors and say hide me – and know if we hid him we might get shot and if we turned him away we would have to remember that for ever. I would like to know which of my nice well-meaning acquaintances would collabo-rate, which would betray, which would talk first under torture – and which would become a torturer. I would like to smell the running bowels of fear, over the English Sunday morning smell of gin and the roasting joint, and hyacinth. I would like to see an English dog playing on an English lawn with part of a burned hand. I would like to see a gas grenade go off at an English flower show, and nice English ladies crawling in each other's sick. And all this I would like to be photographed and filmed so that someone a long way off, safe in his chair, could watch us in our indignity!

At the end of this speech, another actor carries on a box, from which he releases real butterflies into the auditorium. Then he appears to take a last one out and set light to it. The stage direction insists: 'We cannot tell if it is real or false.' The actors freeze, the house lights come on and 'the actors stay immobile until everyone has left the theatre'.[113] There was no curtain, no curtain call, no applause and no closure. As one review put it, 'Their fixed gaze seemed to dare us to go out and not do something about trying to stop the war.'[114]

Inevitably, *US* received very mixed reviews; many were angered by what they perceived as self-righteousness and an anti-American stance. Others found themselves implicated and shattered by the experience of witnessing it. There were debates, too, about what to call it – a play, a documentary, journalism or 'a happening'. For *The Times* it was an 'event [which] conforms to no existing theatrical category and lies outside the scope of conventional criticism'. The Bishop of Woolwich said it was 'a liturgy'. To Harold Hobson, it was 'the noblest and the finest thing done on the English stage in our lifetime'.[115] Brook himself was less satisfied: 'I would say we had done something which is full of bits that are clumsy, thin and bad,' he said. But it was better than nothing: 'The plays do not exist,' complained Brook, 'and this show is a condemnation of the authors who have not produced a single bloody thing on Vietnam.'[116]

Frustration with the failure of the British theatre to engage with the war in Vietnam was not confined to the *US* company. The sense that too many performances anaesthetised audiences to the horrors of the real world (allowing them to hang up their brains in the cloakroom), was the motivation for a coordinated protest organised by the Vietnam Action Group in the month before *US* opened. On 26 September 1966, speakers from the group disrupted performances in six major London theatres (including Wyndham's, the Mermaid, the Palace, the Strand and the Ambassadors) by infiltrating the stage during performances to make speeches attacking the American government's involvement in Vietnam, and the British government's tacit support and complicity.[117]

There were other and less explicit ways in which art and performance were responding to the violence and nihilism of a world teetering on the verge of apocalypse. In September 1966, Covent Garden was the setting for 'Destruction in Art', a symposium to which artists, poets and scientists contributed. This featured contemporary work by artists such as Hermann Nitsch, whose performances took place over several days and involved the ritualised killing of animals and the spattering of audiences with their blood. Other artists introduced the concept of auto-destructive art, with one burning towers of books 'to demonstrate directly his view that Western culture was burned out'.[118] Meanwhile, the RSC revived *The Revenger's Tragedy*, a violent

Jacobean drama barely seen for 350 years. 'The times have caught up with it', said a review of Trevor Nunn's production; 'The representation of a self-destructive society without morality . . . is no longer a neurotic fantasy', and it was therefore 'only logical that the RSC should revive this apocalyptic death-rattle of a play'.[119] Albert Hunt took a different route. In 1967, to coincide with the fiftieth anniversary of the Soviet Revolution, the 'solid Yorkshire city' of Bradford took on the role of St Petersburg in 1917, as Hunt worked with 300 students on 'an experiment in public drama' which involved a 're-creation of some of the events of the October revolution'.[120]

Race

One of the performances disrupted by the Vietnam Action Group was at the Victoria Palace, which for five years had been presenting two performances each evening by the Black and White Minstrels. The show was based on a popular television programme in which white singers blacked up to perform song and dance routines, evoking historical minstrel troupes from the southern United States. 'Musical syrup and costumes exploding with sequins and feathers', as one review described the stage incarnation.[121] While some resented it on account of its politics (not to mention its aesthetics), the television show had big audiences and was successful enough to be scheduled at peak time in Christmas Day programming. Meanwhile, the stage version featured more than once in the Royal Variety evening entertainment. In May 1967, the Campaign Against Racial Discrimination called for the BBC to withdraw 'this hideous impersonation', which 'causes much distress to coloured people' and 'creates serious misunderstanding between the races'. It gave 'a wrong impression to impressionable whites', since 'All it is intended to do is to caricature coloured people and stereotype them'.[122] It would be hard to argue with these claims now, but the BBC did not back down. Indeed, a column in *The Times* which celebrated the arrival of colour television managed in one short paragraph to patronise at least three groups of people: 'The apparent paradox of putting the Black and White

Minstrels in colour is shown to be quite hollow', wrote their reviewer; 'It may sound Irish, but black and white looks even better in colour, and the girls in the show are even prettier (I now know that at least one of the blonde dancers has blue eyes).'[123]

By the time the stage version of the Black and White Minstrels closed in the summer of 1969 it was second only to *The Mousetrap* in terms of consecutive performances, which stood at over 4,300. *The Times* wrote an editorial paying tribute and regretting its passing. Not to worry; within six months it was back again in a new version, guaranteed, as one of its less favourable critics put it, to 'entrance old ladies of all ages and sexes'.[124] There was not much support even in the liberal part of the mainstream media for the objectors: 'Recently there arose a complaint that the show was in some way a slur on coloured people, which would be like saying that Madam Butterfly offended the Japanese', wrote the *Guardian*'s main theatre reviewer dismissively; 'This cant is exposed for what it is by the show, which . . . is animated by affection, not contempt.'[125] Nothing patronising there!

Stage plays addressing racial issues, along with plays by black writers and stage representation of black characters, were few and far between. In 1962 the Lord Chamberlain refused to allow an American revue sketch in which the racist governor of a southern state discovers when he dies that God is black.[126] An exception from the early 1960s was *Nymphs and Satires*, a gently satirical revue set in Africa in which all the sketches and songs focused on issues of racial segregation. In one scene a white American hunter arrives at a hotel in a newly independent African country which is now run by a black majority government, and gradually realises that the rules about who can stay there have been reversed: 'maybe I'm not all *that* white, anyway. Kinda off-white, ya dig me? Sort of used ivory. How about that?' In possibly the funniest scene, a deranged scientist (played by Nigel Hawthorne) performs a long monologue in which he questions assumptions made about the offspring of interracial marriages:

> Is it necessarily true that when a black natural object is crossed or mated with a white natural object, as it were, compromise of colour is the result? . . . Among rocks, black and white

specimens are found in almost overwhelming abundance . . .
What would happen, do you suppose, were we to mate, say,
basalt and moonstone? Can we say for certain that the result
would be a milky basalt or a darker moonstone? . . . Might it
not be an altogether new stone with a marbleised vein in both
black and white.

He then presents examples from the animal kingdom in which black
and white survive separately, culminating with the zebra:

A fifty-fifty usage of the best genes. No mixing-up, no
watering-down, no giving-in . . . Why might we not breed a
whole new race of striped men, marching towards the golden
future, shoulder to shoulder; black shoulder this side, white
shoulder that. White cheek by black jowl, left arm black, right
arm white. Some, God willing, might have stripes running this
way (*demonstrates*) or across (*demonstrates*) or sideways or zig
zagging around . . .[127]

In the early 1960s the Royal Court staged, unusually, a couple of
plays by the Jamaican-born playwright Barry Reckord – though
Skyvers had to be performed with an all-white cast, because the theatre
'could not find any black actors'.[128] As early as 1960, the Court had
produced Reckord's partly autobiographical *You in Your Small Corner*
– 'a slice of life play, set in Brixton, with the slice cut rather near the
knuckle'.[129] In 1965, the RSC presented James Baldwin's *Blues for Mr
Charlie*, a play about race relations in the southern United States,
based on the true story of a murder in Mississippi, and in the same
year Liverpool's Everyman Theatre presented *Jack of Spades*, a musical
about a doomed relationship between a black man and a white
woman written by Norman Beaton, a Guyana-born actor. In 1968
Beaton also wrote and played the lead role in *Sit Down Banna* – 'A
glum play with music' – about a group of immigrants from Guyana
who become involved in a seedy world of abortion, drugs and
extra-marital relationships. It was, said the Lord Chamberlain's reader,
'the worst possible advertisement for racial integration'.[130]

In 1966, Wole Soyinka's *The Lion and the Jewel* received a full production at the Royal Court, given by what the *Daily Telegraph* called 'a Negro Company'.[131] Soyinka had been a contemporary in the Royal Court Writers' Group of Edward Bond and Ann Jellicoe, and this was not his first play to be staged in London; indeed, the Stratford East Theatre Royal production of *The Road* (presented as part of a Commonwealth Arts Festival), had been chosen by the *Observer* critic as one of the best new plays of 1965. On a narrative level, this new play focused on the clash of traditional with imported Western values which are imposed on a Nigerian village. But it was as much the form – which incorporated song, dance and clowning – which broke fresh ground for the Royal Court. *The Times* was enthusiastic for what this brought to the British theatre tradition: 'this work alone is enough to establish Nigeria as the most fertile new source of English-speaking drama since Synge's discovery of the Western Isles', enthused a remarkably fulsome review; 'Even this comparison does Soyinka less than justice . . . to find any parallel for his work in English drama you have to go back to the Elizabethans.' *The Road* was a 'superb comedy' by 'a highly sophisticated craftsman', impressive for 'the sheer ingenuity' of the plot, as well as the 'originality of scene construction'.[132] But other reviewers were made uneasy by the use of 'a lot of near-Shakespearean language' within an African village.[133] Certainly, such fluency was a far cry from the gritty realism and limited language favoured by many plays of the period. The previous year, London's Commonwealth Arts Festival had also presented two plays by another Nigerian playwright, John Pepper Clark. *The Masquerade* and *Song of a Goat* were described as 'wholly indigenous and defiantly unsophisticated', and again the poetic expansiveness of the language was difficult for some people to take: 'Their prime fault is that they beat about the verbal bush and are frequently clogged with metaphor.'[134] By contrast, *The Times* delighted in the 'richly expressive range of speech idioms' in *The Lion and the Jewel*, with its sparring match fought through proverbs.[135] But more typically, Soyinka's play was patronisingly described as 'mild and artless', derivative and reactionary'. It was 'a simple parable', a play of 'naïve and childlike simplicity'.[136]

In an article published in 1967 entitled 'Theatre of Integration',

Michael Billington reported on the achievements of an amateur multi-racial theatre group which had just performed Pinter's *A Night Out*. 'If the Soyinka play helps to gain more recognition for the coloured actor', he wrote, 'it will also have served a useful purpose'; as Billington pointed out, 'the opportunities for coloured artists in this country are pitifully few'.[137] At the end of the 1950s the black American actor Paul Robeson had actually played Othello in London. But in 1964 Sir Laurence Olivier had no hesitation in playing the role for the National Theatre, or with going to extraordinary lengths (including vocal training to lower his voice by an octave and up to three hours of body make-up before each performance) to impersonate a 'Negro' as effectively as possible. Olivier's Othello has gone down in theatre history as one of the most powerful acting performances of the second half of the twentieth century. The film version which survived is less entirely convincing now, and not everyone was persuaded by Olivier's approach even at the time:

> His West Indian accent is totally meaningless. This performance has nothing whatever to do with Othello as Shakespeare wrote it . . . What he gives us is a Notting Hill Gate Negro – a law student from Ghana – and his portrait is made up of all the ludicrous liberal cliché attitudes towards Negroes: beautiful skin, marvellous sense of rhythm, wonderful way of walking . . .[138]

Three years later, the National, under Olivier's stewardship, staged the premiere of Peter Nichols's *The National Health*, 'a comedic dance of death' set in a hospital which also represented 'a microcosm of our society'.[139] The cast includes four significant black characters, but Olivier sought to persuade the play's director, Michael Blakemore, that getting 'the regular girls in the company' to 'black up' would be the best solution: 'Much as I admire the negro races', he declared, 'I'm no great admirer of their histrionic abilities.'[140] Fortunately his advice was ignored, and Cleo Sylvestre became the first black actor to play a leading role at the National Theatre. But even after the production had opened, Olivier was involved in a plan to get one of the black actors replaced by a white one. And it is also striking that even though they were working there, none of the four black actors was cast – or invited to audition – for other plays in the National's repertoire.[141]

The American avant-garde

American companies and artists exerted a crucial impact on the British avant-garde of the late 1960s, both aesthetically and politically. In 1967 the Royal Court staged a controversial (and unlicensed) trilogy of short plays by Jean-Claude van Itallie under the collective and ironic title of *America Hurrah*. First staged in the States by the Open Theatre, they were – according to the playwright – 'about aspects of being alive right here and now in America today – with all the implications that has, including the war in Vietnam and the advertising on the subways and everything else'.[142] Presented as 'the spearhead of a revolutionary movement',[143] it was a fragmentary piece about a divided society – a provocative and sometimes nihilistic attack on the values of contemporary civilisation. 'It does not so much break new ground as smash it', wrote the *Daily Mail*; 'This view of America makes the Congo look civilised.'[144] In the same year at Stratford East, Joan Littlewood staged *Macbird* – a play by Barbara Garson, 'a 25-year-old graduate from the rebellious university of California at Berkeley',[145] which provocatively grafted together the murder of President Kennedy (and the corruption of his successor, Lyndon Johnson) with Shakespeare's *Macbeth*:

> The witches are three agitators, a beatnik, a negro and an anti-Vietnam war demonstrator. They prophesy that Johnson will be Senate Leader (as he already is) then Vice President and finally President. The assassination of Kennedy ... leans dangerously to the opinion that Johnson, if not exactly responsible for it (and the later incidents that befell other members of the Kennedy family), was grateful for it for removing all barriers to his advancement. He dies of a heart attack when he learns that Robert Kennedy (Macduff) has no heart.[146]

The year 1967 also brought the first visit to Britain by La MaMa, an experimental company founded in the early 1960s in New York by Ellen Stewart. Stewart stated at the outset that her company was 'dedicated to the playwright', and it produced plays by writers including Eugene O'Neill, Sam Shepard and Harold Pinter. However, she emphasised her commitment to writers who worked on an audience's subconscious rather than on their conscious or rational minds, creating 'subliminal theatre'. It was an approach she considered more likely to appeal to a younger generation: 'People in their fifties and sixties aren't attuned to this.'[147] In August 1967, La MaMa was both acclaimed ('the sensation of the Festival' – the *Observer*[148] – and 'far and away the most adventurous and exciting offering in this year's Festival drama programme' – *The Times*[149]) and denounced (local magistrates attempted to close the production down) for *Futz*, a play by Rochelle Owens in which a farmer falls in love with his pig, Amanda. *Futz* transferred to London, and although La MaMa was supposedly committed to the voice of the playwright, the spoken text was not necessarily the priority of the production: 'The shouted dialogue is largely inaudible and anyway isn't of prime importance', suggested the *Observer*; 'the stage is awash with gyrating rhythms, ritual eruptions and frenzied coupling'.[150] And *The Times* agreed: 'they use words as much for sheer sound value as for sense, and for much of the time language gives way to barnyard noises and choric rhythms'.[151]

At the same time as presenting *Futz* and three short plays in one London theatre, La MaMa also opened Paul Foster's *Tom Paine*. 'The show is the most impressive demonstration so far of the company's skills', wrote Irving Wardle in *The Times*. 'They have the acrobatic techniques to create a storm-tossed ship, a bear-pit, or a palace interior from a few multi-purpose props.'[152] However, although the title seemed to signal a historical and biographical element, the performance eschewed any responsibility for informing: 'The spectator must draw his own conclusions from what he sees on stage', warned the company's official programme; 'If he knows nothing of the life of Tom Paine he will not learn much from the play.'[153] As Peter Lewis in the *Daily Mail* reported: 'I went in knowing only that Tom Paine was the author of *The Rights of Man* and was mixed up in American independence and the French Revolution. The only extra thing I knew when I came out was that he drank.'[154] But to see this approach in purely negative terms was to fail to understand a new kind of playwriting, as the programme also sought to explain:

> Paul Foster uses the character of the great American patriot as a point of departure for a poetical work . . . [he] does not attempt to propose or develop a theme in conventional, chronological form nor does he try to re-create the man as he really was; he is likewise unconcerned with the events he precipitated or those that befell him . . . What emerges is more a massive prose chorale than a play in any recognisable form.[155]

The golden age

In 1966, Charles Marowitz warned: 'The English theatre has used the past ten years to catch up; now it is in danger of standing still again.' By way of contrast, he cited a festival of experimental theatre he had attended in Frankfurt 'where five out of the six presentations were not plays at all, but events, audience-assaults'.[156] Marowitz had long been arguing that play-based theatre was 'a moribund art-form' – a corpse which audiences and critics treated with an absurd and misguided reverence because they had not noticed the body was dead.[157] Certainly, some of the more striking performances of the late 1960s came from a different tradition. But claims about the death of the play and the playwright were surely exaggerated. In his retrospective analysis, Michael Billington argues that 'the period from 1964 to 1970 looks like a golden age: an equivalent to the first Elizabethan era', and that it produced 'a wealth of new writing'.[158] Leaving aside for the moment Arden, Bond, Pinter and Ayckbourn, this includes the final plays of Joe Orton, some of which reached the stage only after he had been murdered in August 1967; the arrival of Howard Brenton, whose *Gum and Goo*, *The Education of Skinny Spew*, *Revenge* and *Christie in Love* were all staged in 1969; and Peter Nichols's *A Day in the Death of Joe Egg* – a black comedy about bringing up a child with cerebral palsy, which employed a style reminiscent of pantomime and music hall, and which, according to *The Times*, 'significantly shifted our boundaries of taste'.[159]

In November 1968 came Peter Barnes's *The Ruling Class* – a play which used comedy rather than hard political analysis to make its political attack on that class – 'its values and viciousness, its perversions and pernicious charm, the different means it employs to maintain its dominant position'. Again, Barnes's theatre is rooted partly in music hall rather than naturalism, and his savage attacks on the Establishment – 'permeated by class hatred and by a loathing of the social, economic, and religious bastions of Western Society' – were compared to those of Ben Jonson.[160] The play opens with a speech based on John of Gaunt's famous celebration of Englishness in Shakespeare's *Richard II*, as the 13th Earl of Gurney, 'in full evening dress and medals at a banqueting table', calls a toast to the Society of St George:

13th Earl of Gurney Once the rulers of the greatest Empire
The world has ever known,
Ruled not by superior force or skill
But by sheer presence. (*Raises glass in a toast.*)
This teeming womb of privilege, this feudal state,
Whose shores beat back the turbulent sea of anarchy.
This ancient fortress, still commanded by the noblest
Of our royal blood; this ancient land of ritual.
This precious stone set in a silver sea.

Toastmaster My Lords, Ladies and Gentlemen. The toast is
– England. This precious stone set in a silver sea.

Within minutes we are watching the same 13th Earl of Gurney in his bedroom, dressed (or undressed) with the help of his servant, in white tutu ballet skirt, long underwear and sword, making his choice from a selection of ropes with which to 'relax' into a sexual fantasy ('may I suggest silk tonight, sir'), before accidentally hanging himself 'with a lustful gurgle'.[161]

This was nastier than the gentler satire of *Mrs Wilson's Diary*, which nevertheless created its own share of controversy. Based on a weekly column published in *Private Eye* which purported to be a description by the prime minister's wife of events in and around 10 Downing Street, *Mrs Wilson's Diary* seems relatively small beer now. But in 1967 it established a precedent in terms of who could be impersonated and ridiculed on stage, since not just one but most of its characters were well-known national and international political leaders currently occupying real positions of power. Written by Richard Ingrams and John Wells and staged by Theatre Workshop at Stratford East in September 1967, before transferring into the West End, the cast of characters included not only the PM, Harold Wilson and his wife, Gladys, but also the foreign secretary (George Brown), shown (not without foundation) to be more or less constantly imbibing alcohol, the home secretary (and future prime minister) Jim Callaghan and the French president, General de Gaulle. The narrative also involves Lyndon Johnson, the American president, and there is even a phone call from the Queen. The play begins with an announcement that Wilson has described US policy in Vietnam as 'utterly indefensible' and 'a crime against humanity', and that President Johnson's response has been to announce his intention to bomb London that evening. In the end, the Americans drop their bomb on Greenland by mistake, and the Wilsons retire to bed, singing an ode to cocoa as they go. However, the show was presented as 'an affectionate lampoon' (*The Times* said 'the effect is not one of political satire but of a good-natured party') and some critics pointed out that it was likely to persuade people that Wilson was more human and ordinary than he generally seemed in real life.[162]

Another big comic success of the later 1960s was Tom Stoppard's *Rosencrantz and Guildenstern Are Dead*, which focused on two minor characters from *Hamlet* who know little of what is going on, are lied to by those in power and end up dead. The play relied heavily on a sustained almost music-hall-style patter between the principal characters, and in doing so translated into a more widely accessible form some of the elements which had become associated with absurdism; 'at times it seems as if he has put *Waiting for Godot* inside *Hamlet*'.[163] More rooted in everyday reality was Peter Terson's *Zigger Zagger*, written for the National Youth Theatre in 1967, which looked at issues around football hooliganism and disaffected and under-educated working-class youth. Terson's play incorporated songs including 'The Toilets Song' ('We've hung around the toilets our school life'), the 'Youth Careers Officer's Lament' ('I've seen better days than this . . . I've seen when I had respect. Pitmen diggers called me sir/My wife would have fox fur') and the ironic 'Farewell Hymn' on the last day of school ('O God, save our leavers, make them staunch believers . . . Make them pious, make them good/Guide them, lead them, show them, teach them/As they leave our school gates/Peril lurks, achievement waits').[164] Elsewhere, John McGrath's *Events While Guarding the Bofors Gun* also centred on working-class characters, examining the day-by-day build-up of futility and frustration in a group of British soldiers stationed in an army camp in northern Germany in 1954, guarding a gun which is itself obsolete.

Meanwhile, Peter Brook continued to experiment with classical texts in his pursuit of a theatrical form which could combine the holy and ritualistic with the rough and the earthbound and the cruelty of Artaud. In March 1968 he staged a modern-dress production of Ted Hughes's version of Seneca's *Oedipus* for the National Theatre. One striking innovation was the use made of the Chorus, whose members were distributed throughout the auditorium: 'Sometimes one speaker is echoed sotto voce by others, sometimes the rhythm is staccato, sometimes the chorus merely supplies ejaculatory sighs and hisses (rather like characters in the Japanese theatre). A whistle of dismay can shoot around the theatre like a rocket. The sound, in a word, is orchestrated.'[165] Most of the critics found the evening brilliantly inventive and theatrically exciting, though there were more reservations about the final post-tragic scene of Bacchanalian revelry, dominated by a giant golden phallus, and during which the cast surprisingly launch into a rendition of 'Yes, we have no bananas'.

A few months later, Brook and Geoffrey Reeves built on this project in their production of Shakespeare's *The Tempest* at the Roundhouse. The company for this brought together actors from different cultures, languages and theatrical traditions, and pursued 'not a literal interpretation of Shakespeare's play but abstractions, essences, and possible contradictions', as the plot was 'shattered, condensed, deverbalized'.[166] According to Reeves, other RSC directors 'accused us of raping Shakespeare'.[167] Certainly, the original spoken text – and words in general – were decentred in favour of sounds and images, and some critics felt that such experiments really had gone too far:

> The actors mimed with their hands in silence for 10 minutes or so and then a trumpet sounded. After 12 minutes the first words became audible. The word 'blessing' was among them. A Japanese made Noh hisses. Someone said a few words from *The Tempest*. On the fringes, two actors bounced balls. Others rolled on the floor ... Words like Milan and Prince were spoken.
>
> After 43 minutes that section of the audience which had been unwise enough to sit on benches attached to scaffolding were wheeled into the centre of the Roundhouse and gently turned round. 'Here Comes the Bride' was played. The obligatory copulatory movements were made ... Sounds were made and acrobatics performed ... Eventually, after one and a half hours, things stopped.[168]

The Drama Review offered an alternative and less cynical description:

> Before the performance, people mill around the arena ... actors vocalise, dance, play ball, do handstands, turn cartwheels and limber up ... and then begin the 'mirror' exercise ... combined with a low hum that grows louder and louder ... Suddenly the actors 'break the mirror', and run onto the platform ... the actors face the audience and display archetypal masks (made with their facial muscles) and correlative physicalisations. Accompanying these are animal sounds, grunts, moans, howls, whispers, intonations, and gibberish ... Miranda and Ferdinand ... make love in the rocking position. This is homosexually mocked and mimicked by Caliban and Ariel; other members of the cast in turn mirror Ariel and

Caliban . . . Sycorax is portrayed by an enormous woman able to expand her face and body to still larger proportions . . . Suddenly, she gives a horrendous yell, and Caliban, with black sweater over his head, emerges from between her legs . . . Caliban, large and fat, but somehow acrobatic, stands on his head, legs spread; Sycorax . . . stands behind him, her mouth on his genitals. Then they reverse positions. The others follow suit: fellatio, cunnilingus, and other variations of anal and oral intercourse convey a monster-sexuality . . . the 'Garden of Hell' . . . Prospero is pursued and captured. He is wheeled in on a table, and then thrown to the floor. Now the group seems a pyramid of dogs: they are on top of him, they bite him, suck him, and chew him. The leading image is homosexual rape . . . All at once, there are loud obscene sounds – gulping, swallowing, choking, defecating, and farting . . . the scene dissolves into Miranda's and Ferdinand's marriage ceremony, performed in Hebrew-Hippie-Japanese rites. On some nights, the rites are discarded for the Hokey-Pokey dance . . .[169]

Waiting for paradise

Probably the most significant event to occur in relation to theatre in Britain in 1968 was the ending – after some 237 years – of the unique and anachronistic system of control and pre-censorship, whereby a servant in the Royal Household, whose other duties included organising Buckingham Palace garden parties and looking after the Queen's swans, and who was not technically subject or answerable even to parliament – enjoyed unlimited powers to suppress any new play being presented for public performance in Great Britain. The new Theatres Act was passed in the autumn, and suddenly playwrights and managers could go ahead without submitting a script for licensing. But it was a memorable year for other reasons too. Among the new companies to emerge which would become important players in the decades that followed were Red Ladder, Welfare State and the Pip Simmons Theatre Group. Jim Haynes started Drury Lane Arts Lab, Ed Berman launched Inter-Action and the ICA opened at its new site under Michael Kustow. It was also the year in which Jerzy Grotowski's hugely influential *Towards a Poor Theatre* was first published in English.

The first night after the Lord Chamberlain's authority was removed saw the much-delayed West End opening of the rock musical *Hair*. Its messages now seem naive, crude, banal and, perhaps, tame. But with its (actually quite brief) nudity, its celebration of an 'all you need is love' philosophy, of drugs, of dropping out, of burning army sign-up papers ('the draft is white people sending black people to make war on yellow people to defend the land they stole from red people'),[170] of rock music and of sexual freedom, it captured – or at least aped – a mood of youthful rebellion, and a rejection of the old order. In reality – as with so many aspects of the counterculture – we might recognise *Hair* now as essentially a safe, marketed, commercialised and packaged version of rebellion, processed for easy consumption. On Broadway and Shaftesbury Avenue, how could it not be? Yet brilliantly directed by Tom O'Horgan – an experienced member of La MaMa – the show seemed dangerous and threatening to those who felt endangered and threatened by the possibility of youthful revolution. 'Plenty to alarm unwary in hymn to freedom' as *The Times* memorably headlined its review.[171] And as Michael Billington says: 'if you want to understand what the late Sixties was like, you only have to listen to the original cast's recording'.

Billington also notes 'how indebted our alternative theatre was to America for its expression of anti-Establishment values'.[172] At the end of 1966, Charles Marowitz had suggested that

> in a hundred years' time our era will be best remembered, not for its Osbornes and its Pinters, its rediscovery of Brecht or creation of National Theatres, but because a small band of New York actors were harried out of their country and on to the continent where they proceeded to change the shape of conventional theatre.[173]

He was referring to the Living Theatre, the company which had provoked outcries in London earlier in the decade with is productions of *The Connection* and *The Brig*. In the summer of 1969, they returned to London with several productions. An adaptation of Mary Shelley's *Frankenstein* combined the circus with the grand-guignol, containing few words and depending primarily on 'meditation, yoga, calisthenics; writhing, twisting, shaking; howls, grunts, groans'.[174] There was an *Antigone* too, based on Brecht's version of the text. But most controversial was *Paradise Now*, a show which had been closed down in Avignon the previous year. As much a revolutionary ritual as a play, *Paradise Now* really did seek to dissolve the boundaries between the fictional and the real; between the performer and the observer; between acting as pretending and acting as doing. It began with the cast approaching individual members of the audience and listing some of the constraints imposed by society from which they wished to be free ('I am not allowed to smoke marijuana . . . I am not allowed to take off my clothes') and voicing deep frustration ('I don't know how to stop the war'). It ended (if things went to plan) with the cast and audience leaving the theatre together, quite possibly unclothed, to start the revolution beyond – an anarchist revolution which would involve no violence, recognise no laws, and bring peace and freedom to all. It was, you might say, *Hair* uncut. For *Paradise Now* demanded everything:

> To make life irresistible. To feed all the people. To change the demonic forces into the celestial. To remove the causes of violence . . . To work for the love of it and not the money. To live without the police. To change myself. To get rid of the class system. To reinvent love. To make each moment creative . . .[175]

And, as the title suggested, it demanded it now.

London critics were mostly unimpressed – though it was reported that at least one removed his trousers when invited to do so:

> We were waiting for 'Paradise Now' last evening when a man with wild blank eyes and hair to his shoulders came up to me. 'I am not allowed to travel without a passport,' he said, as though bewildered by this, and he said it again and again and

screamed as though he was unleashing years of pent up hate. I looked round and heard his words and his screams echoed by other actors around the auditorium.[176]

Fundamental to the audience experience was 'the way and the degree to which the actors invade us'. As one reviewer described it, 'They swarm among us, hysterical, hectoring, muttering their grand slogans on impotence and despair.'[177] Under the headline 'The Dying Theatre', the *Sunday Times* dismissed the show as 'a collage of humming, moaning, shouting, screaming, writhing and stamping, intermittently varied by incursions into, and physical attacks upon, the audience, amid a stench of sweat and sleetstorms of saliva'.[178] Yet for all the cynicism and anger, the heckling and outrage and walkouts, it is clear that such responses tell only one side of the story. 'As I write now', admitted Nicholas de Jongh in his review, 'the stage and auditorium is crammed with actors and audience, talking, disputing, walking around.'[179]

Conclusion

In his retrospective assessment of the state of British theatre at the end of the decade, Michael Billington sums up the situation as follows:

Examine the work of the period and you get a sharp sense of the political scepticism, youthful disaffection, sexual freedom and spiritual questioning that were part of the times. There is also little doubt that British theatre at the end of the decade was infinitely richer than when it had begun. It combined a corps of first-class dramatists, unequalled in scope since the first Elizabethan age, with a new generation of theatre-makers anxious to subvert the primacy of text.[180]

It is hard to disagree with this judgement, and the 1970s clearly had a rich legacy and an extraordinary potential on which to build. True, the West End was still dominated by long-running musicals, and the

Royal Court had just revived *Look Back in Anger* ('From herald of revolution to respected modern classic in thirteen years'[181]). But not only *Hair* but also Brecht was on Shaftesbury Avenue; regional theatres were on the rise; new playwrights were emerging. There was a National Theatre Company, a vibrant Royal Shakespeare Company, a developing Theatre-in-Education movement and a fringe. And all over the place, new experiments in performance were taking place.

A decade is a long time in theatre – certainly it had been in the case of the 1960s. When it began, stage performances were subject to a law from the 1730s which gave the head servant of the royal household (the Lord Chamberlain) *carte blanche* to ban any play, or parts of a play to which he took exception. Unacceptable phrases in 1960 included 'get stuffed', 'turd' and 'suffering Jesus', as well as the blowing of raspberries and any mention of contraceptives.[182] Before it ended, the press had published photographs of the Queen's eighteen-year-old daughter dancing on stage with the cast of *Hair*, a 'love-rock musical' featuring mass nudity and songs celebrating drugs, masturbation, homosexuality and free love. 'Anne among the hippies', as the *Daily Mail* headline put it.[183] In 1960, the plays of Pinter, Beckett and Ionesco were as far as things went in terms of experimentation or challenges to the conventional well-made play. Artaud was unknown. This had been the decade when not only nudity and sexuality but also violence and cruelty were for the first time thrust 'in yer face'. As a cynical theatre commentator observed somewhere in the middle of the decade: 'In the higher reaches of the theatre, severed heads are becoming obligatory.'

The form and the trappings were changing too. Performances had exploded out of theatres, and 'happenings' and avant-garde experiments were everywhere, with even the boundaries between stage and auditorium, actors and spectators, no longer immutable. In theatre, as elsewhere, the 1960s was a decade when the status quo was challenged, attacked and derided. Often it was the young leading the way, bringing a contempt – perhaps a healthy one – for the world they had grown up in, and for those whom they blamed for accepting it. These sentiments found forceful expression through many cultural anthems of the period, not least in Bob Dylan's 'The Times They are a-Changin" and, even more aggressively, in 'My Generation' by the Who. In 1967, *Plays and Players* reviewed with middle-aged despair and disapproval a series of productions from the NUS Drama Festival which were being presented at the Garrick Theatre.

> Well, this is the world which we, you, created. Youth at the prow and puberty at the helm. The privilege of youth has turned into a bloody great arrogance . . . all of them invoked theatrical devices which, whatever their origins, seemed very up-to-date. The audience were by turns arraigned, insulted and bored. The theatre of contempt seemed to be with us for keeps.[184]

Meanwhile, significant investment by Harold Wilson's Labour government had also ensured that by the end of the decade a number of cities had new and sometimes innovative theatre buildings, with others on the way. One of the most striking was Stoke's revolutionary theatre in the round. For the first time, too, a governmental minister for the arts had been appointed, and a far better endowed Arts Council was spreading its subsidies wider, deeper and more imaginatively. The removal of the Lord Chamberlain's powers of censorship by the 1968 Theatres Act gave more freedom to playwrights and directors, and – since a script no longer had to be sanctioned in advance – opened the door to improvised performance and experimentation. It also encouraged a new emphasis on Theatre of Fact, removing the obstacle to representing or quoting from historical and contemporary public figures and documents. In all sorts of ways, directly and indirectly, theatre sought to engage with important political and real-world issues. By the end of the 1960s, Arthur Miller's famous and much-quoted accusation in the mid-1950s that British theatre was 'hermetically sealed off from life' was surely no longer applicable.[185]

CHAPTER 2
INTRODUCING THE PLAYWRIGHTS

INTRODUCTION TO JOHN ARDEN
by Bill McDonnell

John Arden was born in 1930 in Barnsley, South Yorkshire. Before her marriage his mother had trained as a primary school teacher. His father came from a wine-making dynasty, but rejected the family business in favour of a job managing a glass-making factory.

On the Arden side he came from an impeccable pedigree, able to trace his family genealogy from the Norman Conquest. A distant forebear was Mary Arden of Stratford, the mother of William Shakespeare. Municipal corruption was also in the bloodline. The history of the Ardens took in the Ardens of Beverley, including a Dr Arden, who was six times mayor of the town during the mid-eighteenth century, and, in the spirit of the day, was an enthusiastic and effective briber of voters. The Ardens were not a family of writers, but of talkers: talk imbricated with the English literary tradition. In a memoir, Arden describes his family's 'old-fashioned' ways of speaking, recalling that his mother spoke 'like Jane Arden'. As a child he was obsessed by the great myths and legends of Western literature – British, Arthurian, Roman, Greek and Irish – an 'aspect of European Literature', he later wrote, 'which is now inseparable from my imagination'. As well as a deep love of literature he also imbibed from his parents a reflexive liberalism, which included a determined opposition to British imperialism and its violences. His father was a liberal activist and militant who had 'opposed the colonialist Boer War'. Arden recounts a story about his father's cousin who, at a family gathering, spoke 'with enthusiasm of a day of riot in Cairo, when the British colonial authorities had successfully sent British troops into the "native quarter" to overawe the nominally independent Egyptians'.

Arden's mother had asked incautiously, '"But why should our troops go in? Isn't it the Egyptians' own country?" This remark was not well received.'[1]

Life outside the family home was altogether tougher. Barnsley was a small working-class town in the South Yorkshire coalfields, and had held, since the Industrial Revolution, a central place in the history (and mythology) of labour-movement militancy. Operating in one of a number of solid Labour fiefdoms, local politics was defined by paternalistic egalitarianism and petty corruption, and Arden would regularly mine his birthplace for inspiration. Plays such as *Live Like Pigs*, *The Workhouse Donkey* and *Serjeant Musgrave's Dance* were located in a town very like it. Later he would write of his support for Irish Republicanism: 'My background is that of the northern English industrial communities . . . a wary solidarity with irredentist Irish dissidence comes easier.'[2]

The young Arden was not happy at the local primary school, where he was mercilessly bullied, and in 1939, on the eve of war, he was packed off to preparatory school near York. He boarded there for five years before moving on to another public school, Sedbergh, in Cumbria, where he took English, French and German for his Higher School Certificate. The escape from Barnsley's streets came as a great relief:

> It was impossible to live in such a town without being very conscious that I was a member of the minority party in the 'class war' . . . a little boy going to school in the sort of nice clothes that my mother would provide . . . was quite liable to get attacked in the street.[3]

At Sedbergh, whose theatre is now named after him, the young Arden began work on five plays, none of which was completed, and acted in school productions, most notably as the eponymous lead in Shakespeare's *Hamlet*. Sedbergh also provided occasional opportunities for visiting professional productions in Sheffield and York. However, his first regular exposure to the theatre came with National Service, when he spent twelve months stationed in Edinburgh as a lance corporal in the Intelligence corps. In 1950 he went up to Cambridge to read architecture, graduating in 1953, before moving on to the Edinburgh College of Art to complete his architectural studies. It was here that he wrote his first play, *All Fall Down*, a comedy about the Victorian railway pioneers, and, foreshadowing a life's obsession, a 'pseudo-Elizabethan tragedy on the Gunpowder plot . . . an unsatisfactory mixture of the Elizabethans and T. S. Eliot'. [4] In 1955 Arden secured a post in an architect's office in London, and spent two happy years there, working in his spare time on playwriting projects. It was now that he met his future wife, the Irish actress Margaretta D'Arcy, who became his lifelong collaborator. D'Arcy's influence on Arden's development was critical. Not only was she already known in the theatre circles around the Royal Court, but she also introduced the young playwright to seminal dramatists: 'She gave me a copy of Brecht – a writer I had only heard of . . . Beckett, Strindberg, Toller, Behan.'[5]

From this period came his first radio play, *The Life of Man*, broadcast by the BBC on 16 April 1956. The play is set in 1856 and tells the story of a sailor, Bones, driven half mad by his experiences on a three-day voyage out of Liverpool under the cruel captain, Anthract. Reviewing the broadcast in the *The Listener*, Francis Dillon called it

an exhilarating radio play, radio of a quality we get very rarely these days . . . the crimp gang, the god, devil, or saint shanghaied aboard a cruel coffin ship, tarts, witches, mermaids, a roaring Bible-hard captain, a bunch of fables and parables . . . the talk was taut and authentic; where it broke into verse, it flung itself into the magic winds. [6]

The Life of Man won the BBC's North Region New Play prize, and brought the young playwright to the attention of George Devine, then Artistic Director of the Royal Court Theatre. Devine asked Arden for a play for the Court's series of Sunday-night 'productions without decor'. The first he submitted, based on Arthurian legends – a theme to which he would later return – was rejected. The second, *The Waters of Babylon*, was accepted and was produced at the Royal

Court on 20 October 1957, directed by Graham Evans, and starring Robert Stephens as the protagonist, Krank. The play introduces Butterthwaite, 'a shady Yorkshireman', who would take centre stage in the later *The Workhouse Donkey*. Arden wrote of *The Waters of Babylon* that it was 'part of a sort of North Country tetralogy', which included two plays for television, *Soldier Soldier* and *Wet Fish*, and *The Workhouse Donkey*, in which the same characters appear and reappear. Replete with what would become Arden's signature devices – songs, stand-up, gags and dances – *The Waters of Babylon*, thought Simon Trussler, was 'the first entirely Brechtian play in the language'. [7] And indeed there is something in the play's dramaturgy and ethos of the early Brecht, of *Baal* and *Jungle of the Cities* – a potpourri of seediness, political and moral corruption, anarchic violence and betrayal. Albert Hunt:

> *The Waters of Babylon* plays with staginess. It tells the story of a Polish émigré, Krank, who leads a double life. In the daytime he is the respectable assistant of an architect . . . but at night he runs a lodging house cum brothel. Another Polish émigré, Paul, to whom he owes five hundred pounds, tries to blackmail him into helping him to blow up [Russian leaders] Bulganin and Khrushchev during their visit to London. In an effort to raise the five hundred pounds and so buy himself out of the plot, Krank involves himself with a Premium Bond swindle organized by a former Yorkshire town councillor, Charles Butterthwaite . . .[8]

The plot fails and Krank is accidentally killed by Paul. In an article Arden said of the play: 'I wrote *The Waters of Babylon* as a kind of cross-breed between two Elizabethan pieces – Jonson's *Alchemist* and Chapman's *Blind Beggar of Alexandria*. I wished to treat the complex international life of Notting Hill in terms of traditional comedy.'[9] The critic Kenneth Tynan went to the heart of what would become a recurring trope of London reviews – that Arden over-elaborated, that his writing lacked clarity of purpose: 'The general theme – immigrants corrupted by life in Britain – is obscured by over illustration. A mound of eccentric details, including an entire sub-plot set in an architect's office, stands between us and the author's meaning.' Julius Novick, describing it as 'an odd sort of farce-parable-extravaganza', continues, 'nobody brings in reference to Buchenwald and Auschwitz into a play just for the fun of it . . . but what the point is I have no idea'. [10] But others, such as Trussler, considered it 'a considerable achievement in its complete independence of manner and its control over its own density of matter'.[11] *Waters* was followed by the one-act comedy *When is a Door Not a Door?*, about a factory office strike, which was performed at the Central School of Speech and Drama's Embassy Theatre in Swiss Cottage in June 1958.

Subtitled a 'play in seventeen scenes', Arden's next work, *Live Like Pigs*, premiered at the Royal Court Theatre on 30 September 1958, directed by George Devine and Anthony Page, and starring Wilfred Lawson, Robert Shaw and Margaretta D'Arcy. The play was perhaps the closest that Arden ever came to a documentary-style drama, in content if not in form. It explores the consequences when a family of gypsies is placed in a council-house next door to the 'respectable' Jacksons. The dramaturgy was less flamboyant than that for *Waters*, with the use of ballads to link the scenes the only non-naturalistic device. The Lord Chamberlain's Reader's Report on the play neatly captures the establishment's response to the Royal Court 'revolution', and offers a compelling mix of pseudo-sociological commentary and class snobbery:

> This would have been considered an astonishing play before the advent of the English Stage Company blunted our powers of astonishment. With just enough story to keep it going, it is a detailed, squalid, sour, convincing account of a sprawling, delinquent family group coming from the queer fringe between the actual gypsies and the rough but tolerably respectable fairground folk.[12]

The play's plot turns on a simple enough mechanism: a clash of cultures in which expectations are reversed. The outlaws (Sawyers) become victims of the violence of the law-abiding good people (the

Jacksons). In a comment that would become another trope of critiques of Arden's work, he was accused of amorality, and of presenting a pessimistic and nihilistic vision of human nature. But as Hunt points out, the play 'isn't about human nature. It's talking about a concrete situation. What the play does assert is that if you put people into an unreasonable situation then they are likely to behave unreasonably.' Arden's is not an amoral view, but a deeply political and radical take on a critical social issue, says Hunt. He is 'showing a society whose way of treating people does violence to the way they want to live'.[13]

Arden had taken an actual event (this time in Barnsley) in which a family of squatters had been set on by their neighbours, as the inspiration for the play. His aim in drawing on the real-life crisis, he wrote, was not to write a social documentary, but to create 'a study of differing ways of life brought sharply into conflict and both losing their particular virtues under the stress of intolerance and misunderstanding'.[14] *Live Like Pigs* divided the critics. Kenneth Tynan condemned what he saw as an attack on the Welfare State and on ordinary people, who are portrayed, he argued, as 'stuffy, small-souled hypocrites, inferior, simply *because* they are ordinary'.[15] Eric Keown fulminated in *Punch* at this invitation to 'wallow in filth', agreeing that it was 'powerful', but then 'so is any cartload of dung'.[16] On the other side, Ronald Hayman praised the play's 'absolute clarity and focus',[17] while Robert Hatch celebrated 'a boisterous, driving outburst of human spirit under compression'.[18] Nevertheless, the general critical opprobrium led to a shortened run. And, while the Royal Court had given the Ardens a sense of security, it was always fragile. The response to *Live Like Pigs* was a harbinger of things to come. Dissident voices within the Court were already questioning the wisdom of staging Arden's plays. According to D'Arcy, Council member Ronald Duncan – himself a dramatist belonging to a very different tradition – was heard to say of *Live Like Pigs*: 'This is exactly the sort of play I told the board the Court ought not to be doing'; while newly returned director Tony Richardson looked in at rehearsals and 'groaned, and muttered "student Lorca!"'[19] Arden's relationship with the theatre would be pushed to breaking point by the production of his next play,

Serjeant Musgrave's Dance, whose production and impact is discussed in detail in Chapter 3.

INTRODUCTION TO EDWARD BOND

Edward Bond was born in 1934 in Holloway, north London, his parents having moved there from a rural setting in search of work. On the outbreak of war he was evacuated, first to Cornwall and then to Ely, before returning to London. Bond was not even entered for the eleven-plus examination, and he attended a secondary modern school and left at fifteen with a fairly minimal education. He claims not to regret this: 'Once you let them send you to grammar school and university, you're ruined.'[1] Bond's education – including the political education which made him a confirmed Marxist – was therefore acquired less formally. On the other hand, Bond did have early contact with live performance, since one of his sisters appeared in music hall (she was sometimes sawn in half by a magician) and Bond attended regularly. Probably more significantly, he went with the school at the age of fourteen to see Sir Donald Wolfit's production of *Macbeth* – an experience which he later recalled as 'the first thing that made sense of my life for me', and 'the first time I'd found something beautiful and exciting and alive'.

In the early 1950s, Bond had to undergo two years of military National Service, encountering a world of 'brazen brutality' and deliberate degradation. 'We were turned into automata', he recalled.[2] However, Bond did begin writing, and subsequently submitted several plays for radio, television and the stage, all of which were rejected. In 1958 he sent two scripts to the Royal Court (*Klaxon in Atreus' Place* and *The Fiery Tree*) and was invited to become a play reader and to join the theatre's Writers' Group. Run by Bill Gaskill – who would later become the theatre's Artistic Director and direct Bond's first plays there – the other members included John Arden, Arnold Wesker, Ann Jellicoe and Wole Soyinka. Bond wrote several short plays, 'one of which was rather Beckett-like, and the other rather Brecht-like', but Gaskill was particularly struck by Bond's studious approach to writing: 'he is one of the few craftsman-like writers, who approach their work quite consciously as a skill'. Bond watched as many plays as possible – 'he did literally go to the theatre, to all theatres, night after night' – and analysed carefully how they worked theatrically. An admirer of Chekhov, he chose to study *The Three Sisters* and 'dissected the play's construction in enormous detail'.[3] For all his later desire to interrogate and rewrite the past, Bond has always paid full tribute to his teachers: 'I learned stagecraft from . . . watching how other dramatists dealt with it – some ancient, others modern.'[4]

The Court's Artistic Director at this time was George Devine, the initiator of the new writing revolution whose credits included John Osborne's first plays. According to Bond, he may have been less convinced than Gaskill of this new writer's potential: 'I discovered . . . that in the early sixties or late fifties George Divine [sic] had told a critic privately that there were two people hanging round the Court who he ought to get rid of – but didn't have the heart to – because they would never become writers', wrote Bond, some years later; 'I was one of the two he named.'[5] Nevertheless, at the end of 1962 the theatre gave Bond his first production, a single Sunday-night performance of *The Pope's Wedding*, directed by Keith Johnstone. The script was also entered for a New Play Award, and Bond was paid for an option on a possible full production at the Court, as well as receiving a commission to write another one. It was a breakthrough, and the commission would lead to *Saved*.

The typically elliptical title of *The Pope's Wedding* signified an impossible event, though Bond referred to it in his working notebooks as 'the Tramp play' or 'the Hermit play'.[6] At its heart is the increasingly obsessive fascination felt by Scopey, a young man in his early twenties, for Alen, an elderly and taciturn tramp living in a shack full of empty food tins, who has been vaguely cared for by Scopey's wife, Pat. Scopey and Pat are part of a group of young people who seem to be drifting through life with little to do and little purpose – not a million miles from the group in *Saved*, although the context here is rural rather than urban. Scopey becomes convinced that Alen holds some special knowledge which he could impart, and, presumably out of frustration, he finally murders the tramp and puts on his clothes.

'The old recluse and the young man have been trapped in the same room', explained Bond later. 'Clearly the author intended that they should both look alike – yet not too alike.' And he advised the director of the 1980s revival against staging the final scene in a way which linked the characters too explicitly:

> The old man's face is hidden. If the young man turns his face from the audience, the two men will be all but identical! The image becomes one of Absurdity and says: 'All people are the same, no more than mindless objects in an empty space made even emptier by their presence.'

Possibly thinking of Beckett and Pinter, Bond added that 'There are forms of theatre which make such statements. We should not make them.' A theatre which risked implying that all human beings face the same and inevitable suffering was not what Bond intended, since it reconciles us to despair rather than encouraging us to believe in the possibility of change.

> In the last scene of the play we should be saying to the audience: human beings cannot be reduced to a metaphysical riddle. That nightmarish solution is too comforting. None of us are creatures of fate. Each individual is a possibility of the world being different. Even when they are dead people are still not the same! If we could take you over one of your battlefields we could show you how each of the dead insists on smelling differently!

For Bond, it has always been imperative to keep the message to the fore when making decisions about staging: 'Whenever we're faced with these aesthetic or dramatic problems we must look for the political solution.'[7]

The Court's Sunday-night performances were minimal in terms of resources and commitment, but still attracted national reviews. *The Pope's Wedding* contained sixteen relatively short scenes with no division into Acts, and this was hardly a familiar or comfortable form for most critics: 'The author . . . seemed incapable of sustaining a scene

... for more than a few minutes', complained the *Daily Telegraph*. The inarticulacy of the central character was also problematic: 'Whenever we came to the helpless hermit ... Mr Bond seemed to dry up.' But the author of this 'X certificate Archers' was not without potential: 'It would be wrong simply because he has no skill in plotting to dismiss Mr Bond as neligible. His people hold our attention ... They are alive.'[8] Bernard Levin in the *Daily Mail* was fulsome in his praise: 'this bizarre and unclassifiable piece is an astonishing *tour de force* for a first play', he wrote, with its dramatisation of 'village life in darkest England cut straight down the middle, through pips and all'. The violence and the tragedy were disturbing: 'I would not care to be inside the author's head on a dark night'; but the dialogue and characterisation were 'of a rivetingly compulsive clinical accuracy'.[9]

Bond's next play, *Saved*, had its first, delayed performance in November 1965, with the Royal Court turned into a private club in an effort to avoid prosecution following the Lord Chamberlain's refusal to license the text. In January 1966 the theatre was charged anyway, and in the same month it opened Bond's adaptation of Thomas Middleton's Jacobean city comedy and social satire *A Chaste Maid in Cheapside*. Bond's role was largely restricted to updating some of the language (he also wrote a new ending, but this was not incorporated). However, in talking about the work, he implicitly drew some connections between Middleton's situation and his own. Middleton, said Bond, had been widely accused of amorality and immorality. 'Certainly the present Lord Chamberlain would not license his plays.' But theatre audiences 'must be careful to allow playwrights to be completely honest, even when they use words and actions that the audience might not themselves use, and even when they seem to jeopardise moral values'.[10] The critical response to the play itself was mixed. The *Sunday Telegraph* christened it *Oh, What a Lovely Whore!* but also suggested it was 'like a clownish and caricatured version of *Saved*'.[11] Some were patronisingly dismissive: 'Middleton wrote successfully for an uneducated public in the early seventeenth century, and unsophisticated audiences may still get some fun out of him today', sniffed the *Sunday Times*. 'Many people at the first performance were pleased to find the word "bum" in the text.'[12]

The following year, the Royal Court staged another adaptation by Bond, a version of Chekhov's *Three Sisters*. One critic noted his initial anxiety on discovering that 'Chekhov's only play involving a perambulator was being reworked by Edward Bond',[13] but in fact the playwright's intention was to render rather than reinvent Chekhov, and his version earned respect as 'a new and more than usually vivid translation' which 'emphasised more than I have ever known it emphasised before ... the characters' consciousness of their mortality'.[14] In the second half of the 1960s and beyond Bond also worked on several film scripts (including Antonioni's *Blow-Up*, Tony Richardson's version of Nabokov's *Laughter in the Dark* and Nicolas Roeg's *Walkabout*). Useful though these were financially to Bond, he has always distanced himself from them and insisted that all his significant work has been written for the stage.

Bond's next original play, *Early Morning*, was scheduled for production in early 1968, but was refused a licence by the Lord Chamberlain. Technically, therefore, the first of his plays ever to be seen in full public production was *Narrow Road to the Deep North*, commissioned by Coventry Cathedral for an International Conference on 'People and Cities', and written in two and a half days. The play is set in Japan between the seventeenth and nineteenth centuries and opens with a prologue in which a peasant couple abandon a baby they cannot afford to keep, and the poet Basho, creator of the haiku, chooses to pursue his own search for enlightenment rather than rescue it. When Basho returns some thirty years later, the abandoned baby has apparently become a tyrannical ruler, and the play follows a story of cruelty, atrocities, rebellion, dismemberment and colonial invasion, ending with a ritualised self-disembowelling by a young Buddhist monk. Again, critics found it hard to pin down a precise moral or message, but the power of the writing and the originality of Bond's imagination were widely recognised. By 1969, when the play transferred to the Royal Court, censorship by the Lord Chamberlain had been abolished, and it was presented in a season which also included the first public performances of *Saved* and *Early Morning*.

In 1969 Bond was one of ten writers to contribute to *The Enoch Show*, a political satire directed against the racist British politician

Enoch Powell. The first performance was interrupted by a violent assault on the actors by members of the extreme right-wing National Front movement – an event which was then incorporated within subsequent performances. Two other short plays by Bond preceded the opening of his next full work, *Lear*, both of them verging on the borders of agitprop. *Black Mass* (1970) was written for an event organised by the Anti-Apartheid movement to commemorate the anniversary of the Sharpeville shooting in South Africa, in which white police shot and killed unarmed black marchers demonstrating against racist laws. Bond's play is set in a church where a priest colludes with the security forces and the prime minister against the protesters ('they get pleasure out of causing trouble and giving me a bad name abroad') by shooting them for sport. Christ (played by Bond himself) then descends from the cross and poisons the communion wine, and the prime minister dies while confessing. The priest ejects Christ from the church ('I'm very disappointed in you . . . you've let yourself down'), and instals in his place a young police officer in fascist uniform.[15]

The following year, *Passion* was performed out of doors at an event organised by the Campaign for Nuclear Disarmament. This time the characters included the British prime minister and Queen, along with Christ and Buddha, and a dead soldier. The Queen is due to open a monument to a dead soldier, but accidentally presses the wrong button and fires a nuclear warhead which unleashes worldwide devastation. While neither *Passion* nor *Black Mass* is as subtle or rich as Bond's previous work, they both contain a recognisable and unnerving mixture of satire, anger and horror. Nor do they lack for theatrical imagination or horror. As Christ declares in *Passion* when he looks at what is going on in the streets of South Africa: 'This is a hell worse than anything my father imagined.'[16]

Interviewed in 1971, Bond declared that 'art must have a social function', and that his work as a whole constituted 'an examination of what it means to be living at this time'. How, then, could it be anything other than dark? 'It would be very silly to think you could write about our society and not write about violence. It's a violent century.' Nor was it the role of plays or stage characters – even Christ

– to bring peace. As Bond insisted, 'the answer to the violence must be found by the audience'.[17]

INTRODUCTION TO HAROLD PINTER

I can take nothing you say at face value. Every word you speak is open to any number of different interpretations.[1]

Harold Pinter was born in Hackney in the East End of London in 1930, his Jewish grandparents having fled from persecution in Eastern Europe. Anti-semitism was rife in parts of Britain, and the threat from Fascism was by no means confined to Hitler and the Nazis. Like Edward Bond, Pinter was evacuated to Cornwall at the start of the Second World War. He returned in 1942 and attended Hackney Grammar School, where he encountered an inspirational teacher of English, Joseph Brearley, who became an enduring mentor, friend and touchstone. Pinter read widely in literature – he was particularly fired by Dostoyevsky, Eliot and Kafka – and took a keen interest in avant-garde culture; but he was equally ready to engage directly with the tough political environment of post-war Britain: 'When the Hackney fascists, newly released from war-time internment, were harrying us down the back streets of Dalston, he would turn and fight, or chat them to a standstill', remembers Henry Woolf, another lifelong companion.[2] The threat of imminent nuclear confrontation was equally terrifying, following the dropping of atomic bombs on Japan by the Americans and the developing Cold War with the Soviet Union. In 1948, Pinter was called up for National Service but declared himself a conscientious objector (though he said he would have fought against Hitler). He refused to go, and, after a series of court cases, was fined.

At school, Pinter had taken major acting roles, including those of Macbeth and Romeo. He subsequently attended RADA, but disliked it so much that he faked a nervous breakdown and left. In the early 1950s he joined a professional company touring Shakespeare through Ireland (roles included Horatio in *Hamlet*, Macduff in *Macbeth*,

Edgar and Edmund – presumably not simultaneously – in *King Lear*, and, for one performance only, the title role in *Hamlet*). From 1953 to 1954 he worked at Hammersmith with Sir Donald Wolfit's company (a Knight in *King Lear*, Second Murderer in *Macbeth*, Officer in *Twelfth Night*, etc.), and then spent several years acting under the name of David Baron in regional repertory companies, often playing slightly sinister parts in predictable dramas. One way of viewing Pinter's own early plays is to see them as traditional and old-fashioned scripts which have somehow slipped off kilter, or from which a number of pages have gone missing. Perhaps Pinter was taking revenge on behalf of David Baron for all those Agatha Christie plays. Although it would be as a writer that Pinter would become best known, he would always remain an effective and powerful performer – and not just of his own plays. Moreover, an actor's experience and perspective were vital to his ability to write dialogue and character. 'Nobody wrote better lines for actors: clean, hard, intoxicating . . . like a grenade going off in a Rolls.'[3]

In 1956, Pinter married the successful repertory actress Vivien Merchant. He wrote poetry and a novel (*The Dwarfs*) before producing his first short play, *The Room*, supposedly written in three days (some say less) at the request of his lifelong friend and fellow actor Henry Woolf, then a student at Bristol University. Woolf later recalled the impact of the performance: 'I remember the audience waking up from its polite cultural stupor and beginning to enjoy itself. Something special was going on. Something very funny and at the same time rather menacing. A new voice was speaking, and English theatre was never going to be the same again.'[4] The setting and the language of *The Room* are hardly removed from the everyday; but the events are less predictable, and it is a normality seen through a glass darkly, resembling more the reality of a dream: a woman insistently warns her husband about driving his van on icy roads; a couple arrive and claim her room is free and that they are moving in; the landlord can't remember how many floors his property has; a blind 'Negro' tells the woman her father wants her to go home; the husband assaults him; the woman becomes blind. The elements could be fragments from a dimly remembered repertory thriller, dozed through by an audience who miss the key scene which explains it all. There are no obvious signals of comedy, and yet the dialogue is strangely amusing. The atmosphere is tense and uncertain, perhaps even sinister, but it is hard to locate the danger or to know if it is substantial. As Harold Hobson wrote in the *Sunday Times*: 'The play makes one stir uneasily in one's shoes, and doubt, for a moment, the comforting solidity of the earth.'[5]

The Birthday Party, Pinter's next play, had similarities in terms of style, language and atmosphere – and perhaps even in narrative. In a run-down southern seaside boarding house, a woman talks insistently to her husband about breakfast before he leaves for his day's work as a deckchair attendant; her single lodger, Stanley, is visited by two strange and unsettling figures who seem to have been looking for him; they insist on holding a party for him, at which they deliberately smash his glasses and interrogate him with quickfire and apparently random questions; the next day, they take him away – a broken man – and no one intervenes. *The Birthday Party* would later be recognised as one of Pinter's most important works, but London at the end of the 1950s was not ready for its absurdities and non-sequiturs. Only Harold Hobson detected a level of meaning below the surface: 'Mr Pinter has got hold of a primary fact of existence. We live on the verge of disaster.' Hobson found echoes of Henry James and *The Turn of the Screw*, and understood that the play's 'spine-chilling quality' lay precisely in the fact that the threat could not be named:

> It breathes in the air. It cannot be seen, but it enters the room every time the door is opened. There is something in your past – it does not matter what – which will catch up with you. Though you go to the utter most parts of the earth and hide yourself in the most obscure lodgings in the least popular of towns one day there is a possibility that two men will appear. They will be looking for you, and you cannot get away.[6]

In *The Dumb Waiter* – first performed in Germany but opening in London in 1960 on a double-bill with *The Room* – two hired killers wait in a room for instructions on whom to murder next. They could almost be the intruders from *The Birthday Party*, but this time the twist is different, for it transpires that one of them is to be the victim. Again, the play could have been a chilling thriller, and at times it is. But the edge of comic absurdity and the sometimes Beckettian triviality of the men's arguments as they wait for something to happen makes it more treacherous than that. *The Lover* (1963) was equally disconcerting, as a suburban husband and wife double as their own illicit and secretive lovers by day. They are – or are they? – the same couple.

The Lover was shown on television before it was staged, and in the late 1950s and early 1960s Pinter wrote several other texts for television and radio. He also contributed short sketches to revues and wrote screenplays for two darkly compelling films directed by Joseph Losey – *The Servant* (1963) and *Accident* (1967). In 1969 he wrote a film adaptation of L. P. Hartley's *The Go-Between*. Meanwhile, Pinter's acting roles included Mick in *The Caretaker* (1961) and Lenny in *The Homecoming* (1969), while he also appeared in a televised version of Jean-Paul Sartre's *Huis Clos* (1965).

Pinter's early plays were often dismissed as derivative attempts to jump on to a passing bandwagon. 'It's all very well to imitate Ionesco and Beckett provided you have something else to offer beside the pastiche', disparaged the Lord Chamberlain's Reader; 'Mr Pinter imitates both without anything more to add – and my God! How boring he is.'[7] Later in his career, when his involvement with political issues became explicit, critics began to read back into these early plays a politics which had been largely missed. Pinter himself had always known it was there. Speaking in 1960 of the unexpected intruders in both *The Room* and *The Birthday Party*, who arrive 'out of nowhere', he commented: 'I don't consider this an unnatural happening. I don't think it is all that surrealistic and curious because surely this thing, of people arriving at the door, has been happening in Europe in the last twenty years. Not only the last twenty years, the last two to three hundred.'[8] Yet Pinter also refused a request from the director of the original production of *The Birthday Party* 'to clarify, to put a final message into the play so that everyone would know what it was about'. The play, explained Pinter, showed 'how religious forces ruin our lives'. But to spell this out would have been entirely inappropriate: 'Who's going to say that in the play?' asked Pinter; 'That would be impossible.'[9]

Before long, Pinter's style was termed 'Pinteresque', and he in turn had his imitators. His genre was branded as 'the comedy of menace', and his use of silence and – especially – the pause identified as trade-mark features. Pinter sometimes bemoaned the rather lazy critical obsession; it is perhaps as well that he couldn't know that the headline of his *New York Times* obituary would label him as 'Playwright of the Pause'. For Pinter, the pauses had never been particularly complicated or mysterious: 'All I was talking about was a natural break, when people don't quite know what to do next', he told one interviewer; 'But this damn word "pause" and those silences have achieved such significance that they have overwhelmed the bloody plays.'[10]

However, he also knew their weight as 'part of the body of the action' which the actor had to locate:

> The pause is a pause because of what has just happened in the mind and guts of the characters . . . if they play it properly they will find that a pause . . . is inevitable. And a silence equally means that something has happened to create the impossibility of anyone speaking for a certain amount of time – until they can recover from whatever happened before the silence.[11]

'I don't care for the didactic or moralistic theatre', Pinter declared in 1961; 'I object to the stage being used as a substitute for the soapbox, where the author desires to make a direct statement at all costs, and forces his characters into fixed and artificial postures in order to achieve this.' Revealingly, he described such manipulation as 'hardly fair on the characters'.[12] For it was crucial to Pinter's approach to writing that he should follow where the characters went, rather than dragging them around behind him. 'Characters always grow out of proportion to your original conception of them, and if they don't, the play is a bad one', he insisted.[13] Moreover, they are under no obli-gation to reveal themselves fully to the writer: 'My characters tell me so much and no more.'[14] That being the case, the author can hardly be expected to explain what his characters do or say. 'Something is being said, but the playwright isn't necessarily saying it.'[15] The result was a form of theatre which, for all its strangeness, bore a closer resemblance to real life than the neat constructions of the traditional well-made play. 'My situations and characters aren't always explicit', acknowledged Pinter in 1960; 'Well, I don't see life as being very explicit.' The lack of definition was in contrast to the conventional roles embodied by David Baron: 'Our personalities are too complex to be cut and dried and labelled.'[16]

One review of *The Birthday Party* commented – with some perception – that 'No character has any grip on his identity.'[17] The *Daily Telegraph* theatre critic put it differently – and more pejoratively: 'The author never got down to earth long enough to explain what his play was about, so I can't tell you.' Henry Woolf, the director of *The Room* and one of Pinter's long-surviving friends, remembers that the playwright's early work created a kind of panic among critics, who 'savaged' it 'in an extraordinary display of collective venom'. Precisely because Pinter's work was 'so different from anything that had gone before' they tried to shut it out and 'did their best to kill him stone-dead'.[18] By the early 1960s, it was clear they were not going to succeed.

INTRODUCTION TO ALAN AYCKBOURN

Born in Hampstead in 1939, Alan Ayckbourn had a childhood that was neither straightforward nor particularly happy. His father was a professional violinist with the London Symphony Orchestra, and his mother a prolific fiction writer for popular women's magazines. They never married and finally separated when Alan was only five. He spent his early years as the only child in a predominantly female environment, and from the age of seven, when his mother married someone else, he was sent away to boarding school. Inevitably, the tendency for Ayckbourn's plays to focus on dysfunctional marriages and warring families has often been linked to his own experiences.

Ayckbourn's secondary education was at Haileybury, a boys' public boarding school to which he won a scholarship. Here, he became heavily involved in theatrical activities, including writing plays for his 'house', and appearing in school Shakespeare productions which, remarkably for the 1950s, toured as far afield as Holland, Canada and the United States. He left school at seventeen, and worked briefly as an assistant stage manager with the company run by Sir Donald Wolfit, a powerful performer and an intimidating figure whose approach harked back to a pre-war theatre world dominated by imposing actor-managers. Ayckbourn went on to act in a number of regional repertory theatres, and it was as a performer – and perhaps a director – rather than as a writer that he seemed likely to develop his career. In 1957 he took up a position at the Library Theatre in Scarbrough, a venue founded two years previously by the pioneering Stephen Joseph, who had created the country's first professional theatre-in-the-round company. Joseph had also experimented with developing scripts through improvisation, and planned to go further by building on the traditions of commedia dell'arte and presenting shows which were partially improvised in front of audiences. This, however, was prevented by the Lord Chamberlain who decreed that any performance which failed to keep to a script he had previously authorised would be automatically illegal and liable to prosecution. Joseph became an important friend and mentor to Ayckbourn until his premature death in 1967.

Ayckbourn's own acting career at Scarborough in the late 1950s included appearing in the role of Stanley in the second production of Harold Pinter's *The Birthday Party*, in which he was directed by the playwright himself. Ayckbourn recalls that his own initial response to the play was to assume that its author was 'barking mad', and that he struggled to get to grips with the role or how to approach it: 'I remember asking Pinter about my character. Where does he come from? Where is he going to? What can you tell me about him that will give me more understanding? And Harold just said, "Mind your own fucking business."'[1] On the other hand, Ayckbourn has also acknowledged the significant influence of Pinter on some of his own early work.

Ayckbourn had written a number of plays while still at school, but his professional writing career officially began in 1959 with *The Square Cat*, a script created while he was working on *The Birthday Party*, and produced in response to a challenge from Joseph that if he wanted better acting roles he should write them himself. *The Square Cat* appeared under the pseudonym 'Roland Allen' – a name which acknowledged the contribution of Ayckbourn's first wife, the actress Christine Roland, whom he had recently married. *The Square Cat* was staged at the Library Theatre in the 1959 summer season under Joseph's direction, with Ayckbourn appearing in the part of rock'n'roll star Jerry Wattis, a character whose identity, when not performing, is that of the awkward and bespectacled Arthur Brummage. The play's title exploits a period-specific pun, further highlighted by the subtitle 'a cool comedy': the protagonist is simultaneously an edgy 'cat' and a safe 'square'. The part of Wattis/Brummage requires the actor to switch repeatedly between these two alter egos in line with the expectations of different characters: the play thus reveals in Ayckbourn an already keen interest in farcical situations and the potential of a complex interweaving of multiple 'realities'. *The Square Cat* proved a considerable success for the Library Theatre (unusually, its run was extended to a second week), although once he had become more firmly established as a playwright, Ayckbourn commented in interview – perhaps only partly in jest – that he had since tried 'to destroy all known copies'.[2]

After this promising start, Joseph immediately commissioned a further play from Ayckbourn: this became *Love After All*, staged at Scarborough in the autumn season of the same year. Complex construction was again a feature of this play (also by 'Roland Allen'), another farcical work that heavily exploited the twin motifs of disguise and mistaken identity. In this instance the plot was borrowed: Ayckbourn based the play principally on Pierre Beaumarchais's eighteenth-century comedy *The Barber of Seville*, although the context (the Edwardian era) and tone of the whole is also somewhat reminiscent of P. G. Wodehouse. Ayckbourn was not involved in the original production, but in a revival six months later he played the main part of Peter (originally Jim) Jones, a young man who eventually acquires a bride, as well as no fewer than three dowries from a miser, Scrimes.

Throughout the play, Scrimes is fooled as to the identities of both groom and bride: the latter is not – 'After All' the plot's twists and turns are resolved – his own daughter.

Peter Jones is a virtuoso role designed to allow the actor to demonstrate his flexibility. In the premiere Jones was played by the actor Barry Boys; Ayckbourn had always intended to take the part himself but was prevented from doing so because he was called up that month for National Service. Paul Allen, Ayckbourn's biographer, details his various attempts to avoid this duty, for example by deliberately ticking wrong answers on a multiple choice test and emphasising that he fainted at the sight of blood. Despite such tactics he was assigned to the RAF, but his 'service' ended after just two days. By chance, the medical officer who examined him was also a writer, and after a brief discussion of literature, the medic announced that it would be irresponsible to take Ayckbourn on with his 'bad knee' and dismissed him with an exit visa, apparently while other men – some with genuine health problems – were being told they were 'perfectly fit'.[3] Ayckbourn's own account of this exceptionally brief period of duty indirectly reveals that class privilege coloured his experience throughout. Perceived by those in command to be 'an educated sort of bloke', he was singled out immediately and told to 'see that these lads' in his billet '(got) on with their work'.[4] Undoubtedly, the armed forces were at the time still marked by insularity and snobbery; arguably, they remained a relative stronghold for the privileged even as increasing social mobility through the 1950s and 1960s continued to undermine the country's old class-based system more or less everywhere else.

In 1961 Ayckbourn directed *Gaslight* at the Library Theatre, and 'Roland Allen's' *Standing Room Only* – a play set on board a bus stuck in a traffic jam in Shaftesbury Avenue, and which imagines a Britain in the later twentieth or early twenty-first century where overpopulation has led to the roads becoming permanently gridlocked – was one of the successes of the season. (By coincidence, the same idea was picked up nearly fifty years later as a plot for a *Doctor Who* story.) In 1962, however, Ayckbourn and Joseph moved to Stoke to join with Peter Cheeseman in setting up the country's first permanent professional theatre-in-the-round venue (the Library Theatre had been seasonal rather than full-time). Two of Ayckbourn's plays had their first performances at Stoke. *Christmas V Mastermind* in 1962 was a seasonal show aimed at children, in which Ayckbourn himself appeared as 'The Crimson Golliwog', an unpleasant character who seeks to ruin Christmas by provoking industrial unrest and revolution and blowing up Father Christmas's factory with a bomb hidden inside a teddy bear. Ayckbourn describes the play as 'a broad, jolly farce', but also as 'the most disastrous play I've ever done' in which 'we died the death'.[5] In November 1963 Ayckbourn himself directed his own *Mr Whatnot*, an out and out comedy of mistaken identities and confusions, in which the central character is mute. The performance drew heavily on the sorts of visual gag and physical dexterity associated with classical silent films and comedians admired by Ayckbourn, including Charlie Chaplin and Buster Keaton, as well as the contemporary French performer Jacques Tati. The play was well received in Stoke, and the *Guardian* described it as 'extremely funny' and 'an unusual, and unusually effective piece of theatrical experimentation'; it was, said the reviewer, 'goonery with overtones of social comment', and he speculated as to whether this might set the tone for a new genre.[6] But when it transferred to London in the summer of 1964 the production was slated by almost all the critics, to an extent which nearly led Ayckbourn to abandon writing altogether.

By now, Peter Cheeseman had become focused on the idea of developing documentary and musical dramas from local history, with scripts which were not the work of a single author but emerged through a creative process involving the entire company. This was not a model which interested Ayckbourn, and he became a full-time producer with Radio Leeds. However, he also continued his own writing – he has always been able to produce texts remarkably quickly – and to have his plays produced in Scarborough. In 1965 he directed his own *Relatively Speaking*, which transferred to London with great success, and in 1967 *The Sparrow*, a slightly darker comedy about relationships and exploitation, which was linked by some of the theatre critics to the work of Harold Pinter. *The Sparrow* received good national reviews during its Scarborough run, but failed to follow *Relatively Speaking* into the West End.

Following the death of Stephen Joseph in 1967, Ayckbourn was one of a group of people who committed themselves to keeping the Library Theatre going – not least in tribute to what Joseph had achieved. In 1970 he felt able to leave his job with the BBC in order to focus fully on writing and directing, and in 1972, he began what would become a remarkably long and successful career at the Library Theatre (renamed Stephen Joseph Theatre in 1996) as Artistic Director and resident playwright.

CHAPTER 3
PLAYWRIGHTS AND PLAYS

JOHN ARDEN
by Bill McDonnell

In 1978 John Arden, one of the finest dramatists of the twentieth century, gave up writing plays for the British and Irish stage. This, despite the fact that in *Serjeant Musgrave's Dance*, *The Workhouse Donkey* and *Armstrong's Last Goodnight*, three plays considered here, he had written some of the most powerful and innovative dramas of the late 1950s and early 1960s. More than any of his contemporaries he has divided critics and audiences alike. Two narratives define orthodoxy on Arden.

The first describes a considerable theatrical poet, who produced in *Serjeant Musgrave's Dance* one of the great post-war dramas, and who then went off the rails, got caught up in the great causes of the radical Left in the 1960s: Vietnam and the liberation struggles of Africa and Latin America, black liberation and, above all, the neo-colonial war in Ireland. Driven on by his wife, the radical intellectual, writer and actress, Margaretta D'Arcy, he became detached, it was argued, from the wellspring of inspiration that had driven him, his art compromised by a naive activism, a great talent wasted on polemics. The second narrative also recognises his greatness, but sees it as coterminous with the politics, with ideological passion and theatrical brilliance nourishing each other. Director William Gaskill thought him the closest modern writer to Shakespeare, while Michael Billington designated him Britain's Brecht. For Fintan O'Toole he was the last of the sixteenth-century dramatists, a designation which neatly caught Arden's deep sense of tradition – the radical conservatism of his dramaturgy. For his great advocate, Albert Hunt, Arden was a twentieth-century theatre revolutionary, 'one of the greatest dramatists in the English Language for several centuries', and an instinctive political radical.[1]

What all can agree on is that he and Margaretta D'Arcy had an increasingly turbulent relationship with the mainstream theatre and, with the exception of occasional pieces for political campaigns, this potential colossus of post-war theatre wrote no more works for the stage after *Vandaleur's Folly* (1978), focusing instead upon radio plays and novels. For some this seemed an appropriate choice: where his plays were weak, say his critics, was in an excess of language, theatrical elaboration and imagery. His was a novelistic imagination. Perhaps he overwrote, argued his advocates, but he also produced great dramatic works of an exuberant visual density, in which politics and theatricality, poetry and commitment, existed in mostly fruitful tension – part Brecht, part Rabelais, part medieval minstrel and part activist. Writing nourished by an eclectic mix of classicism and the carnivalesque, Shakespeare and Jonson, Dickens and Defoe, cowboy westerns and the folk traditions of British popular culture.

Where critics saw a falling away in the later years, a materialist reading sees, beneath the necessary turbulence of lives, of shifts in thinking and writing, a developing political, ideological and artistic commitment. We can distinguish, between 1958 and 1978, a movement from a generalised and liberal concern with social injustices, state violence and war, to a radical commitment to revolutionary change. Or, in Arden's words, a movement from a play like *Serjeant Musgrave's Dance*, 'which does not come to any very positive conclusion' to a more interventionary and didactic form, 'affirming from his own hard experience the need for revolution and a Socialistic society'.[2] It is tempting to read the earlier works forward into the later, to see in *Serjeant Musgrave's Dance*, for example, a clear foretelling of the later radicalism. Yet this is to disengage the plays from their personal, theatrical and historical contexts, and to ascribe to Arden a clarity of political purpose which he refutes. 'Twelve years ago I looked on at people's struggles, and wrote about them for the stage, sympathetically, but as an onlooker. Without consciously intending it, I have become a participant.'[3]

In exploring the seminal Arden plays of the 1960s, then, this essay will view them neither as the (considerable) detritus of a once-promising career, nor as self-evident harbingers of revolutionary commitment, but rather as the expression of an encounter between a rich and instinctually liberatory theatrical imagination and the contingencies of post-war imperial and economic history. It will pay particular attention to the political events which inspired the plays, seeing them not as incidental, as many critics have, but as central to understanding how the Aldermaston protester became the political dissident and exile.

Serjeant Musgrave's Dance

In the post-Suez period the slow unravelling of the British Empire gathered pace. On the foreign news pages of *The Times*, Arden and his generation read of imperial crises in Cyprus, Malaysia, Hong Kong, Kenya, Nigeria, Aden and more. One of the more intractable was Cyprus, which Britain had annexed in 1925 from a disintegrating Ottoman Empire, and which had a population composed of Greek and Turkish nationals. In 1955 a guerrilla movement, the EOKA or Ethnikí Orgánosis Kipriakoú Agónos (National Organisation of Cypriot Struggle), began a military campaign to end British rule and achieve unification with the Greek mainland. Greek Cypriot irredentism was fierce, if short-lived, and the British response was equally ferocious – beatings, torture, extra-judicial killings and internment were among the strategies employed by the British colonial administration. Arden's play draws on a particular incident.

On 4 October 1958, a Mrs Cutliffe, wife of a British soldier, was shot by two young EOKA fighters as she walked along Famagusta's high street. In response the army rounded up every male Greek Cypriot aged between fifteen and thirty, confining them in 'emergency interrogation pens'. As *The Times* noted in a careful understatement: 'Troops in the grip of sheer cold rage . . . were in no mood to use kid glove methods.'4 Over 150 Greek Cypriots were hospitalised and a further 100 badly injured; a little girl was one of five Cypriot fatalities. The incident was the inspiration for Arden's most famous play, *Serjeant Musgrave's Dance*, first produced at the Royal Court Theatre, London on 22 October 1959. The production was directed by Lindsay Anderson and designed by Jocelyn Herbert with music by Dudley Moore. Ian Bannen played Musgrave.

Musgrave is set in a small mining town in the late nineteenth century, not unlike Arden's home town of Barnsley, the hub of the South Yorkshire coalfields. Albert Hunt offers a summary of the play's actions:

> The story of *Serjeant Musgrave's Dance* has the simplicity of a ballad. Four deserters bring the body of a dead soldier back to his home town, a mining community in the grip of a coal strike, and cut off by the winter snow. Their leader plans to hold the town at gunpoint, while, in a public meeting, he presents the dead soldier's skeleton and brings people face to face with the truth about war. But things go wrong. One of the soldiers, Sparky, tries to run away with a barmaid called Annie, and is accidentally killed. At the climax of Musgrave's meeting Annie produces Sparky's body. The meeting collapses, the snow thaws, the dragoons arrive, and one more of the deserters is killed. At the end of the play the town celebrates its escape, while the two remaining soldiers, Attercliffe and Musgrave himself, wait to be hanged.[5]

It is around this basic tale that Arden weaves his anti-imperial narrative. The text was influenced by his fascination with cowboy films, in particular an American Civil War western, *The Raid*, in which disguised Confederate soldiers arrive in an isolated Northern town. The play has three acts, broken down into eight scenes which, following the dramaturgy of *The Raid*, show a slow unfolding and complicating of relations between the soldiers and the town before the dramatic denouement. Musgrave, in his thirties, commanding, rigid, messianic, was drawn from images of the Crimean sergeant who fought with gun and Bible: 'I began with the scarlet uniforms for purely theatrical reasons.' [6] The other soldiers began as types 'surly', 'angry' and so on, and were given names only during rehearsals:

Attercliffe, a fifty-year-old seasoned soldier; Hurst, in his twenties, quick-tempered and impetuous; Sparky, the 'baby' of the group, is emotional, vulnerable, easily led. The Mayor is also the coal-mine owner, the Parson another stock type. Of the play's composition Arden writes: 'I did not plan much beyond the middle of act two . . . I knew the climax was the production of the skeleton . . . I had three main visual images – the big marketplace scene, the scene with the soldiers in the stable at night, and the soldiers' arrival in the town.'[7] These scenes are the cornerstones of *Musgrave*'s architectonics, an analysis of which can help us elucidate the play's themes and the dramatic strategies which embody them.

'The revelation'

In Act 1, scene 3 the soldiers meet at sunset in the churchyard. They have returned from scouting the town, and as Musgrave asks each man what he has seen, their responses form an arresting series of cine-matic vignettes, the western motif alive in each. The repetition adds to the accumulating atmosphere of latent fear and hostility, of cold and emptiness:

> Hardly a thing. Street empty, doors locked, windows blind, shops cold and empty. A young lass calls her kids in from playing in the dirt – she sees me coming so she calls them in / Hardly a thing. Street empty, no chimneys smoking, no horses, yesterday's horse dung frozen on the road. Three men at a corner post, four men leaning on a wall. No words: but some chalked up on a closed door – they said: 'Soldiers go home.' (pp. 28–9)

But for the cold it could be another colonial enclave, with the soldiers as an occupying force. Hurst makes this connection explicit in the scene's first revelation, that the soldiers are deserters on the run and bent on some retributive act. He himself has killed another soldier, though we do not know why. This act, blamed on 'rebels', binds him to Musgrave, whose messianic rhetoric he rejects, but whose purposes he supports.

Hurst I thought when I met you, I thought we'd got the same motives. To get out, get shut o' the army – with its 'treat-you-like-dirt-but-you-do-the-dirty-work' – 'kill him, kill them, they're all bloody rebels, State of Emergency' . . . It's nowt to do with God. I don't understand all that about God, why do you bring God into it! You've come here to tell the people and then there'll be no more war . . .

Musgrave Which is the Word of God! . . .

Unlike Hurst, Musgrave is not intent on pacifistic agitation, but revelation and retribution. He is a man of specifics and terrifying logic. When Attercliffe tells him that 'All war is sin', he brushes him aside:

Musgrave I'm not discussing that. Single purposes at a single time . . . one night's work in the streets of one city, and it damned all four of us and the war it was part of. We're each one guilty of particular blood. (pp. 33–4)

The 'one night's work' being, as in Cyprus, a bloody repression which has brought them to this moment. These experiences have given them common cause with the strikers: 'their riot and our war are the same one corruption', meaning colonialism, the ultimate expression of 'dishonour and greed, and murder for greed' (p. 36). The soldiers are in the town, Musgrave tells them, to purge it of corruption, 'to stand before the people with our white shining sword and let it dance' (p. 36). There will be, or so the iteration of the word 'dance' implies, an ecstasy of retribution, a 'Judgement against mercy and Judgement against the blood' which will absolve the deserters of 'the murders we have done' (p. 36). Musgrave, Sparky will later tell the barmaid Annie, is God, 'and it's as if *we* were like his angels' (p. 37). They are avenging angels, driven mad by war and the suffering of war. They are planning something terrible, but we do not know what. Arden called Act 1, scene 3 the 'revelation', and rewriting went on during rehearsals, focused on clarifying the soldiers' purposes without revealing their intentions. Audiences, caught up in the tense emotion of the soldiers' debate, remained puzzled.

'Wild woolly mad!'

Act 2, scene 3 opens with the soldiers settling to sleep in the public house. Musgrave sleeps in the main building, while the others bed down in the stable; as audience we can see both spaces. It is a night of dramatic emotional turmoil and tragedy, of nightmares and violence, evoked in a series of striking stage images. Earlier in the evening the barmaid Annie had arranged to come to Hurst's bed. She does so, but is painfully rejected, first by Hurst and then by Attercliffe. In desperation she turns to Sparky, responding to his vulnerability and fear. The two plot to run away but are overheard by Hurst, who confronts Sparky, bayonet drawn. Attercliffe intervenes, and in the ensuing mêlée Sparky is accidentally stabbed to death. Musgrave acts to cover the death, telling Mrs Hitchcock to lock Annie in a cupboard; Sparky's body is thrown into the pub's midden. Now the Bargee comes to tell them that the colliers have their Gatling gun. Just as the strikers and their leader Walsh are apprehended, the Constable and Mayor arrive. The snow is thawing; they have called out the Dragoons, who will be there by midday. There is an urgency now to Musgrave's plans. He tells the Mayor to call a public meeting the next morning: the soldiers will recruit, and the beer and money will help contain further militancy.

'A judgment against mercy'

Act 3, scene 1 is the great climactic scene in the market place. The small town, cut off from the outside world, is a microcosm of England under Empire. The iterative tropes of the play, 'empire', 'colonial', 'rebels', 'killings', are more insistent now. The choreography of the scene is intricate, and hinges on two moments of dramatic complexity. Mistaking Musgrave's intent, the Mayor and Parson begin by praising army life, urging the strikers to join up: 'The Empire calls! Greatness is at hand!' (p. 79). Following these vacuous hypocrisies, the soldiers take out the Gatling gun, praise its murderous capacity, and set it up facing the people and, behind them, the audience. It is a brilliant theatrical gest. Then this troupe of performing avengers stage a furious *coup de théâtre* as, to frantic drumming, Hurst throws a rope over a lamp bracket and

Flings open the lid of the big box, and hauls on the rope . . . the
rope is attached to the contents of the box, and these are jerked up
to the cross-bar and reveal themselves as an articulated skeleton
dressed in a soldier's tunic and trousers, the rope noosed around the
neck. The **People** *draw back in horror.* **Musgrave** *begins to dance,*
waving his rifle, his face contorted with demonic fury. (p. 84)

As he dances he sings: 'Up he goes and no one knows/How to bring
him downward' (p. 84). The song's refrain hints at a nihilistic fatalism,
a ritual of rage and despair, prefacing Musgrave's planned murderous
act of retribution. 'I am', Musgrave had told the soldiers earlier, 'in
this town to change all soldiers' duties' (p. 37). The violence of the
colonial wars is to be brought back to its source, 'to work that guilt
back to where it began' (p. 37). Those who send others to kill will be
killed, violence will be cured with violence. The dance over, he
beckons the people forward, telling them, on pain of death, not to
move from the market place.

After the manic energy of the dance the soldiers, like a fractious
Greek chorus, tell a story: how local boy Billy Hicks had died, shot by
a 'terrorist', and how the soldiers had gone on the rampage as they had
in Cyprus: 'It's easy, they're all in bed, kick the front doors down,
knock 'em on the head, boys, chuck 'em in the wagon' (p. 87). At the
end of the reprisals five are dead, including a girl, and twenty-five are
injured.[8] The sequence is the most perfect compression of the
dynamics of counter-insurgency. The insurgents got away, but the real
killers are here, in the market place, where young men are raised and
sent off as cannon fodder in imperial wars, generating a cycle of
violence. For each dead Cypriot Musgrave will kill five people. That is
Logic, he says, and 'Logic is the mechanism of God' (p. 91). This is
the act of messianic retribution prefigured in the dance. It is at this
moment that his authority drains away. It is left to Hurst to refocus
the mission:

Hurst   We've earned our living by beating and killing folk like
yourselves in the streets of their own city. Well, it's drove us mad
– and so we come back here to tell you how and to show you what

it's like. The ones we want to deal with aren't, for a change, you and your mates, but a bit higher up. The ones as never get hurt. (*He points at the* **Mayor**, **Parson** *and* **Constable**.) Him. Him. Him. You hurt them hard, they'll not hurt you again. And they'll not send us to hurt you neither. But if you let them be, then us three'll be killed yes – aye and worse, we'll be forgotten – and the whole bloody lot'll start all over again!

Hurst's speech is a call for revolutionary violence, a plea for class solidarity between soldier and worker. His warning of the consequences of a failure to seize the moment is prescient. Two of the colliers are sympathetic: 'These are just the same as us. Why don't we stand with 'em?' (p. 95). Yet Walsh, the militant, demurs – the soldiers are part of the state's repressive armoury and he does not trust them. The revelation of Sparky's death a moment later distracts the plotters, the Dragoons arrive, Hurst is shot dead, and the old order is reinstated after a temporary, if dramatic, lacuna. The reassertion of order is encapsulated in a series of stage images as striking as those surrounding the raising of Billy's skeleton, and which go to the heart of the play's dramaturgy. Musgrave's dance is now mirrored by another. It is a visual, scenic representation of the defeat not only of Musgrave's project, but of the colliers, as the strikers are ritually reabsorbed into the community. The Bargee invites all to drink and dance:

He gives out the mugs in the following order: the **Mayor**, the **Parson**, the **Slow Collier**, the **Pugnacious Collier**, the **Constable**. Each man takes his drink, swigs a large gulp, then links wrists with the previous one, until all are dancing around the centrepiece in a chain, singing.

Annie has climbed the plinth and lowers the skeleton. She sits with it on her knees. The **Dragoons** remain standing at the side of the stage. **Musgrave** and **Attercliffe** come slowly downstage. The **Bargee** fills the last two tankards and hands one to **Walsh**, who turns his back angrily. The **Bargee** empties one mug, and joins the tail of the dance, still holding the other. After one more round he again beckons **Walsh**. This time the latter thinks for a moment, then bitterly throws his hat *on the ground, snarls into the impassive face of the* **Dragoon**, *and joins in the dance, taking the beer.*

The scene closes, leaving **Musgrave** *and* **Attercliffe** *on the front stage.* (p. 99)

This remarkable tableau integrates the personal and political, the emotional and the social. Walsh's absorption was seen by some as a defeat, yet it is tempered by the knowledge that the community still exists: the oppressions that motivated Musgrave and the strikers still obtain. Arden tells us to look to the women for the message, and it is Mrs Hitchcock, not Walsh, who goes to the heart of Musgrave's failure. Mocking his attempt to 'end the world' she goads him, 'In control, you!' (p. 102). Control, duty, logic, these were Musgrave's mantras. His is the logic of terror, individual or state: the logic of colonial oppression and of the Gulags, of Stalin's Russia or Cambodia's Killing Fields. If the individual death is 'not material' as he says of Sparky and the little girl, then any violence can be done in the name of a projected greater good. It is also Hitchcock who recognises the fragility of the new accord. Musgrave despairs as he watches the people: 'and all they dancing – all of them – there' (p. 102). To which she replies:

Mrs Hitchcock   Ah, not for long. And it's not a dance of joy. Those men are hungry, so they've got no time for you. One day they'll be full, though, and the Dragoons'll be gone, and then they'll remember.

Human life is short, but history is long, she is telling him; you are lost, but your cause is not. This is the message of Arden's play, and of another great anti-war play, Brecht's *Mother Courage*. And, like *Mother Courage*, Arden's play refuses banal solutions to intractable historical problems. Walsh's question takes on special resonance in this context:

Walsh (*with great bitterness*)   The community's been saved. Peace and prosperity rules. We're all friends and neighbours for the rest of today. We're all sorted out. We're back where we were. So what do we do? (p. 99)

Revolutionary change, as the great Polish Marxist Rosa Luxemburg insisted, is not the product of a single moment, but is a long and circuitous historical process, defined by fruitful failures as well as successes. Therefore Walsh, we recognise, is wrong. We are not back where we were. The order that is reasserted is not the same order: people have been changed. Here, as in his other works, Arden worked complexity from simplicity: a simple tale is rendered through its dramatic elements into a complex (for some confusing) political and moral drama about war, colonialism and capitalism. Arden was correct to reject the idea that *Sergeant Musgrave's Dance* was a 'nihilistic play', a symbolist drama, or that it advocated violent revolution. It is an anti-war play. Arden wrote: 'I have endeavoured to write about the violence that is so evident in the world', through a character whose actions we can deplore while understanding his motives: 'the sympathies of the play are clearly with him in his original horror, then turn against him and his intended remedy'.[9]

That Arden did not approve of Musgrave's action is implicit in the play's conclusion, but also in its formal features. Musgrave's grand seriousness is constantly undercut by farce. For example, at the conclusion of 1.3, as Musgrave prays, he is parodied by the Bargee. The parody is a distancing device: a type of alienation. Throughout the play the Bargee will play the people's Fool, acting as a 'fugleman', disrupting empathy, revealing the author's hand at work. Or we may look at the 'Fred Karno' sequence at the beginning of 2.2. as the Bargee drills the drunken colliers in a parody of the soldiers. It is he who suggests the colliers steal the soldiers' gun, and who arrests Musgrave and delivers him to the Dragoons before initiating a return to a known community. These are complex theatrical devices, and their effect is to deny Musgrave and his mission its full tragic solemnity. Commentators say this is Brechtian; it is not, it is Shakespearean.

Serjeant Musgrave's Dance divided the critics, as all his plays would. Many found the play too slow, blamed variously on Arden's lack of discipline ('overwriting'), its poor dramatic structure (the first two acts were overlong) and Lindsay Anderson's direction. Harold Hobson called it 'another frightful ordeal', fulminating that 'it is not the principal function of the theatre to strengthen peace, to improve morality or to establish a good social system . . . it is the duty of the theatre not to make men better, but to render them harmlessly happy'.[10] Phillip Hope-Wallace felt it was 'something short of a great play', but all in all a 'highly original and challenging experiment'.[11] Felix Barker, writing in the *Evening News*, enthused: 'That last scene with its breathtaking change of pace and mood and the blinding flash of understanding that came with it produced a tremendous theatrical explosion.'[12] Overall there was a sense of a flawed but disturbing work. What the reviews shared was a deeply political evasion of *Musgrave*'s critique of colonialism, which led Arden to insert the following into the programme for the 1965 revival:

> Please don't attach too much weight to the drama critic of *The Times* who says, 'When this play first appeared, its sidelong references to the Cyprus troubles overshadowed the main content . . .' Cyprus may be a solved problem. May be. Aden? Malaysia? Do I have to list them? Rhodesia was once a Victorian Imperialist adventure. Vietnam has never been a British colony of course, but . . . 1965–6 is an ugly year's-end as was 1958–9, when this play was conceived and written.[13]

Hobson would later revise his opinion, but in that moment his response seemed decisive for *Musgrave*'s commercial success. It played to third-full houses, and cost the Court its entire Arts Council subsidy for 1959. Arden's next play would address a very different theme, municipal corruption.

The Workhouse Donkey

The Workhouse Donkey – a Vulgar Melodrama was commissioned by the English Stage Company, but was 'farmed out', in Arden's words, to the Chichester Festival Theatre, where it was directed by Stuart Burge, in July 1963, with Frank Finlay in the lead role. The Court's rejection hurt, and not just because Chichester was an unsuitable venue. According to D'Arcy the decisive break with the Court had come earlier, with the 1960 production of *The Happy Haven*, which had been taken off after two weeks: 'That was the end of Arden at the Court. Indeed the board seems to have vowed "No more Arden ever again!"' For a long period after the 'humiliation' of the *Happy Haven* débâcle, D'Arcy writes, Arden was in a state of 'collapse and depression'.[14] One fruitful side effect was the remarkable month-long community arts festival which the couple organised in their home in the Yorkshire village of Kirbymoorside in 1961.

For the moment, however, Arden turned again to his birthplace, Barnsley, for inspiration. In an autobiographical fragment, Arden writes of his home town that it was 'run by a self-perpetuating mafia of Labour Party demagogues', its politics dominated by Labour politicians whose ideology was in many respects 'humane and excellent' but whose secure hold on local government had led to a 'highly complacent local politics', and culture of complacent low-level corruption:

> I wanted to set on the stage the politics, scandals, sex life, and atmosphere of Barnsley as I remember shocked Conservative elders talking about it in my youth . . . certain key incidents – the burglary at the Town Hall, the incident at the Victoria, the politics of the art gallery, and so on – belong in not so veiled form to the politics of Barnsley.[15]

Arden's text, a sprawling, Rabelaisian comedy about local town-hall corruption, focuses on the downfall of 'the Napoleon of the North', Alderman Charlie Butterthwaite, nine times lord mayor, and a character last seen by audiences in *Live Like Pigs*.

Although *The Workhouse Donkey* could not be more different in ethos to *Serjeant Musgrave's Dance*, it opens with a bustling public scene which, Arden says, is an attempt to link it with the older play. The plot focuses on the fall of Butterthwaite, the workhouse donkey of the title, who has risen from extreme poverty to dominate his local Labour Party and the town. A swaggering, charismatic, manipulative scoundrel, he has a gambling addiction, which is bankrolled by the Machiavellian, but self-aware, Doctor Wellington Blomax: 'I am a corrupted individual; for every emperor needs to have his dark occult councillor: if you like, his fixer, his manipulator – me. I do it because I enjoy it' (p. 17). It is this relationship which has maintained Butterthwaite's power, and which will undermine it. Leading the local Conservative Party is Sir Harold Sweetman, a local brewer, art lover and (undeclared) investor in the town's Copacabana strip-club. The play opens with Butterthwaite laying the foundation stone for a new police station. During the ceremony the new chief constable is introduced, the 'incorruptible' Colonel Feng, fresh from colonial service: 'An extremely different locality where the prevalence of violent crime was such that only the firmest of firm hands could eliminate it. It has been eliminated' (p. 14). Labour leader Councillor Boocock has appointed Feng to try and cleanse the town of the systemic corruptions of Butterthwaite's reign, corruption which extends to the highest levels of the police, embodied in Superintendent Wiper, who is having an affair with Gloria, the manageress of the Copacabana. She becomes pregnant, and to secure her situation, secretly marries Blomax. The plot is driven by the intent of both political groupings to enlist Feng's support in exposing and undermining their political opponents. When Sweetman sets him on to investigate after-hours drinking by Labour councillors, Butterthwaite retaliates by accusing the chief constable of political bias: 'He has wrapped himself up, neck and navel, to an unscrupulous political minority. I am preparing a full exposure' (p. 71). An exposure which will include revealing Sweetman's involvement in the Copacabana Club. Gloria and the Tory leader's wife, Lady Sweetman, hatch a plot to bring the great man down, enlisting the support of Blomax, whose daughter is in love with Maurice Sweetman. He can, they tell him, support his own class and abandon the workhouse donkey – or face being struck off for selling prescriptions. Blomax folds. He presses the impecunious Butterthwaite for the repayment of a £500 loan. Butterthwaite burgles the town hall safe in order to pay his debt. His attempt to pass the theft off as a burglary fails, and he is exposed and publicly shamed. Feng is sacked. As in *Musgrave*, the final scene tends to a surface resolution: the corrupt but powerful stay in place, class inequalities and state and civic power structures remain.

The play bursts at the seams with great set pieces: the visit of

Butterthwaite and the Labour councillors to the Copacabana club: the burglary, and its Keystone Kops-inflected aftermath: Feng's inept attempt to woo Ms Wellesley; and so on. The play is a rumbustious melodrama, and for the Chichester production a band sat on a balcony in full view of the audience, providing the musical accompaniment for the songs and dances which are woven into the fabric of the action. Arden asked for a scenographic simplicity to allow the actions to flow, remarking that the production should observe 'the limits of visual extravagance normally adhered to by the artists of seaside picture-postcards'.[16] He described the play as 'a straightforward classic comedy in structure ... Jonsonian', a potent mix of social comment, music hall and pantomimic forms, with a complex plot which is 'not realistic but fantastic'.[17] The play's theatrical force derives from the prodigious energy which is applied to what are, in the scale of human wrongdoing, minor transgressions. This energy flows in part from Arden's dramaturgy, in part from language. Part of Arden's break with naturalistic modes lies in his characters' linguistic facility: his characters are wordsmiths, poets, major or minor, capable, like Butterthwaite, of a striking eloquence. He is a Falstaffian character, whose speech is imbricated with borrowings from Shakespeare and the Bible, the demotic argot of Barnsley blended with the grand rhetoric of tragedy. 'Making strange' in Arden is first and foremost an effect of language.

In the final Act, as his world collapses following the discovery of the theft, this rhetorical richness is married to a potent, visual and 'Ardenesque' theatricality. The setting is a civic reception to celebrate the opening of Sweetman's art gallery. The epic register is set with Boocock's remonstration to the fallen hero: 'Charlie, I don't know why you've done this, but your last remaining friends can do nowt for you now. You have pulled your own self down' (p. 124). Seated on a table, drunk, holding a bottle of champagne as a weapon, caressing the head of a supporter, a Carnival Lear with his Fool, bereft of support, his speeches are defined by a superlative grandiosity and a wonderful visual density:

> Oh, oh, oh, I have lived. I have controlled, I have redistributed.
> The Commonwealth has gained. The tables have been spread.

Not with bread and marge you know, as they used to in the workhouse, but with a summation of largesse demanding for its attendance soup-spoons in their rank, fish knives and forks, flesh knives and forks, spoon for the pudding, gravy and cruet, caper sauce and mayonnaise . . . and I by my virtue stood the President of the Feast . . . Philosophy be damned . . . We piped to them and they did not dance, we sang our songs and they spat in the gutter. (*He pats the little Demonstrator's head.*) I was the grand commander of the whole of my universe. (p. 125)

He wraps the tablecloth around him like a shawl, takes a paper chain and hangs it around his neck, and places a ring of flowers that had garnished the buffet on his head. He is a prophet abandoned:

In my rejection I have spoken to this people. I will rejoice despite them. I will divide Dewsbury and mete out the valley of Bradford; Pudsey is mine, Huddersfield is mine, Rotherham also is the strength of my head, Osset is my law giver, Black Barnsley is my washpot, over Wakefield will I cast out my shoe, over Halifax will I triumph. Who will bring me into the strong city, who will lead me into the boundaries of Leeds? Wilt thou, oh my deceitful people, who hast cast me off. And wilt thou not go forth with Charlie?

His ejection from the community is symbolic. He has overreached himself: he is a scapegoat who must be sacrificed, a fallen king. The sequence is, says Arden, 'meant to refer to the medieval character, the Lord of Misrule. This is what he has become.'[18]

Reviews were, for the most part, extremely positive. Michael Billington thought the play a masterpiece, one that had yoked Shakespeare and music hall, demonstrating that it 'was after all possible to unite passion, politics, poetry, sex and song in a living theatrical form'. And while Bamber Gascoigne was less impressed, finding it too rambling and cliché-ridden, Philip French was enthusiastic: 'Why the piece hasn't been recognised as one of the half-dozen best British plays of the last decade is a mystery.'[19]

The play, says Arden, was 'conscientiously historical,'[20] a fact reinforced when, in 1974, former Newcastle City Council leader T. Dan Smith was sentenced to six years in prison for corruption. Born into a mining family, Smith had been council leader between 1960 and 1965, and had overseen the redevelopment of the city, clearing its slums and providing good housing and social and cultural amenities for its people. Known as 'Mr Newcastle', he was a charismatic, ambitious, combative politician. He was also corrupt, holding pecuniary interests in firms which received council contracts. Smith was one of a generation of Labour Party politicians who came to power in the 1950s and 1960s, who had been shaped by the experience of the General Strike and the Depression, and who, while they had flirted with Communism, were socialists of an instinctive, ideologically pragmatic and tribal kind. While not all were as corrupt as Smith, *The Workhouse Donkey* was prescient in its satirical but affectionate dissection of this historical phenomenon. Butterthwaite celebrates the type in a typically vainglorious manner:

> I turned tramcars over
> In the turmoil of twenty-six,
> I marched in the hungry mutiny
> From the north to the Metropolis,
> I carried the broken banner.
> When hungry bellies bore no bread,
> I dreamed of my dinner
> In the wasted line of dole,
> And by fundamental force of strength
> I fetched my people through it.
> Call it the Red Sea, call it
> The boundaries of Canaan,
> I carried them over. (p. 92)

Butterthwaite, for all his flaws, was a socialist in the mould of T. Dan Smith. He had presided over a flawed and corrupt but warmly human polity. We have, says Arden, more to fear from the 'ferocious integrity' of a Feng than from the cupidity of a Butterthwaite.[21] Boocock is clear-sighted about the corruption which pervades all classes and all relations, and yet – and this is the play's point – there is a type of venal harmony here, which produces schools and homes even as it traduces civic ethics.

Given Arden's later flirtations with revolutionary Marxism, and his commitment to Republican irredentism, the play may seem to lack ideological freight, its critique of class inequalities too light, and its vision of an ideal order too liberal. Butterthwaite's lament as he is dragged away to prison could be construed as a warning about the vulnerability of democracy in the face of entrenched class interests, the comic counterweight to Mrs Hitchcock's counsel to Musgrave:

> Out he goes the poor old donkey
> Out he goes in rain and snow
> For to make the house-place whiter
> Who will be the next to go?

Yet, despite the political sources of these plays, in none of them does Arden propose a different order of society, or even suggest that one is possible, or explore how it might be achieved. This has led some to accuse him of a naive romanticism. Clearly a committed internationalism and anti-imperialism went hand in hand at this stage with a pre-lapsarian vision of human community. In the preface to *The Workhouse Donkey* he extolled the virtues of Dionysus, including in them generosity and lasciviousness, but also corruption and ease. His vision for the perfect production of *The Workhouse Donkey* was of an all-day durational performance, with interludes, with audiences free to wander among fairground stalls, play and eat, returning to the theatre as they chose to pick up the narrative. This was close, he acknowledged, to Joan Littlewood's concept of the Fun Palace, but also to Breughel's paintings, such as 'Lenten Fair', where we find a similar celebration of social existence, of a flawed but energised humanity. For the pre-1968 Arden the ideal human community is more likely to be found in the paintings of the medievalists Breughel and Cranach the Elder than in the school of Soviet socialist realism. Talking about the 'tradition' of comic theatre, he sums up his purposes in *The Workhouse Donkey* as follows:

Theatre consists of plays which must be organic events – to get hold of their audiences by laughter, by pain, by music, dancing . . . people must be able to laugh, not only at other people but at themselves, and at the things that hurt them. The social purpose of theatre is to bring men and women together in a secular Eucharist.[22]

It is an emancipatory text, a carnivalesque dissection of political mores, a gentle political satire, not a political manifesto.

Armstrong's Last Good Night

Albert Hunt sees *Armstrong's Last Good Night* as a sequel to *Musgrave*: 'Like *Musgrave* it deals with an attempt to stop violence, and like *Musgrave* it springs from an historical situation, this time the war in the Congo.'[23] The Congo's independence from Belgium, achieved in June 1960, was part of the broader anti-colonial liberation movement which was redefining sub-Saharan Africa in the period. The pre-independence elections were won by Marxist radical Patrick Lumumba, who became its first prime minister. Alarmed by the threat to its neo-colonial economic strategy posed by Lumumba, Belgium and its indigenous proxies acted to protect their interests, and Lumumba was faced within weeks by an army revolt and the secession of Katanga, a mineral-rich area, under the leadership of Christian and anti-communist opposition leader Moise Tshombe. On 10 July Belgium sent in troops to support the secessionists and secure the mines. Lumumba appealed to the UN, who sent a peace-keeping force under special envoy Conor Cruise O'Brien, who was mandated to negotiate the ending of secession and the removal of Belgian troops. When the rebels refused to obey, O'Brien ordered the UN troops in. Western pressure on UN secretary general Dag Hammarskjöld led to O'Brien being removed from his post. The CIA supported a Tshombe-led coup, during which Lumumba was assassinated. O'Brien wrote a book about his experiences, *To Katanga and Back*, which Arden had read, and which came to inform the play's political argument.

The play's plot was derived from the sixteenth-century ballad 'Johnnie Armstrong', which details James V's assassination of the Scottish warrior during the 1530 suppression of the Borderlands. Arden took this moment in late-medieval history to create a subtle political allegory on the themes of political and cultural colonisation. While the ballad gave the play, in Arden's words, 'its climate', its political and ideological argument drew once again on contemporaneous colonial struggles. Inspired by Arthur Miller's creation of faux-seventeenth-century speech patterns in *The Crucible*, Arden fashioned what he termed 'a Babylonish dialect', a pastiche of modern and late-medieval Scots, which, he hoped, would 'prove practical on the stage and yet still suggest the sixteenth century'. The invented dialect provided a linguistic bridge between past and present, historical fact and poetic metaphor. During rehearsals for William Gaskill's production Arden worked with the actors, helping them come to grips with the demands of the language. For the setting he turned again to tradition: 'The play is intended to be played within the medieval convention of the "simultaneous mansions". These are three in number and represent the Castle (for the Armstrongs), the Palace (for the court) and the Forest (for the wild land of the Borders).'[24]

Arden insisted that the mansions retain the formality and emblematic qualities of the medieval source. What the audience see are two power centres contesting a middle ground: two conflicting cultures and conceptions of nation explored in a dynamic and fluid dramatic space. The mansions allow for visual complexity – we see the journeys between the centres, as when Glass and the two women walk out into the Forest and then into the Palace: we see Lindsay seeing Armstrong claim his lover: characters do not always see what is close, but can sometimes see what is out of sight. In Arden, moral complexity is expressed through visual complexity.

In the opening scene Lord Commissioners from England and Scotland are negotiating a peace accord. England is ruled by Henry VIII, Scotland by the child-king James V. The accord is being threatened by the freebooting outlaws of the borderlands, whose 'masterless raids from Scotland into England' (p. 150) invite English invasion and risk Scotland's existence. Accompanied by his secretary, McGlass,

John Lindsay, poet, diplomat and tutor to the young James, is sent to bring the 'maist ferocious of these thieves', Johnny Armstrong of Armstrong, 'intil the King's peace and order' (p. 151). Lindsay, 'ane very subtle practiser' of the diplomatic arts, prized for his urbane charms and 'discreet humanity' will seek a rational solution to the war using 'Policy, nocht force' (p. 151).

> As ane man against ane man
> And through my craft and my humanity
> I will save the realm frae butchery
> Gif I can, good sir, but gif I can. (p. 153)

Lindsay likens the situation to a Gordian knot, which must not be cut, but subtly unravelled. At the Scottish court he must reckon with the powerful Lord Maxwell, 'ane tyrannous and malignant peer . . . and ane constant threatener of rebellion. Nae Armstrong rides against England outwith his implicit permission' (p. 153). Maxwell's urge to power would be served by an English invasion to unseat James. Lindsay offers Armstrong the title of Warden of Eskdale and Free Lieutenant if he 'will follow the course of war ahint nae other banner than that of King James' (p. 48). Armstrong, impetuous, sensuous, a warrior king, is delighted: 'Ye are the King's Herald: ye bring the offer of the King. Acceptit. I am his officer' (p. 177). In return for his fealty, the King promises to imprison Lord Johnstone, protector of his borderland rivals, the Wamphreys. Later Armstrong will seduce Lindsay's mistress, a deliberate provocation. Lindsay's plan is undermined by Maxwell, who, jealous of his own status, refuses to allow Armstrong's elevation. In fury, Armstrong organises another raid into England, losing Lindsay his influence with the King, who is faced with the threat of invasion. When the Herald goes to see Armstrong he finds him in the (apparent) thrall of a Lutheran Evangelist. He warns the warrior that 'the English are preparen war' (p. 228). When McGlass berates the Evangelist for sanctifying Armstrong, 'that murderer in all verity with the words of the Gospel!' (p. 233), he is stabbed to death with his own knife. The act feels arbitrary, echoing the death of Sparky in *Musgrave*. Lindsay returns to Armstrong a third time, carrying a free pardon and safe conduct from the King, and inviting him to join the royal hunt. Flattered, and trusting Lindsay, he goes with him. But the invitation is a trap. The King, disguised as a soldier, meets Armstrong, hidden soldiers disarm him and his men, and, after a violent struggle, the outlaw is hanged from a tree.

While the play is subtitled 'an exercise in diplomacy', it bodies out Clausewitz's famous dictum that 'war is the continuation of politics by other means'. Lindsay's error – and Arden stresses this – is to assume that his belief in human discourse and rational dialogue could survive the Machiavellian imperatives of either court. He and Armstrong are both pawns, guilty of political naivety. The one is led astray by impetuousness, the other by a lack of seriousness. For Lindsay diplomacy is a game, and one he thinks he is very good at. Disdainful of Alexander the Great's need to cut the Gordian knot ('could he no be a human man instead and sit down and unravel it?', p. 154), he finds to his cost that power always seeks the shortest route to its object. Diplomacy is long but political necessity is short – 'the urgency is merciless' (p. 154), the Scots clerk tells him in 1.2. Later his secretary McGlass, dying from the fatal stab wound, goes to the heart of Lindsay's problem:

McGlass   Ye did tak pride in your recognition of the fallibility of man. Recognise your ain then, Lindsay: ye have ane certain weakness, ye can never accept the gravity of another man's violence. For you yourself hae never been grave in the hale of your life! (p. 222)

Treachery is not a breach of this moral order, but its binding principle. Armstrong states it most clearly: 'There's nane that may in a traitor trust/Yet trustit men may be traitors all' (p. 159), and just before he lures his enemy Wamphrey into a trap, and has him brutally murdered. Yet it is Lindsay, who decries covert treachery, who will be the agent of the play's greatest betrayal. Arden is clear in the moral equivalences he sets up: the murder of Wamphrey is paralleled by the murder of Armstrong. Treachery and violence emanate from both sides: expediency, material need and a cruel pragmatic violence is the currency of power in a complex and ever-shifting political landscape. Armstrong's power is fragile, but so too is Lindsay's, who panders his mistress, only for jealousy to bleed into policy and render him vulnerable. We are not meant to see the resolution as a good. Accused of condoning Lindsay's expediency Arden responded:

> I find the whole sequence of events in the play so alarming and hateful (*and at the same time so typical of political activity at any period*) that I have, perhaps rashly, taken for granted a similar feeling amongst the audience . . . My views on the Armstrong story are positive enough – Lindsay was wrong.[25]

Lindsay's tragedy was to realise the seriousness of his situation only at the point when he had already lost his power in James's court. Arden wrote of the plot: 'I've tried to present a situation in which everything is linked to another factor, until you can hardly get through the thicket of it all. There is no simple answer, which is the natural situation in life.'[26] Yet there is a moment in the third Act when Lindsay sees a way out of the 'thicket', proposing to McGlass a solution based on 'the manner of mountain cantons of the Switzers as I hae observit them, on my travels. Nare heriditaire nobility, nae theft, nae feuden . . .' (p. 222). The solution was not continuous domination and occupation, but a federation of equals which respected cultural and national autonomy, and brought an end to war. Armstrong also envisions an independent Borderland, and Lindsay will promote the idea again later as 'ane practicable rational alternative . . . he is ane potential magnificent ruler of his people' (p. 226). The play's climax is also foreshadowed here:

> **McGlass**   It is ridiculous and unpractical. England wad never consent to it – why, it wad mean peace! (p. 222)

The irony of McGlass's comment is overlapped by a deeper irony as, told that the King wanted Armstrong dead, Lindsay retorts:

> **Lindsay**   King Henry has preoccupations. Religious, financial, amorous. I trow he craves for peace – sincerely.

McGlass   He craves for the execution of Armstrong and I think we hae no choice but to gie it him.

Lindsay   What way, man? Whaur's your army, whae's your hangman – you? Wad ye mak your name ane byword for tyranny and coercion . . . (p. 222)

It is at this point that diplomacy is unravelled by Armstrong's renewed raids, which put Lindsay, as his advocate, in peril. Now *he* must cut the Gordian knot. Outmanoeuvred, he colludes in the murder of his antagonist, and the withered tree on which Armstrong is hanged becomes, in Lindsay's final speech, a symbol and warning: 'ane dry exemplar to the warld: here may ye read the varieties of dishonour' (p. 248).

Within its intricate, poetic structure *Armstrong's Last Good Night* addresses one of the most critical questions of colonial and neo-colonial political diplomacy: the use of a parallel policy of military force and diplomacy. These questions arose in the last colony, Ireland, and in the slow resolution of contemporary wars in Iraq and Afghanistan. While the events in the Congo did not map neatly on to the play's plot, Arden would draw attention to the parallels in a detailed exegesis in a programme note:

> Tshombe of Katanga was a threat to the central government of the Congo if he remained a separatist leader . . . He was backed by Belgian mining interests and also by foreign governments whose activities at the United Nations bear a certain resemblance to the activities of Maxwell and his friends in Edinburgh . . . the UN brought Dr O'Brien into a society where intrigue . . . was no less common than violence in its most naked form.[27]

Arden makes clear that Lindsay does not represent O'Brien just 'as Armstrong does not represent Tshombe, nor Wamphrey Lumumba'.[28] A more accurate reading of the historical parallels would have Lumumba as James V seeking to contain the secessionary impulses of Armstrong, whose actions were manipulated by both indigenous forces (Maxwell et al.) and the external pressures of the predatory colonial power (England). While the play was not a 'roman à clef', in yoking this late-medieval crisis to contemporaneous neo-colonial conflicts, Arden was pointing to certain imperial and historical continuities, including the violation of subaltern cultures. Its political themes are articulated in a poetic, visual and panoramic play full of dense theatricality, beautifully summed up by Penelope Gilliatt:

> There is a clump footed reel that looks like a Breughel, an almost cinematic shot of a girl lugging the corpse of her untrue lover into the woods, a hanged body that turns like a salmon on a hook . . . sweet love scenes and swift treacheries, a sense of tragedy that is cool and rather chaste.[29]

Armstrong's Last Good Night and *Serjeant Musgrave's Dance* are post-colonial texts in their concerns with the great themes of liberation and oppression, cultural imperialism and militarism, but they are not didactic texts or historical documentary dramas about colonialism. Indeed, *Armstrong* is not historically accurate in any sense – its main protagonist, Lindsay, was not involved in King James's war against the Armstrongs, and the Reformation, represented by the Evangelist, was still a century in the future.

The play received its first performance at the Glasgow Citizens Theatre in May 1964, before being revived for the Chichester Festival in July 1965, where it was co-directed by John Dexter and William Gaskill for the National Theatre Company. Albert Finney played Armstrong and Robert Stephens, Lindsay. Although it was, perhaps inevitably, well received in Scotland, reception in England was mixed. Hobson thought it a 'rag bag of clichés old and new',[30] while Tom Milne considered the play 'as rich and full blooded as anything seen on the English stage for years'.[31] For some the invented language proved a barrier, seeming dense and incomprehensible, with even as sympathetic a critic as Frances Gray consoling herself by focusing on the beauty of the actors. When it was revived, again in a production by Gaskill, at Edinburgh in 1994, critics pointed now to its relevance to the unfolding peace process in Ireland, where diplomacy went hand in hand with the continued threat of state and Republican violence.

Gaskill was a great admirer of Arden's work and was bemused by his lack of commercial success, given that 'he seems to be the one who comes closest to writing a kind of English popular theatre'.[32] He thought Arden a writer

> a bit like Shakespeare in his approach in that the writing not only has to convey the dialogue of characters speaking together, but also has to carry the sense of the social environment, and the texture of people's lives; in addition it has to carry the writer's attitudes and his philosophies about the situation.

This calls for a special kind of writing, one that combines scholarly erudition with a refined poetic imagination, qualities Arden has in abundance. Directing a play like *Armstrong's Last Good Night*, Gaskill said, is 'like doing a symphony by Mahler or Bruckner – you have to be prepared for the length of it . . . with Arden you have to absorb the entire experience from start to finish before you understand'. In comparison with a Pinter or Beckett, Arden was, he thinks, 'very Shakespearean', a playwright who 'wrote in full flood, and the shape merging as he wrote it . . . I think he is unique in being so.' It was the plays' scale and poetic density which affected their reception, a point iterated by Geoffrey Reeves, who blamed the conservativeness of the British theatre system, in particular its actor training, which left it unprepared for and unable to translate Arden's demanding plays adequately to the stage. He makes a striking comment: 'If he is performed within the framework of the system, the system feels a great jolt – and so does the play.'[33] Later Arden would dismiss the Court 'revolution' as a myth, which had left the basic and conservative power structure of the theatre intact. As the 1960s progressed, such issues would come to the fore as part of a broader ideological critique of Western society driven by the emergent alternative theatre movement.

Britain's Brecht

Michael Billington has called Arden the British Brecht, a comparison which he accepted, albeit with the important qualification 'I would have written as I did without Brecht'.[34] Citing *Mother Courage* as the one play he wished he had written, Arden praised Brecht's view of the theatre: 'he believed that it was a potential instrument of social progress, and that the playwright, by reflecting in his work the true image of human society, assisted by members of that society to diagnose the defects in the image and thence to improve the reality'. He admired Brecht's theoretical rigour, noting that a poor theatre is poor only in so far as it is not 'possessed by any ideological purpose'. What he was not was a slavish imitator: he and Brecht arrived at roughly similar perceptions because they shared a rejection of naturalistic forms, and a patrimony of ballads, Shakespearean and Jacobean drama, and popular culture(s). Where Brecht drew selectively on popular traditions to reinforce a core dramaturgical model, Arden raided the tradition for models: commedia dell'arte for *Happy Haven*, music hall for *Live Like Pigs*, medieval dramaturgy for *Armstrong's Last Good Night* and melodrama for *The Workhouse Donkey*. These borrowings and reworkings are a trope of his dramaturgy, but also go to the heart of his politics. Each method helped to create the distance he wanted, the imperative to reveal theatre as a 'material fiction, an artificial contrivance'.[35] It is in this sense that he is a dialectical playwright, who found in traditional forms a fruitful tension between conserving and radical impulses

Conclusion

Between 1965 and 1970 Arden produced one more single-authored work, *The True History of Squire Jonathan* (1968). The five years marked a paradigmatic shift in his thinking about theatre and politics. His partnership with D'Arcy, which began with *The Happy Haven*, would now come to define his theatre writing. Visits to New York in 1967 to work with the anti-Vietnam movement, and to India in

1969, where they witnessed poverty and oppression on a scale unparalleled in the West, reinforced their critique of Western economic imperialism. From 1965 onwards there would be an accelerating concern with how theatre could speak to the age, and in particular to the post-colonial condition of Ireland and the Third World. Their confrontations with the mainstream theatre, notably with the ICA during a production of *The Hero Rises Up* (1968) and with the Royal Shakespeare Company over the production of *Island of the Mighty* (1972), reinforced a growing disenchantment. While left-wing playwrights produced through the moment of '68, the likes of Brenton, Hare, Edgar and Griffiths, would gravitate from the fringes into the centre of the British theatre establishment, Arden and D'Arcy moved inexorably in the opposite direction. This was reflected in their 1968 collaboration with socialist theatre CAST, for whom they wrote *Harold Muggins is a Martyr*, a play exploring the corruption scandals then embroiling the Metropolitan Police, and which premiered at Unity Theatre on 14 June 1968. The production signalled a shift in Arden and D'Arcy's conception of political drama, from a focus on plays about political subjects to plays written for political contexts, a change brought about by the historical crises of the 1960s. Arden:

> In 1968 many things had come to a head. There was the revolt of the students and workers in France, with all the consequent excitement exported abroad from it . . . There was the Russian invasion of Czechoslovakia . . . There was the prohibition by Stormont Unionists of a perfectly reasonable Civil Rights March in Derry . . . the savage attack on the marchers who had the nerve to defy the ban, and the inexorable slide of the largely forgotten Irish problem into the maelstrom of blood and bitterness which to this day swirls wider and wider.[36]

Their work from *The Royal Pardon* onwards had mined history for its metaphorical power, its oblique and suggestive political exemplars for the present. As the 1970s progressed there would be a shift to a more direct interventionary style and didactic engagement, in plays which dealt directly with the neo-colonial war in Ireland, and which took a more didactically Marxian approach to history. Texts such as

The Ballygombeen Request (1972), the *The Non-Stop Connolly Show* (1975) and *Vandaleur's Folly* (1978) would accelerate their rejection by the mainstream, not because they were bad plays, Trish Dace argues, but for being plays containing an 'indictment of what Britain has done to the Irish'.[37]

What changed Arden from a liberal to a radical, then, was history, in the shape of the moment of '68, and in particular the Irish Troubles. This is not to say that the earlier works were not deeply political in their concerns with imperialism and its many violences – including economic and cultural – but that they were not the expression of a fully formulated political philosophy, as for example, we find with Edward Bond. Arden's radicalisation is explicable, but it was not inevitable. Although he would later commit to revolutionary socialism, his political and social philosophy as expressed in these three plays is emancipatory, not revolutionary. A deep and continuous concern with history and human oppression and liberation is expressed through a rich theatricality, capable of both stark realism and a poetical and sensual beauty. If there is a consistent political theme to these plays, it is that ideological rigidity and dogmatic thinking repudiate the essentially improvised nature of all social life, and of revolution itself, and deny the radical uncertainty that is the wellspring of change. Imperialism, war, economic exploitation, moralisms of all kinds, are the enemies of a human world because they are the enemies of an emancipated, self-determining, creative and necessarily disordered human polity.

Although Arden did (briefly) describe himself as a Marxist, he more properly belongs in the great dissenting tradition of English literary radicalism, with Hazlitt and Paine, Shelley and Blake.

EDWARD BOND

There's nothing complex or difficult in the things I am writing about. It's a very common-sense, straightforward assessment of what's wrong with the world, and what one ought to do about it. There's nothing profound in what I say.[1]

In 1965, *Saved* heralded the arrival of a completely different voice to the British stage, unlike any that had gone before. There had been anger. There had been violence. But nothing that had disturbed or seemed so threatening as this. The censors who decided what could and could not be seen and said in British theatre were genuinely anxious about the impact it might have – particularly the notorious scene in which a group of youths assault and murder a baby in its pram:

> At the Royal Court it is unlikely that anyone got more than a sadistic thrill from the scene . . . It is my opinion however that this scene acted vividly by well cast characters, with all the appropriate props and business and before a different type of audience, which included a proportion of the gangs that now exist, could be a direct incentive to some of the sub-humans who now associate in gangs, to perpetrate a crime of this kind.[2]

Most critics denounced the play. Even one of the play's champions reported that she 'spent a lot of the first act shaking . . . and thinking I was going to be sick', while the murder was 'watched by the audience in utter silence' – a silence in which 'Nobody dared move . . . for fear of vomiting.'[3] If anyone had thought of the term, they might have called it 'in-yer-face theatre'.

All the plays on which this chapter focuses contain shocking and brutal images. Bond was often accused of revelling in such violence – even of celebrating it:

> The whole play, whilst allegedly designed to illustrate the squalor of ugly lives has a secondary, perhaps unintentional theme . . . the glorification of the teenage gangster and . . . his utter callousness and immorality . . . Since the Royal Court Theatre glories in the fact that its offerings are didactic and not entertainment, this play is designed to teach, and to teach what may well be asked.[4]

Bond would later claim that he wrote about violence as inevitably as Jane Austen wrote about manners – it is at the centre of the world we inhabit.[5] Those seeking to keep it off the stage had ulterior motives: 'The censors are themselves military men, they are trained to use the bayonet in anger . . . when a soldier says that violence must be curbed one should at least always have the freedom to ask if in practice that means conserved.'[6] In Bond's view, the majority of people living under capitalism are controlled by 'inhuman institutions whose task is systematically to destroy them'. Society has violence as its bedrock: 'They destroy people because . . . our society could not exist unless we were destroyed. A human being was not designed to work in a factory . . . as a tool. You're not made to stand at a bench day after day doing these mechanical things.' When a society depends on a system which involves doing violence against its citizens, it is inevitable that some of those citizens will themselves commit violent acts. 'If you take a dog and you chain it up from the moment it is born, the dog will become vicious. Now this is in fact what we do with human beings.'[7] Moreover, how could it be reasonable to attack a playwright for showing an enactment of violence while ignoring the real thing? 'Only a Philistine can be revolted seeing the stoning of a doll on the stage and reconciled with the fact that children are being starved to death.'[8] A perception which almost exactly pre-echoes a sentiment expressed thirty years later by Sarah Kane – whose work was in turn defended by Bond – in the face of the critical assault on her play *Blasted* at the time of the Balkan war:

> The thing that shocks me most is that the media seem to have been more upset by the representation of violence than by violence itself . . . While the corpse of Yugoslavia was rotting on our doorstep, the press chose to get angry, not about the corpse, but about the cultural event that drew attention to it.[9]

By contrast with *Saved*, the violence in Bond's other plays of this period is perpetrated either by, or at the behest of, those in authority. And often it is carried out calmly and professionally – even dutifully. For another of Bond's key insights is that many of the greatest crimes against humanity are committed not out of hate but out of love; that, as he says, 'We are as likely to be destroyed by "good" as by "evil".'[10]

Yet he maintains that we are not, as a species or as individuals, inherently violent or evil. Rather, we have constructed a society which makes us so. Therein lies the hope for humanity, and while these plays may at first appear nihilistic, they all offer the possibility of a way out. For all their horrors, these are not plays of despair. Not even tragedies. All we've got to do is to change the world. Above all, then, these are political plays. The task is to show that change is necessary.

Saved: 'Yer can't call it livin' . . .' (p. 123)[11]

No, I've never heard of a baby being stoned to death but I have heard of babies being bombed to death.[12]

Saved had not arrived from nowhere. In the late 1950s Bond had been part of the Writers' Group nurtured at the Royal Court, and his first performed play, *The Pope's Wedding*, had been given a Sunday performance there in 1962. This led directly to the commission which would result in *Saved*, the script of which had been gathering dust in a drawer in the theatre until Bill Gaskill took over as Artistic Director and immediately decided to produce it. The Lord Chamberlain's Office refused to issue a licence ('this revolting play . . . ought not to be shown on any stage'[13]) without more than fifty cuts, including two entire scenes, and the resulting confrontation has often been credited – not least by Bond himself – as the key weapon which detonated under the 230-year-old system of theatre censorship and brought it crashing down: 'It was either the censor or me – and it was going to be the censor.'[14] Thumbing its nose at the censors, the theatre announced that it would constitute itself as a private club for fourteen performances, with admission restricted to members only. The Lord Chamberlain promptly advised the Director of Public Prosecutions that he doubted the club would be 'genuine', and that this was 'disguised public performance';[15] but although the theatre was taken to court and fined on the grounds that its 'private' performances were effectively public, the financial penalty was tokenistic and the censor's authority had been fatally wounded.

The 'private' production opened in November 1965. 'REVOLTING IF IT WASN'T RIDICULOUS', was the *Sun* headline (in the days when that newspaper still went to the theatre). 'PAST THE LIMITS OF BRUTALITY' said the *Sunday Times*, while under 'EVEN THE ROYAL COURT REVOLTED', the *Daily Mail* described the 'the waves of shock' which had run through the theatre and 'the smack of seats being vacated'. Although Bond's play had public supporters – including Sir Laurence Olivier – he was widely accused of indulging in 'filth for filth's sake', 'squalid fantasy', 'sadistic antics'; of taking a 'gloating approach to moments of brutality and erotic humiliation', of 'reducing the theatre to the equivalent of 20th Century bear-baiting or cock fighting', and taking theatre to a new low: 'was there ever a psychopathic exercise so lovingly dwelt on as this?'[16]

Saved focuses on the impoverished lives of working-class characters in south London. Bond intended to raise questions about what drives them to behave as they do; about the values and structures of a society which permits people to grow up like this. But what made the play difficult for many of the critics to accept was that no one within the play voices such questions or attacks the system which has imprisoned them. That is what Bond required his audiences to do – for the characters in the play lack any political consciousness. A newspaper review of the Royal Court's revival of the play at the end of the 1960s which toured to Belgrade and Eastern Europe recognised the point; the characters of *Saved* are 'trapped in a world from which all exits are barred'; they are 'players in a brutal and cruel game which they do not understand', and can do nothing but 'knock their heads irrationally and furiously against the walls'.[17] But most members of the British critical establishment were unable – or unwilling – to spot this, and longed instead for a character or a speech to clarify the playwright's message, so that they would know where they were. Bill Gaskill (the director), acknowledged the problem: 'The lack of overt didactic statement in the play has misled people into failing to grasp this essentially moral design of the author', he admitted; *Saved*, he said, was 'written for an audience who could see that these people were impoverished'. As Michael Billington shrewdly observed: 'Mr Bond has chosen a difficult task: to try and dramatize the lives of the inarticulate.'[18] Those who attacked the play criticised them as 'a bunch of brainless, ape-like yobs';[19] 'moral imbeciles'; 'foul-mouthed, dirty-minded, illiterate . . . barely to be judged on any recognizable human level at all'.[20] Bond agreed they were 'hooligans', suffering from 'moral illiteracy'. But he located the root of their illiteracy not within the individuals, but in society. It was, he said, 'the disease most people are being left to rot of', and the education system was doing the leaving: 'There's really no difference between our State prisons and our State schools', he wrote; 'They function in the same way, and they are organized, in the same way, to serve the same purpose.' And that purpose was the deliberate production of 'zombies' – in other words, 'alienated slaves, who will fit into our society, at least to the extent of consenting to it'.[21] Writing in the programme, Bill Gaskill also challenged the easy demonisation of the characters: 'Some of the critics of *Saved* talk of the people in the play as if they were freaks or psychopaths', he noted, 'but to me they are absolutely ordinary people with whom it is very easy to identify.' By labelling and separating, he said, 'you avoid responsibility'.[22]

One of the more positive and perceptive reviews of *Saved* was written by Penelope Gilliatt in the *Observer*. Gilliatt wrote primarily about film – a medium which frequently puts less into words and invites us to read behind what we see and to extrapolate meaning. She had no problem in seeing the implications of the play:

Edward Bond has planted a foul piece of social evidence in our files . . . The play is about English thuggishness; it is our Fascist document, the one we don't want to know about. 'Gangs all over the place,' says the murderer in the play . . . 'police don't do their job.' It wasn't my fault about Belsen, I only worked there.[23]

The scene on which the controversy centred occurs towards the end of the first half when Pam leaves the baby, which she never wanted, in the charge of a group of young men in the park, one of whom, Fred, is probably its father. Over the next ten minutes – for no real reason other than because they can – they dare each other into an increasingly vicious attack, which culminates in throwing stones at the baby from close range, and placing lighted matches in its pram. At the end of the scene Pam returns and pushes the pram away, without even noticing what has occurred. It was (and is) an intensely shocking and disturbing scene, and many pronounced it the most nauseating and repellent they had ever witnessed. 'The important thing', said Bond in relation to his own unmade screen adaptation of *Saved* in the 1980s, 'is to explain the cultural poverty and thus the murder.'[24] The key question an audience must face is why the act is committed: 'The young people murder the baby in the park to regain their self respect', explained Bond in 2011, when the play was revived; 'If you do not understand that you do not understand the times you live in.'[25] Sean Holmes, the director of the 2011 production, again emphasises the fact that the murder – and what it stands for – should not be seen as inevitable, or blamed on inherently anti-social individuals, but as something which is preventable, but which no one prevents:

> if you follow that scene through there are a couple of hundred moments which would prevent it happening. It's not a *Clockwork Orange* thing in that they get up in the morning ready to go out and commit an act of savage violence. The last thing on their mind is killing a baby. Tiny things happen that lead towards that act which are also symptoms of something enormous about the world they live in.[26]

Such was the level of misunderstanding and hostility directed towards *Saved* in 1965 that the Royal Court organised a 'Teach-In' at which the playwright, the director and several critics and cultural commentators debated some of the issues raised. Bond admitted he had been taken aback by the accusations made against him:

> one assumes that if you are going to show a murder on the stage one doesn't have to get up or make one of the characters say before or after – this is horrible and ought not to happen. That is self evident and a writer must be able to rely on his audience to some extent.[27]

Yet he was also clear that he had meant the play to disturb. 'It is shocking and intended to shock', proclaimed the leaflet advertising the Teach-In; 'The intentions of the author are unquestionably serious', it insisted, 'and though he offers no moral solution, he poses the problem in such a way that one knows a solution must be found.'[28] Bond himself stirred things up further by describing the violence as 'a typical English understatement', since the murder of a single baby was 'a negligible atrocity' when compared, for example, with the British air-strikes on German towns at the end of the Second World War.[29] 'I wanted to evoke the heartlessness of all violence', he wrote, 'the aftermath of an air raid, the atrocities in Africa, the garrottings and firing squads in Asia.' For Bond, the killing of a single baby was also 'insignificant' if set alongside 'the cultural and emotional deprivation of most of our children'.[30]

The way in which the killing is actually staged is also critical, as Gaskill explained at the Teach-In: 'if I wanted to give an audience a vicarious thrill to their masochistic instincts I should have done it much more successfully', he declared; 'It's not a difficult thing to do, I promise you.'[31] Curiously, some of the reviewers who objected most had also complained that the killing had not been theatrically convincing ('I knew there was no baby in the pram, just as I could see there were no stones in the actors' hands'[32]). In fact, Gaskill's intention had been to present it in such a way that the audience could watch it 'with great detachment'. It was on the men and not the baby that the audience should focus, and Gaskill's staging promoted this – as some critics appreciated:

It was a stroke of genius on the part of Gaskill to turn the baby into an object, so that the main emotions and reactions are determined not by the cruel murder of the innocent baby but by the way the murderers experience it . . . it transpires in the end that the baby in the pram is an ordinary doll. Not even crying is heard to support the illusion. And so it happens that our attention is diverted from the sufferings of the baby to the intense feelings bursting from the young murderers.[33]

For Bond, it was vital that the play should not just be a photographic slice of life: '*Saved* isn't naturalistic', he insisted; 'Naturalism asks: what? Realism shows what and asks: why?'; crucially, he added, 'this has implications for the performance, since the "why" obviously determines the way the "what" is shown'.[34]

In some respects, *Saved* focuses less overtly on the causes of the murder and more on its consequences. At first, it may appear that these are also few or non-existent. There is no repentance or regret, no clear sign of anyone learning lessons or changing their lives – everyone and everything seems to carry on largely as before. Fred is convicted, but expresses no guilt or remorse either before or after his imprisonment. 'It was only a kid', he says without irony, accepting no blame and even accusing Pam of having 'ruined my life' (pp. 83–5). In Bond's own words, 'Fred regards going to prison as a middle-class boy would regard going on one of the Duke of Edinburgh's Outward Bound courses – as an initiation and something to boast of.'[35] Nor do we see any direct evidence after his release that Fred has faced up to what he has done. Perhaps even worse is the fact that Pam appears equally unconcerned about the baby she has lost; she remains as obsessed with Fred as ever, and it seems hardly to occur to her to blame or question him for what he has done. Some reviewers thought this must be the point Bond was making: 'His purpose, if I understand it, is to show that even this can happen and life goes on as before.'[36] This was a misreading of the playwright's intentions:

I wanted to show that violence and what you could call misdirected sex cannot be indulged in – in an interlude from normal life – and then forgotten: the agent is affected as well as the victim. These effects change the structure of his life in less obvious but more far-reaching ways than the effects of social exposure or punishment. They force compromises and give psychological wounds that often turn the remainder of his life into tragedy.[37]

For it is not true that nothing changes. Superficially, Fred may seem the same when he emerges from prison, but Len reports this differently: 'Yer ain' seen what it done t' 'im. 'E's like a kid. E'll finish up like some ol' lag, or an ol' soak. Bound to. An' soon. Yer'll see' (p. 126). And in a devastating scene towards the end of the play Pam finally breaks down into uncontrollable crying and suicidal despair, realising the hopelessness and poverty of her existence: 'Whass 'appenin to us? . . . All my friends gone. Baby's gone. Nothin' left but rows. Day in, day out. Fightin' with knives . . . I'll throw myself somewhere . . . I can't go on . . . Yer can't call it livin' . . . I can't stand any more. Baby dead. No friends . . . 'No 'ome. No friends. Baby dead. Gone . . .' (pp. 122–3).

According to Gaskill, 'Everything about the play is planned and organized so that the audience's experience will pass from the shock of violence to an understanding of its causes and finally to a statement which is positive rather than negative.'[38] True, there is no revelation or redemption, no sudden vision of a better world. But to resolve such profound problems on the stage would be manifestly dishonest – and would also let the audience off the hook, since it is they who must take the responsibility to try and initiate change. 'If I had written a meretricious, modest little piece, with a facile panacea in the last scene, I could have had the critics clapping their hands off', claimed Bond – and he was probably right.[39]

Bond emphasised that while *Saved* 'leads up to tragedy', yet 'it doesn't fall into tragedy'.[40] Indeed, he famously described the play as 'irresponsibly optimistic'.[41] The most obvious manifestation of the positive is invested in Len – a deeply flawed character, hardly more able than anyone else to articulate or perceive what is wrong within the world of the play, but someone who at least aspires to a code of moral values, and who consistently tries to help others. For Bond, Len was the centre of the play – a point which most critics failed to identify: 'Hardly one of them has noticed that the play is about a liberal, although he is in every scene, and about his attempts to pacify his environment. These attempts fail, and not only because of his personal failings. He is finally captured by his environment.'[42] Len, says Bond, is 'naturally good, in spite of his upbringing and environment'. Yet he is 'not wholly good or easily good because then his goodness would be meaningless'.[43] The fact that he observes the stoning of the baby without intervening makes him as guilty as anyone else. Indeed, Bond called Len's inaction 'a worse crime', characterising it as one 'which has, for the liberal position, much worse implications'. Probably these implications extend to a Royal Court audience which observes the performance and then does nothing about the world it sees. Yet Bond also insists on 'the tenderness, humanity and decency of Len', explaining: 'That is why I did not leave him, or his liberal position, without hope.'[44] In conversation with Fred, Len at least shows some recognition of culpability: 'I didn't know what t'do. Well, I should a stopped yer' (p. 86). He at least has the capacity to ask questions and make judgements about the behaviour and situations of others – such as the non-relationship of Pam's parents, constructed entirely on a basis of hatred and revenge. Moreover, even after Pam rejects him, Len offers care for both her and the child. In the near-silent final scene – a devastating image of non-communication described by Gilliatt as 'the most horrific thing in the play' – Len, alone, is doing something constructive.[45] While Harry completes his football coupons, Pam leafs repeatedly through the *Radio Times*, and Mary tidies the room or just sits, he is mending a chair. Moreover, when he discovers his repair has not worked, he returns to the task again. There are no big speeches, no profound changes, but here, at least, is some possibility of change. As Bond put it: 'Clutching at straws is the only realistic thing to do.'[46]

Olivier said of the final scene that 'Chekhov himself would have purred his approval.'[47] In fact, the play often focuses on the everyday and the trivial. 'Many of the scenes are very slow', observed Gaskill, each with its own 'very separate identity'; some were 'funny', some 'tender', and others 'just representative of the infinite lethargy and boredom of people's lives'. The crucial point, says Gaskill, is that the violence 'comes out of the apathy'.[48] Indeed, arguably more distressing than the stoning is the prolonged scene of dysfunctional family life, throughout which we hear the crying of a baby that no one wants to look after. Another disconcerting aspect of *Saved* is that it is often balanced on the edge between darkness and comedy. The moment when Mary is provoked to strike her husband produces blood and pain; yet there is an almost absurd comedy about the use of such a domestic weapon, and about the husband's self-pity. As Bond once commented in relation to his dramaturgy: 'I like them [i.e. the audience] to laugh in my plays when they want to feel tragic.'[49]

While it is sometimes difficult in looking at the impact a performance had in the past to grasp what all the fuss was about, nearly fifty years after *Saved* was first staged, and in spite of our familiarity with violence graphically depicted on stage and screen, Bond's play still shocks. 'It's going to get worse', he warns; 'I don't know what will happen, but I do know that we are driving straight at that brick wall.'[50]

Early Morning: 'Perhaps we needn't be like this' (p. 211)[51]

I wrote this play very carefully, it was very carefully put together; it was about a year or more. It was not an unimpassioned play, but it was a very calculated play . . .[52]

While *Saved* has retained its status as one of the iconic plays of the 1960s, Bond's next play has been largely forgotten – other than for its distinction of being the last play banned in its entirety by the Lord Chamberlain. With its cruel satire against such pillars of historical respectability as Queen Victoria and Florence Nightingale, it might have been designed to get up the noses of the establishment. But it is much more than just a rude and provocative gesture, for one of Bond's starting points is that the values established in the nineteenth century continue to dominate in the second half of the twentieth. This was not, then, a play that was only about the past.

While most critics saw *Early Morning* as a grotesque and sick fantasy, Bond describes it as 'social realism', and 'a simple and lucid record of history'.[53] 'The statement 'This play is true' was inscribed in large print both on the title page of the published text and in the programme, though the narrative offers a nightmarish dystopia and a series of extreme events which, on a literal level, are impossible fictions. There are, of course, other levels on which fictions can be true. The notes Bond kept kept while writing *Early Morning* propose the possibility that Victoria gave birth at the age of fifty-three, ten years after she had been widowed, and that this 'so shocked and dismayed the British public at large, that every inhabitant of these islands took a formal vow that they would not tell their children about these events'. To ensure it remained hidden, he imagines that 'history books, almanacs and newspaper record copies of these events were rewritten', and 'a fictitious past was substituted for the actual past'. In all of this, 'the Empire co-operated'.[54] If, as some historians have recognised, history is always fictional, and constructed so as to justify and preserve the present, then Bond's re-writing is simply an alternative – and, in his view, a truer fiction. The programme featured a detail of Goya's painting of Saturn – a monstrous but recognizably human figure – devouring his own child. Not only is eating other people a literal feature of this play, it is also, on a metaphorical level, what the characters in *Saved* are doing to each other.

Rarely performed it may be, but *Early Morning* is surely one of the most remarkable and distinctive achievements of any playwright during the 1960s. At first sight, it seems a complete contrast to *Saved*. Where the earlier play had been broadly realistic in style and set absolutely in the present and among society's underclass, this one was set in Victorian England among its rulers and shakers. Moreover, its style crosses into the surreal, drawing on such diverse precedents as Strindberg's *Dream Play*, the films of Buñuel, the nonsense writings of Lewis Carroll and Edward Lear, and the art of Bosch, Goya, Magritte and Blake. Yet there were obvious parallels between the plays in the way the characters behaved. 'In *Saved* Mr Bond seemed to be saying that brutalization can reach a point at which people can perform any violent act and slip back into apathetic indifference ... In *Early Morning* he says the same thing about our rulers.'[55] The actual dialogue remains generally reliable and realistic; it is the plot and the actions which take us closer to the world of *Ubu Roi* than to Chekhov. Queen Victoria, for example, has Siamese twins, murders her husband and rapes Florence Nightingale (who is engaged to one of the twins); her husband, Albert, has previously plotted to assassinate Victoria with the help of Disraeli, who sometimes shares a bed with Gladstone and Florence Nightingale; and the Lady of the Lamp's distinctive method of tending wounded soldiers at the front involves having sex with them just before they die. Later, Nightingale sets up a brothel, and disguises herself in a kilt and an appalling Scottish accent as John Brown, the Queen's 'special' companion. In effect, Bond is undermining the conventional view of Nightingale as an exemplary Victorian heroine and 'angel of mercy'; from another perspective she is simply the acceptable face of a brutal political war machine, and one which helps to legitimise it. The violent abuse perpetrated on her by Victoria is itself a metaphorical 'truth'.

Often in *Early Morning* dead characters refuse to lie down. They may return as ghosts, or simply come back to life as though nothing has happened. One of the conjoined sons, George, is reduced to a decaying skeleton attached to his twin, Arthur, and the final Act is set in a Heaven (or possibly a Hell), where the characters constantly consume (and are consumed by) each other ('Victoria: I'm working out a roster for the order in which we're eaten' – p. 223). In the final moments of the play, a Christ-like Arthur is resurrected and ascends to Heaven. The macabre feast continues till the end of the play – a last and eternal supper for the Victorians, perhaps – and it is surely not by chance that the final line ('Pass us that leg' – p. 223) is spoken by an eighteen-year-old working-class character – whose name just happens to be Len.

Early Morning does not so much argue its vision as embody it through image and metaphor. In fact, the use of cannibalism as symbol for how capitalism functions has a long history, going back at least to Marx, with those at the top growing fat as they consume the bodies, minds and lives of the workers. On one level the play can be read as a satire (much of it is potentially very funny) which attacks the myths and hypocrisies of an era which, in Bond's view, still held sway. 'I'm all for holding trials in secret and executions in public', declares Bond's Lord Chamberlain; 'That simplifies government and satisfies the people' (p. 143). And again: 'If you don't go into battle neat and clean you never win', says the Lord Chamberlain with a typically absurd British arrogance; 'One guardsman with polished boots is worth fifty American rockets' (p. 163). But the humour is also mixed with a disturbing sadism: 'Shall I put my foot on him, ma'am?' asks the Lord Chamberlain as Albert is dying: 'Let him crawl', replies the

Queen; 'it circulates the poison' (p. 161). Indeed, with its plotting and counter-plotting, its characters who act only in self-interest, its mingling of the lust for power with sexual appetite, and its sense of a world on the edge of anarchy, the atmosphere and the view of humanity are more reminiscent of a Jacobean tragedy than a play by Chekhov:

> The animals would blush to call him brother. The earth isn't his – he stole it, and now he messes in it. Even lice crawl off him, like rats abandoning a doomed ship. He has no pity. He can't see further than his own shadow. He eats his own swill and makes his own night and hides in it. (p. 189)

Although the setting is historical, *Early Morning* is littered with anachronisms that invite us to reconsider a more contemporary world:

> Our kingdom is degenerating. Our people cannot walk on our highways in peace. They cannot count their money in safety, even though our head is on it. We cannot understand most of what is called our English. Our prisons are full. Instead of fighting our enemies our armies are putting down strikers and guarding our judges. (p. 144)

And while much of the play concentrates on the ruling elite, other classes feature in their calculations – as when Albert propounds the ominous vision inspiring his dream of power: 'The people are strong. They want to be *used* – to build empires and railways and factories, to trade and convert and establish law and order,' he insists. 'I know there'll be crimes, but we can punish them' (p. 141).

When he was asked about the last scene of *Saved*, and Len's action of 'doggedly repairing the chair', Bond not only confirmed the significance of Len's action but added: 'it was because of that he was able to appear as Arthur in the next play'. As he explains, there is 'a central character who runs all the way through my plays', and according to Bond the whole of *Early Morning* was 'written from his point of view'.[56] Arthur starts the play physically attached to George, and with little knowledge of the world. Even Bond's choice of name jokingly refers to this – Arthur, as in 'half a'. But by the final act, Arthur has profound insights into the nature of society, and is able to communicate these to Florence Nightingale: 'Most people die when they're still babies or little children', he tells her; 'A few reach fourteen or fifteen. Hardly anyone lives on into their twenties' (p. 209). He could be thinking of the characters in *Saved*. During the middle section of the play, Arthur's view of human beings is excessively nihilistic. Even Beckett might have been proud of his perception: 'That's what's wrong with the world: it's inhabited.' Or his discovery that 'Live is evil backwards' and 'also an anagram of vile' (p. 189).

One extraordinary speech explores Bond's perception that 'good' people may cause as much harm and damage to others as those who are conventionally recognised as evil: 'Hitler gets a bad name, and Einstein's good. But it doesn't matter, the good still kill. And the civilized kill more than the savage. That's what science is for, even when it's doing good. Civilization is just bigger heaps of dead' (p. 186). Elsewhere, Bond has cited as 'probably the most interesting thing that's been said this century' Himmler's insistence 'that he gassed the Jews "out of love"'.[57] In his madness in the middle section of *Early Morning*, Arthur celebrates Hitler for his encouragement of the human deathwish: 'Hitler had vision. He knew we hated ourselves, and each other, so out of charity he let us kill and be killed' (p. 186). Arthur observes cynically that so far 'The world's been lucky' because 'there's always been enough dictators to ease its misery'. This is a profoundly depressing reading of history, but Arthur takes it further, suggesting that Hitler 'had his limitations', because his aim was to kill only some people rather than everybody: 'What we need now is the great traitor: who kills both sides,' he declares; 'It lets you kill twice as many' (p. 187). Arthur himself achieves this at the end of the second act, when, in an image easily read as a metaphor for nuclear holocaust between America and the Soviet Union, he engineers the mutually assured destruction of two sides in a tug of war contest in which everyone falls over the edge of a cliff.

Bond had a clear concept charting Arthur's development through the three sections of the play:

> In the first Act, he can't see what the correct sort of political action for him ought to be either. He doesn't know whether he ought to join the Revolution . . . In the second Act . . . he goes mad . . . he swallows the Victoria line, that's the law and order bit, completely and he says, So we are violent, so . . . we must have law and more law and law enforcement . . . just to keep the animal in control, and then he says, well, if this is true what is the point of life . . .

The crucial switch comes at the end of the second act:

> at the supreme moment of his madness he has this illumination . . . his vision is clarified and he is no longer seduced by the trappings of society . . . he says if you really want to see the way you're behaving, well, you're behaving like cannibals . . . he says, this is your heaven, you've got everything you want, you've got your civilization . . . and in that act he sees clearly what his position is and is then able to act . . . he wants to get out of heaven and escape from society.[58]

Arthur not only refuses to join in the cannibalism, but his vision convinces Nightingale to see the world differently: 'Why didn't you tell me this before?' she asks; 'perhaps we needn't be like this' (p. 211).

There was never much likelihood that *Early Morning* would receive a licence for public performance, and the Royal Court planned two open dress rehearsals on successive Sundays. However, some senior figures within the management withdrew their support, and the second one was cancelled. The performance which did take place was attended by most of the major critics, but according to Bond was 'a disaster' because it was completely under-rehearsed.[59] The *Daily Telegraph* was 'not much amused' and suggested Bond's writing was ineffective and impenetrable: 'He clearly means much more than he is saying but seems unable to say it with theatrical coherence.' The *Daily Mail* found it 'obscure, inconsistent, pointless and boring'. Under the headline 'Don't ban this play, just let it fade away', the paper urged the Lord Chamberlain to 'let it just fall flat out of its own sheer tedium'.

In *The Times*, Irving Wardle agreed it was 'muddled and untalented', and that it exposed 'the author's lack of technique'. The *Sunday Times* called it 'a baffling enterprise', written 'in words of ludicrous simplicity', with 'no organization; no formal development; no characterization; no sense of artistic probability . . . no grace, no beauty, thoughtfulness, or . . . effective ferocity of speech'. Ronald Bryden in the *Observer* was more positive, suggesting that the picture in *Saved* of a world in which people knew only how to take and not to give, had been developed: '*Early Morning* extends the same image of Britain into a gargantuan Swiftian metaphor of universal consumption: a society based on cannibalism, in which all achievement, power, and even love consists of devouring other lives.'[60]

The play had its first full staging at the Royal Court in 1969, but reviews were not much better. Milton Shulman – who left before the final act – called it 'silly, self-indulgent and pretentious' and dismissed Bond with absolute contempt: 'his construction is clumsy, his language is uneven, his wit is jejune, his metaphors are trite, his philosophy is adolescent'. Harold Hobson guessed that the play must have 'a savage moral purpose', but he couldn't quite locate what it was. 'It is like a nightmare dreamed by an overheated child whose head is a jumble of misunderstood fragments.' In the *Financial Times*, B. A. Young made a telling and condescending link with the contemporary and widespread protests and demonstrations against the establishment: 'Mr Bond is like those students who think they are fit to take over the world when they haven't even the patience to finish their education', he declared. 'Like them, he has not the ability to let us know clearly what the hell it is he wants.'[61]

The challenge of finding an appropriate performance style and aesthetic for *Early Morning* is considerable. The Lord Chamberlain's Office had compared it to a farce, and before the play opened, the press reported that the part of Queen Victoria had been offered to John Bird, a comic actor who had already taken the role in an award-winning television satire, *My Father Knew Lloyd George*.[62] On the other hand, Gaskill's full staging of the play was praised for its 'Goya-like quality'.[63] In 1969, a production in Zurich by the German director Peter Stein combined elements of expressionism and abstraction with a heightened realism; acts of violence were made as convincing as possible, with actors using protective padding and blood capsules, but Albert had a swastika on his belly and Florence Nightingale wore a bikini and see-through plastic mac. In the opening sequence, Albert and Disraeli moved towards each other across an empty stage 'as though tracing their way through a labyrinth' – a stylised way of symbolising the elaborate scheming of the characters.[64] Gaskill, however, found such stylisation and expressionism detrimental to the clarity, opting for a more Brechtian approach and striving to be 'clinically accurate'.[65] *Early Morning* has many moments of brilliance and many opportunities for different approaches. Could it work in performance today? One longs to see more directors test it.

Lear: 'We'll make the society you only dream of' (p. 99)[66]

Lear was standing in my path and I had to get him out of the way. I couldn't get beyond him to do other things that I also wanted, so I had to come to terms with him.[67]

Bond's attitude to Shakespeare has always been ambivalent. He calls Stratford-upon-Avon 'a shrine of philistinism',[68] complaining that the Royal Shakespeare Company 'trivialises and vulgarises Shakespeare in a way that is truly barbarous'[69] and that because the organisation uses its resources 'mummifying Shakespeare's corpse' it has 'nothing left with which to feed the living'.[70] As for *King Lear*, Bond acknowledged he had 'learnt more from it than from any other play', but objected to its appropriation: 'I very much object to the worshipping of that play by the academic theatre, which I dislike very much because I think it is a totally dishonest experience ... It's nice and comfortable. You don't have to question yourself, or change your society.' In Bond's view, any potential the play had to make audiences examine their society or think about how to live had been removed by its status: 'As a society we use the play in the wrong way', he argued; 'and it's for that reason I would like to rewrite it so that we now have to use the play for ourselves, for our society, for our time, for our problems.'[71]

Bond's *Lear* departs from its *ur*-text too radically to be considered a rewriting or an adaptation. At the heart of it is a massive wall designed to enclose the kingdom; its construction is begun by Lear but subsequently carried on by successive regimes as they usurp power. Lear believes it will protect his people from external attack, making them safe; it becomes a prison and a symbol of oppression, a source of discontent which he brutally and casually suppresses. The Berlin Wall constructed by the Communist East German government a decade earlier hovers somewhere in the background. Lear's two daughters, Bodice and Fontanelle, form alliances with their father's enemies and inflict military defeat on him. However, their regime is even crueller than his had been, and the peasant and pregnant Cordelia – in Bond's play no relation to Lear or his daughters – is viciously raped by their army, which also kills her husband for sheltering the fleeing Lear. Cordelia in turn leads another violent revolution which defeats Bodice and Fontanelle, both of whom she imprisons and kills. She then establishes a government which claims to be forging a better world, but which becomes yet another dictatorship, unable to tolerate opposition or debate. The failure of Cordelia's regime to institute real change is symbolised by her insistence on maintaining the wall, and the cycle seems endless. Lear, accompanied by the ghost of Cordelia's dead husband, gains insight into his own crimes and the world he has helped create. 'How do most men live? They're hungry and no one feeds them, so they call for help and no one comes. And when their hunger's worse they scream – and jackals and wolves come to tear them to pieces' (p. 95). Yet even in this despair he manages to reject the ghost which, like Arthur in the middle section of *Early Morning*, sees the logical extension of Lear's insight as being total nihilism and widescale annihilation: 'Let me poison the well' (p. 95). Lear takes a different route. In the final moments of the play, he begins to physically dismantle the wall, until he is shot dead by a passing soldier.

A few years earlier, Peter Brook had placed *King Lear* at the core of his Theatre of Cruelty experiments and linked it to Samuel Beckett's *Endgame* as a forerunner for an absurdist vision of the futility and hopelessness of human existence. In one sense, Bond could be seen as

155

responding to Brook. But the problem lay also with the original text, and what he saw as Shakespeare's readiness to give in to despair. From this perspective, *King Lear* reflected the position Arthur has reached in the middle section of *Early Morning*, and that was a counsel of pessimism. 'Shakespeare does arrive at an answer to the problems of his particular society', claimed Bond, 'and that was the idea of total resignation, accepting what comes, and discovering that a human being can accept an enormous lot and survive it.' This was an 'inadequate' response for art to make: 'Acceptance is not enough. Anybody can accept. You can go quietly into your gas chamber at Auschwitz, you can sit quietly at home and have an H-bomb dropped on you.'[72]

Yet as we might expect, Bond's own *Lear* provides no catharsis or easy resolution. Most reviews of the original Royal Court production in 1971 saw its view of humanity – the unspeakable things people do to each other, and the failure of every attempt to break the cycle – as profoundly negative: 'a long scream of pain and horror', 'no optimism whatever', 'the bleakest play I have ever seen'.[73] Bond's world was a 'hell on earth', filled with 'Goya-like enormities' and located in 'a monochrome dungeon where terrified and merciless insects enact an endless cycle of political atrocity'.[74] Crucially, none of the male characters generally associated with virtue in Shakespeare's play – Kent, Edgar, Albany, Gloucester – survives into Bond's text, while Cordelia, the virtuous and innocent daughter in the original, becomes – whatever her justifications and positive instincts – as ruthless and repressive as every other dictator. Despite this, and like *Saved* and *Early Morning*, *Lear* carries seeds of hope. Lear himself may start as a monster, but he learns and changes – albeit only when he has lost his power. In Cordelia's prison, Lear encounters the ghosts of his two daughters as children, and is suddenly able to imagine a better world in which 'We won't chain ourselves to the dead, or send our children to school on the graveyard. The torturers and ministers and priests will lose their office. And we'll pass each other in the street without shuddering at what we've done to each other' (p. 54). This is hardly Utopia. It is a description of what will be absent rather than present. But as grounds for optimism it will do to start with. Perhaps Utopia can be imagined best by thinking of what will not be there, rather than what will. In another strangely beautiful prison scene which picks up on a proposal in Shakespeare's text to 'anatomise' one of his dead daughters, Lear watches as an autopsy is carried out on the body of Fontanelle. What he discovers is that the evil has no physical or actual existence – is not, as it were, hard-wired in:

Lear   Where is the . . . Where . . .?

Fourth Prisoner   What is the question?

Lear   Where is the beast?

And he experiences an almost religious revelation – what Bond himself calls 'a Blake-ian vision of the orderliness and structure of nature' – in realising for the first time the simple, physical fact of how the human body is constructed: 'So much blood and bits and pieces packed in with all that care . . . I have never seen anything so beautiful' (p. 173).

One of the key issues that *Lear* dramatises is the way in which violent revolutions against an unjust society replicate the crimes and systems they set out to overthrow. Bond acknowledges the Soviet Union and Stalinism as a primary inspiration – and one which all advocates of a socialist alternative had (and have) to face up to. Many of the Royal Court costumes evoked the Russia of 1917 – though the costumes of Cordelia's army suggested a contemporary Latin American revolution. For Bond, as a committed socialist and Marxist, the issue of revolutions which become as oppressive as the regimes they have replaced was of vital significance. As he says, the question which underlies the play is: 'Given, then, that you want to change society, and if you don't there isn't much future for human beings, how do you make a revolution? That's the question which, as a society, you've got to answer.'[75] The easy route to take in starting from Shakespeare's text might have been to allow Cordelia to embody the answer. But such a solution would have been unconvincing and would have taken the responsibility away from the audience. Bond's Cordelia was based in part on arrogant moral campaigners such as Mary Whitehouse, the self-appointed guardian of Christian morality who, as founder and first president of the National Viewers' and Listeners' Association, campaigned endlessly for tougher censorship to be imposed on the arts and media. 'She always has the word "good" and "justice" on her lips', but 'I very much wanted to convey through that figure that the people who have manipulated and taken over the language of ethics in our society are in fact very violent and destructive people'.[76] Or as Lear says to Cordelia in the final Act: 'Your law always does more harm than crime, and your morality is a form of violence' (p. 99).

Bond's Cordelia is driven by a ruthlessness in the pursuit of her ends which allows her to treat people as objects. When she is urged by a colleague to let a prisoner join their army, she chooses instead to have him shot: 'To fight like us you must hate', she declares; 'we can't trust a man unless he hates. Otherwise he has no use' (p. 58). Similarly, she abandons a badly wounded soldier to die alone rather than risk damaging her overall strategy. Such decisions may be correct on political and military grounds, but they are less than human. 'When we have power these things won't be necessary', she insists (p. 59). Certainly, Cordelia has a vision of a better world that she wishes to create: 'We'll make the society you only dream of', she tells Lear; 'we won't be at the mercy of brutes any more, we'll live a new life and help one another' (p. 99). One wants to believe her. But can good come from bad? Peace from violence? Not according to Bond:

> The simple fact is that if you behave violently, you create violence, which generates more violence. If you create a violent revolution, you always create a reaction . . . Lenin thinks for example that he can use violence for specific ends. He does not understand that he will produce Stalin . . . So a violent revolution always destroys itself . . .[77]

The on-stage violence in *Lear* is probably even more disturbing to watch than in the earlier plays, and it takes many forms. However, even where it is carried out by ordinary soldiers it is usually those at the top who command it. The first sustained example – the vicious torturing of Warrington in scene four – is performed by an unnamed soldier, but at the behest of Bodice and Fontanelle. As the soldier says to his victim when he leads him away afterwards: 'Don't blame me, I've got a job t' do' (p. 30). This may not excuse him, but is an accurate recognition of the reality of the situation – and the soldier knows it could easily be his turn to suffer the following day. The rape and atrocity at the end of the first act is all too reminiscent of invading armies – probably at the time of the play's first performance of the Americans in Vietnam – but equally sickening is the blinding of Lear, carried out by a scientist proudly demonstrating his latest piece of pioneering medical equipment. 'With this device you extract the eye undamaged and then it can be put to good use', he tells Lear proudly; 'Understand, this isn't an instrument of torture, but a scientific device' (p. 77).

Like Arthur at the end of *Early Morning*, the Lear of the last act understands at last. He speaks publicly and to whoever will listen as an oppositional force against Cordelia's government, and warns her not to make the same mistakes he has made. He may not convince her ('You are like my conscience', she says, p. 97) but he refuses to be silenced or to give in to despair. In the final, short scene, the three shovel loads of wall we see Lear extract before he is shot may seem to represent no more than a pointless and individual gesture. But to understand what Bond wishes the scene to say it is necessary to look at the staging more precisely. It takes place in 'clear daylight' – a visual metaphor which sets the scene apart. And crucially, Lear's gesture is witnessed – not only by the theatre audience, but by a small one on stage. As he begins dismantling the wall, 'a group of workers come on and stare at Lear'. After he has been shot, some of them go towards the body in curiosity, but are quickly moved on. However, while most of the workers dutifully turn their backs and walk away 'quickly and orderly', a direction tells us 'One of them looks back' (p. 102). That, perhaps, is where the change might begin. Of course, the action has also been witnessed by us, and the closing image includes not only the dead body of Lear but a wall which has been partially dismantled, and implements – not only the shovel Lear has been using, but 'a stack of tools' that are beside the wall. They are ready, perhaps, for us to take up and carry on what Lear has begun. For tools can build, but they can also pull things apart.

Conclusion: 'Plays stretch from the kitchen table to the edge of the universe – or they are not dramas'[78]

'What period are the characters in?' Bond was asked by the director of an American production of *Saved* in the early 1980s: 'Our own', he replied, 'and perhaps those of our children.' And he advised: 'I shouldn't bother about setting it in the sixties.'[79] In 2011, Bond gave permission for a major London revival of *Saved* – the first time he had done so for over twenty-five years. One reason was the connection he saw with the riots which swept across Britain that summer, mostly perpetrated by the young, who were, in turn, often condemned and demomised in the same language applied to the characters in *Saved*. In a newspaper article published under the headline 'My play predicted the riots', Bond spoke about the play's continuing relevance: 'Those girls out there, those guys – were they acting politically? You have to say "No – they don't understand their political situation." They didn't find out where the bankers are living – they turned on their neighbours. They started destroying themselves – and that's what happens in this play.'[80] Ironically, he is also convinced – probably rightly – that 'If I sent *Saved* or *Lear* to the Royal Court now they would reject them.'[81]

Everything Bond writes is informed by his strongly held and unwavering political position as a Marxist, and his conviction that Western capitalist society is fundamentally unjust and needs to be transformed if we are to survive as a species. For all the horrors of our history, humanity is not inherently evil, he believes; we have the possibility of saving ourselves, and there are always grounds for optimism and reasons for hope. A fundamental idea which frequently surfaces when Bond talks about his work is the wish that his plays will be 'useful'. And one of the qualities of his writing which gives his theatre power – certainly in these early plays – is that they do not deal in abstract political ideas but in the human. As he says: 'You need to relate to politics, economics, history, society, and then perhaps to one shoe abandoned on the sea shore or to say the crumbs lying on the edge of the universe. The play must enact the inter-relation between self and society.'[82]

But there is another element in Bond's writing from the 1960s which is striking. Too often in bad political plays it is the messages – the slogans – that are likely to be shoved 'in yer face'. For all the convictions that may lie behind them, these texts never do that. 'I think that art is very often ambiguous', said Bond in 1965 in relation to *Saved*; 'I think the play is open to several interpretations.'[83] Looking back now at his early work he acknowledges that when he wrote these plays 'I didn't – in an analytical sense – know what they were about.'[84] Strangely, perhaps that, too, is a crucial source of their continuing power.

HAROLD PINTER
by Jamie Andrews

As the 1960s dawned, Harold Pinter – itinerant actor, occasional writer for radio and author of the celebrated flop *The Birthday Party* (1958) – could have had little reason to suspect that within less than six months he would be fêted as one of the country's most admired, and commercially successful, new writers. However, the familiar narrative of what Pinter termed the 'total disaster' of *The Birthday Party*,[1] subsequently redeemed two years later by the triumph of *The Caretaker*, masks the importance of Pinter's iterative development across genres, and of the recirculation of his earlier work through revivals and adaptations. Indeed, if *The Caretaker*'s opening on 27 April 1960 at the Arts Theatre was an immediate critical triumph – and soon became a commercial success when it transferred to the Duchess a month later – Pinter's first great success of the 1960s had been the broadcast of *The Birthday Party* on the commercial television station Associated Rediffusion on 22 March 1960. The broadcast reached an estimated 11 million people, and was enthusiastically received by the critics, conspicuously framing their enthusiasm in the context of its initial rejection ('Stage Flop is a Big Hit'[2]). At the same time, his double-bill of *The Dumb Waiter* and *The Room* was playing at the Royal Court Theatre, to which it had transferred after opening in January at James Roose-Evans's Hampstead Theatre Club.

Meanwhile *A Night Out*, which Pinter had originally developed for television during 1959, was broadcast as a radio adaptation on the BBC Third Programme on 1 March 1960, before being televised by ABC's *Armchair Theatre* on 24 April.

The line that leads from the closure of *The Birthday Party* in under a week in 1958 to the triumph of *The Caretaker* in 1960 is therefore more nuanced than a straightforward, and glorious, reversal of fortune. Pinter's reception in the capital developed dialectically along-side enthusiastic reception in the provinces, in amateur theatre and abroad (*The Birthday Party* received a number of acclaimed profes-sional and amateur productions throughout 1959, and *The Dumb Waiter*'s world premiere took place in Frankfurt in February 1959); while his reputation in the theatre was bolstered by popular and crit-ical approbation for his broadcast work. Pinter himself recalled the importance of the BBC for sustaining his career in the early days – 'I don't think anyone's received a worse body of reviews than I did in 1958, but in actual fact it was a very good education for me . . .The BBC actually came to my rescue'[3] – and it is worthwhile equally acknowledging the importance of commercial television in this respect.

Pinter and his work were, therefore, far more familiar to audiences and reviewers by April 1960 than had been the case two years earlier, and *The Caretaker* now appeared to resonate with a particular cultural moment. The week that saw *The Caretaker* opening at the small Arts Theatre also saw the first English production of Eugène Ionesco's *Rhinoceros* at the larger Royal Court. The ambitions for the produc-tion of *Rhinoceros* were signalled by the choice of director Orson Welles, and by his casting of Sir Laurence Oliver. In the event, reviews for *Rhinoceros* were underwhelming, but the conjunction of the two openings facilitated identification of Pinter with the Theatre of the Absurd. Most reviews took for granted that *The Caretaker* must be understood in relation to Ionesco. Alan Pryce-Jones claimed that 'the two plays can be discussed together, since both inhabit that looking-glass world of which Ionesco is a prime inventor'[4] – an assumption that spread beyond critical discourse, as noted by the young poet and keen theatregoer Ted Hughes ('Everybody's full of

Harold Pinter. He has a play on at the Arts with which everyone is clubbing *Rhinoceros*[5]).

The Caretaker

The Caretaker is set over a few weeks in a junk-strewn west London flat, to which the apparently slow-witted Aston has brought an irascible, grasping tramp, having rescued him from a fight. Davies inveigles his way to being offered first tobacco, then shoes, and finally a bed, all the time offering scant appreciation for Aston's charity. By Act II, Aston has offered the tramp the job of caretaker, and closes the act with a lengthy monologue describing his forced electric shock treatment. Davies leaps on these admissions as a source of weakness, and in Act III attempts to play Aston off against his older, more streetwise brother, Mick, who sneeringly also offers Davies the position of caretaker. By now convinced that he has the upper hand over Aston, Davies attempts to push home his advantage by mocking the former's incarceration; however, Aston calmly informs the tramp that 'I think it's about time you found somewhere else' (p. 53),[6] a position backed by Mick after hearing Davies call his brother 'nutty' (p. 57). The play ends with the abject defeat of the tramp, who rails against his expulsion – 'What shall I do (*Pause.*) where am I going to go' (p. 61) – as Aston remains immobile, his back to the tramp, staring out of the window.

From this brief summary, it is apparent that the play is not without narrative drive and structure. However, a number of elements – in particular the unnervingly dislocated dialogue – lead to the ready identification of the play with the Absurd. The halting non-sequiturs were felt by Pryce-Jones to be divorced from an identifiable external reality ('talk has the zany destructiveness of the scorpion turning inwards upon itself'), while the abject world portrayed by Pinter was seen as one of tragedy and emptiness. Yet in many respects, it is apparent that *The Caretaker* marked an increasing realism in Pinter's work, a rejection of the more overt symbolism and mystery of his earlier plays, at the same time as maintaining a degree of accommodation with the prevailing assumptions of mainstream West End theatre that allowed an apparently puzzling work to find an audience for over four hundred performances.

Pinter himself later recognised how his early work, from his debut in 1957 until 1965, could be seen as a gradual attempt to write through his early attraction to a heavy-handed symbolism and crude violence. This tendency was apparent at the climax of his first play, *The Room*, when a blind black man bursts into the eponymous room with a prophetic message for its occupant, Rose, followed immediately by the entry of Rose's husband, who proceeds to beat the man to death in what Martin Esslin terms a 'near parody of a death-symbol'.[7] Such a laboured ending was initially repeated in Pinter's next performed play, *The Birthday Party*, which originally ended with a similarly grotesque recourse to violence when Stanley is struck on the side of the neck by McCann, and knocked out (p. 110).[8] When he came to draft *The Caretaker*, Pinter explained in an interview that his original idea had been 'to end the play with the violent death of the tramp. It suddenly struck me that it was not necessary.'[9] This single decision points to the development of Pinter's dramaturgy apparent in *The Caretaker*, described by Pinter in the same interview as 'a particular human situation, concerning three particular people and not, incidentally, symbols'.

For all the potentially alienating obtuseness of the verbal exchanges, this 'particular human situation' is rooted in a reality evident both in- and outside the terrain of the room over which they all compete. *The Caretaker*'s characters inhabit a recognisable locale, a situation taken to its extreme in Mick's chronicling of inner-city London: 'His old mum was still living at the Angel. All the buses passed right by the door. She could get a 38, 581, 30, or 38a, take her down the Essex Road to Dalston Junction in next to no time' (p. 23). This line, of course, operates at different levels, and is equally a tactical claim to territory in front of the itinerant Davies; yet despite the giddy accrual of topographical detail, it is rooted in an identifiable and coherent reality, the same reality that Pinter explored as a young *flâneur* in his walks across east London with his teacher, Joseph Brearley ('From Clapton Pond to Stamford Hill/ And on/ Through Manor House to Finsbury Park/ And back/ On the dead 653 trolleybus'[10]).

Interventions by Pinter himself have tended to shape consideration of the way that the world of *The Caretaker* drew from the
playwright's own experiences. As early as 1966, he had suggested a
model for the tramp, Davies – 'I think there was one particular one
[tramp] . . . I bumped into him a few times, and about a year or so
afterward he sparked this thing off'[11] – and he elaborated on this
anecdote for the first time in interviews with Michael Billington in
the early 1990s. In this more detailed account, Pinter recalled the
house in Chiswick where he lived with his wife, actress Vivien
Merchant. The house was owned by a builder, whose introverted
brother brought back a tramp one evening. Pinter recalls that 'the
image that stayed with me for a long time was . . . the two men
standing in different parts of the room doing different things . . . the
tramp rooting around in a bag and the other man looking out of the
window and simply not speaking'.[12]

Pinter himself recognised the danger that the single-room theatrical set might have masked the degree to which *The Caretaker*
operated within a carefully constructed reality – 'they [the critics]
often assumed it was all taking place in limbo, in a vacuum, and the
world outside hardly existed'[13] – and he remedied this by the introduction of a number of exterior shots when adapting his play for the
cinema in 1963. However, the importance of Pinter's rejection of the
'limbo' identified by many early critics lies less in the accumulation of
recognisable topographical and social details, but rather in the way
that the play's characters act on and among each other. Unlike Stanley
in *The Birthday Party*, who embodies the struggle of the individual to
remain isolated from society, *The Caretaker* proposes the challenge of
the individual to establish his place within more complex societal
structures.

If Mick is able to dismiss the challenge of the potentially nauseating excess of objects that accumulate in the flat – 'All this junk here
. . . It's just a lot of old iron, that's all. Clobber' (p. 47) – the relations
between the three characters prove less easily resolved. Each attempts
to dominate the other by denying his subjectivity, and in dramatising
this ontological dilemma, Pinter draws closer to the very real analyses
of human relationships of Sartrean existentialism. From this

165

perspective, we may find that the junk-strewn room resembles less a Beckettian void than it does Jean-Paul Sartre's Second Empire drawing room in *Huis Clos* (1947); Pinter played the part of Garcin in 1965 on TV. In both plays, three characters confined in a single room are trapped in a perfect circle of mutual torture, each trying to dominate the other, but equally only able to achieve self-affirmation through them. Just as Davies's stories of future legitimacy in Sidcup need Aston's willing acceptance, so Mick's ludicrously detailed plans for the renovation of the house (often assumed to be an example of grotesquely aggressive humour) require the tramp to give them credence. Even Aston's monologue describing his forced EST intervention in the hospital requires a credulous audience (both Davies, and the play's spectators) to respond to what is usually played as an unproblematic moment of emotional sympathy, despite Pinter's own warning that 'it isn't necessary to conclude that everything Aston says about his experiences in the mental hospital is true'.[14] When in *Huis Clos* the characters are given a sudden opportunity to escape, they are no more able to assume this terrifying liberty than Davies to make good his regularly repeated promise to travel to Sidcup to claim his papers. Indeed, while the play appears to suggest that Davies has been finally ejected from the house, in fact the concluding stage directions simply show the three characters fixed in place (p. 61), the implication being that the infernal machine can only begin anew.

A particularity of *The Caretaker* is the way that its characters attempt to navigate the complexities of these social exchanges through an emphasis on contractual relationships. 'It's a fine legal point, that's what it is' (p. 56), explains Mick, and references to contractual rights and responsibilities proliferate throughout the play. In the opening moments of the play, Davies recounts the violence done to his employment rights by the café – 'nobody's got more rights than I have' (p. 5) – while later conversations with Mick about taking on the position of caretaker and decorator revolve around a parody of complex contractual negotiations. The play equally engages with less specific contractual bonds, such as the fraternal bond between Mick and Aston, which ultimately triumphs over any negotiated bond with Davies, or the haplessly general appeal by Davies 'Let's have a bit of fair play' (p. 5) in the face of any number of real and perceived slights. As Austin Quigley demonstrates, this process of constant renegotiation of social contracts at the micro-level of individuals is often repeated in Pinter's work in the 1960s, and even when Pinter later addresses more explicitly political structures and ideologies, it is still most often done at the level of local relationships.[15] *The Caretaker* marks the beginning of this exploration of realistic social relationships through what Pinter terms 'a particular human situation', and as such this new realism places it at some distance from both his own earlier work, and from the early critical expectations of an Anglophone Absurdist.

Nonetheless, in considering the play and its popularity in 1960, its incorporation of recognisable West End conventions must not be forgotten. Pinter the actor had spent much of the 1950s in regional rep, and an element of *The Caretaker*'s appeal was rooted in his exploitation of classic repertory tricks, the 'cabaret turns and blackouts' that Pinter claimed, in an interview with Kenneth Tynan, to have left behind.[16] The scene in Act II (33), when Davies enters the room and, unable to switch on the lights, fumbles on the floor for some matches, is reminiscent of the blackout scene in *The Birthday Party*, with added menace provided by the sudden irruption of the Electrolux.

Alongside these elements of more traditional stagecraft, the other attribute of Pinter's play highlighted by critics was its humour. The linguistic excesses of much of the dialogue, for instance the grotesque poetry of consumerism in Mick's plans for a table 'in afromosia teak veneer, sideboard with matt black drawers, curved chairs with cushioned seats, armchairs in oatmeal tweed' (p. 47), contains a significant element of humour, but the real specificity of Pinter's dialogue lies in its invocation of what director Peter Hall identifies as 'piss-taking':

The basis of Harold's drama isn't anything to do with Beckett: it's piss-taking, the cockney phrase ... The essential thing about piss-taking is that, as I mock you, you should not be sure that I am mocking you, because if you can see that I am mocking you then I have lost. The whole of Harold's drama is based on that in one form or another.[17]

This 'piss-taking' is apparent in practically every exchange between Mick and Davies. However, for all the humour generated by the incongruity of Mick's amazement that the tramp is no 'experienced first class professional interior and exterior decorator', and thus unprepared 'to fit teal blue, copper and parchment linoleum squares and have those colours re-echoed in the walls' (pp. 56–7), such exchanges mask a disconcerting violence; for Hall, 'the piss-take actually hides violent emotions', and as Pinter wrote, the play was 'funny up to a point. Beyond that point it ceases to be funny, and it was because of that point that I wrote it.'[18]

In *The Caretaker*, Pinter maintains some of the more exaggerated stage effects of his early work, but grounds them in a new and more intricate realism: not a social-naturalistic 'Royal Court' realism ('I liked the Royal Court . . . but I simply didn't fit in'[19]); and not simply realistic to the degree that the work draws from real-life experiences; but thanks to the play's consideration of more complex human inter-relations. Following the success of *The Caretaker*, Pinter's short stage plays would continue to investigate the contractual nature of social relations, most notably in the context of marriage. *The Collection* was presented for the stage by the Royal Shakespeare Company in June 1962 following a television version, and charted an evolving love triangle between a husband and wife, the wife's suspected lover, and the latter's older male 'protector'. Meanwhile, a year later *The Lover* (played with Pinter's adaptation of his unpublished novel *The Dwarfs*) staged the intricacies of a permanent renegotiation of the marriage bond between a husband and wife who spend their afternoons with each other, each pretending they are conducting an illegitimate affair with another lover.

Early audience response; or 'A bloody pain in the neck'

If the only tool usually available to judge audience responses to histor-ical theatrical performances is the response of a critical elite, whose tastes sometimes ran ahead (and sometimes far behind) public appe-tites, supplementary evidence in the Pinter archive demonstrates the responses of a broader range of audience members.

As noted above, Pinter's early radio work in 1959 to 1960 was, alongside the television broadcast of *The Birthday Party* in March 1960, key to preparing the ground for the stage triumph of *The Caretaker*, and BBC Audience Research Reports[20] allow us insight into audience reception to his three early radio plays: *A Slight Ache* in 1959, and *A Night Out* and *The Dwarfs* in 1960. Only *A Night Out* scored above the 'average Appreciation Index', while *The Dwarfs* (2 December 1960, seven months after the opening of *The Caretaker*), appeared to present the greatest challenge to audiences. The latter's Appreciation Index score of 35 (against an average of 63) was one of the lowest recorded for a BBC Third Programme play, and sample comments attested to not only the incomprehensibility of the work, but in particular to its consequent futility: 'meaningless rubbish' and 'disgusting to no apparent purpose'. Others were keen to engage with the content, but – in the words of an anonymous Farmer (longer comments were identified by occupation) – concluded that 'as a form of dramatic art it gets nowhere, and throws no further light nor penetrating thought on any human problem'.

Despite the intervening television broadcast of *The Birthday Party*, and mainstream coverage afforded *The Caretaker*, these comments and ratings represented little advance on those for Pinter's first radio piece of 29 July 1959, *A Slight Ache*. The play's Index of 45 was still significantly below the average, although its audience was, unsurprisingly, smaller than that for *The Dwarfs* (0.1 per cent of the Daily Audience as opposed to 0.3 per cent a year later). 'Subtopian Beckett' typified the views of 'many listeners', while the non-appearance of the silent match-seller who terrorises the husband and wife frustrated audience expectations: 'Most people would have switched off if they had known they were "Waiting for Nobody"' (A Teacher), and 'I would have forgiven everything if the dénouement had been interesting' (An Insurance Clerk). In contrast to the pleasure expressed by some audience members in working to make sense of *The Caretaker* in the theatre, quoted below, over half of the sample audience for *A Slight Ache* expressed 'positive dislike', their complaints coalescing around the 'intense frustration' (A Repertory Actress) of 'words that do not mean anything' (A Research Botanist).

The only radio play to exceed the Appreciation Index average was the arguably more conventional *A Night Out* (1 March 1960), which recorded an audience of 0.2 per cent and a rating of 65. The accessibility of its (albeit) 'dreadful realism' was highly rated, listeners able this time to incorporate the 'repetitive banalities and fatuities' through their relation to a recognised reality: 'real people talking real language' (A Clerk in Insurance). The identification of an accessible theme underpins the play's positive reception, eliciting an assimilation of the work to the listener's own circumstances: 'After hearing this play I made a vow never to nag my husband or son' (A Housewife/Former Civil Servant).

Meanwhile, what is most striking about much of the early unsolicited correspondence relating to the 1960 television broadcast of *The Birthday Party* and the staging of *The Caretaker* is the ease with which audience members were able to identify with plays that still mystified professional critics, and relate them to their own lives. If Pinter often referenced his antagonistic designs in relation to the audience ('I tend to regard the audience as my enemy'[21]), many audience members apparently responded to the challenge of this assault: 'But I get it all right – bang in the guts' responded one viewer on 28 March 1960. Others related their ease in incorporating apparently disconcerting events to the quotidian (in a letter one audience member described how 'I saw an incident of this on our local bus'), or a willingness to work to make independent sense of the plays: 'I am writing to ask if you will let me know if I have solved the riddle of *The Caretaker*', asked another spectator in a letter of 28 January 1961. Professional hierarchies appear far from unassailable ('Ken Tynan is incorrect . . .', Pinter was told in a letter dated 5 June 1960), and the contrast between the glamour of West End openings and the reality of reception is encapsulated in one letter of thanks dated 27 March 1960 following the broadcast of *The Birthday Party*: 'It gives middle-aged housewives something to think about as they plod to school with the children in the mornings.'

The Homecoming

Having directed *The Collection* in 1962 at the Aldwych Theatre, Peter Hall – Artistic Director of the nascent Royal Shakespeare Company, and the man who had introduced Samuel Beckett's stage work to London in 1955 – was keen to claim Pinter's next major work for his company. Not only did Pinter add to the lustre of Hall's ambitions for the RSC to stage challenging new work, but his small casts were also financially attractive to the company's management in comparison to major Shakespearean revivals. As Hall admitted in a letter to future prime minister Margaret Thatcher, MP, dated July 1965, in response to an audience complaint about the play being produced by a publicly funded company, Pinter could easily be commercially produced, but: 'Plays like *The Homecoming* are, in fact, a great help to us. They do not cost much to do, they relieve our company on some nights, as they have small casts, and their modern interest is such that they boost our general Box Office take.' For all the trangressive possibilities of Pinter's theatre, it should not be forgotten that he was nurtured in the commercial sector, and that by the mid-1960s, his work was arguably needed by the subsidised sector to a greater degree than he was reliant on that sector to have it produced.

The Homecoming opened on 3 June 1965, and its early acclaim has been matched by a sustained level of critical and popular interest that makes it, in Peter Hall's words, 'his greatest and biggest play'.[22] The play is set in an old house in north London, to which philosophy professor Teddy brings back his wife, Ruth, to meet his family for the first time after several years living in the United States. The ageing patriarch, Max, is a widower, whose two other sons – middle brother, Lenny, a brutal pimp; and the youngest, Joey, a boxer – also live in the house, along with Max's chauffeur brother, Sam.

While Max at first welcomes the arrival of his new, previously unknown, daughter-in-law, the two younger sons respond to Ruth's suggestive hints about her life before meeting Teddy. Lenny begins to dance with her, a declaration of physicality that leads to Joey embracing her, and Teddy abruptly packing to leave for the States – intending to take Ruth back with him. At this point, Ruth asserts herself, ordering the sons around, and dragging Joey upstairs to the bedroom. Downstairs, Max and Lenny discuss a different kind of homecoming, proposing that they invite Ruth to stay and 'put her on the game' (p. 73).[23] Teddy joins the conversation, acquiescing in the proposal, as does Ruth, subject to closely negotiated 'conditions of employment' (p. 78). As Teddy prepares to leave, Sam suddenly collapses, revealing that Max's widow, Jessie, had been unfaithful with MacGregor in the back of his car. The play concludes with a *tableau vivant*, and the family understands that Ruth appears to have gained the upper hand: at the curtain, she remains seated, as if on a throne, with Sam's body still on the floor, Joey's head in her lap, while Lenny stands to one side, watching, and Max desperately beseeches her: 'Kiss me' (p. 83).

In his *Paris Review* interview, Pinter explains that 'the only play that gets remotely near to a structural entity which satisfies me is *The Homecoming*. *The Birthday Party* and *The Caretaker* have too much writing. I want to iron it down, eliminate things.'[24] The play can therefore be seen as the culmination of Pinter's project to write through his earlier dramatic excesses to attain a structural unity that, through rigorously maintained internal tensions, attains an almost tragic conception. The clash of wills between all the characters is dramatised in all its complexities – significantly, *The Caretaker*'s privileging of contractual relationships is revived in Ruth's insistence near the end of the play that 'all aspects of the agreement and conditions of employment would have to be clarified to our mutual satisfaction before we finalised the contract' (p. 78) – but never fully resolved; in this way, the play ends not with a violence that would overwhelm the characters' interrelationships, but with a horrific tableau that Pinter's French translator, Eric Kahane, glossed as the playwright's acceptance of his characters' 'fundamental and insoluble divergences'. The Oedipal nature of the way the younger sons embrace Ruth as a substitute mother-figure made to act the whore is matched by the overt symbolism of Max's walking stick, but we may feel that the true debt owed to Greek tragedy is less psychological than aesthetic in its unsparing structural unity, and rigorous maintenance of internal tensions between the characters.

However, it cannot be forgotten that the formal beauty of this 'elegant shell of the writing'[25] covers an animalistic, 'ugly brutality'.[26] Hall describes Pinter's exploitation of a similar device to that employed in *The Caretaker* – 'the phrase always on our lips when we were doing this play was "taking the piss"' – but in a more 'cruel and bitter' way than in the previous play.[27] Evidently, this amoral jungle in which the characters operate was bound to shock not only audience members, but also some reviewers; the latter included Harold Hobson, who attempted to negate the absence of 'any moral comment' regarding Teddy's abandonment of Ruth by denying that the characters were ever really married.[28]

The position of Ruth at the play's denouement has been the source of particular debate, with the degree of true agency apparent in her decision to remain in the household uncertain. Penelope Gilliatt suggested that 'she looks on her body rather as a landlord would look on a corner site; the moment she has apparently been exploited sexually, she really has the advantage because she owns the property',[29] and yet despite later critical concern at the degree to which the male gaze conditions Ruth's actions, Michael Billington is unapologetic in seeing *The Homecoming* 'as an implicitly feminist play', with the power at its conclusion entirely vested in Ruth.[30] It should, not, however, be forgotten that the degree of violence suggested towards women in the play is hardly confined to the family's arrangements with Ruth; soon after Teddy and Ruth arrive, Lenny relates the story of an old woman who asked for help to move a heavy iron mangle, only to be told to 'stuff this mangle up your arse' and given 'a short-arm jab to the belly' (p. 33), while the brothers later trade tales of picking up 'birds' during late-night trawls of the seamier sides of north London (p. 67).

However Ruth's decision is interpreted, it is nonetheless clear that Pinter's portrayal of the family is – despite the overtly vicious narrative – extremely complex in its presentation of competing subjectivities that give the lie to the facility of Teddy's contention that 'You're just objects' (p. 62). No more than in *The Caretaker* can individual consciousness be reduced to the level of objects or junk; rather, as Lenny details in a discarded monologue from the first full draft, the play presents a social unit 'made up of . . . various and not entirely similar component parts, which, put together, make up a whole. An organism which, though we're not exactly a sentimental family, we recognise as such.'[31] In *The Homecoming* Pinter has combined the nuanced fraternal and conjugal (and extra-conjugal) pairings of *The Caretaker*, *The Lover* and *The Collection*, to create an epic portrait of a family; 'the one I was issued with and the one I escaped to' (p. 244), in the words of the protagonist of *Forget-Me-Not Lane* (1971) by Pinter's contemporary Peter Nichols. When Pinter was asked about the meaning of *The Homecoming*, he replied that he was 'dealing with love',[32] a description that does not deny the reality of the terrible choices that the family members make, but reminds us of the desperation of Max's curtain line, delivered on his knees, his body sagging at Ruth's feet: 'Kiss me' (p. 83).

We have seen how the more nuanced presentation of complex social interaction in *The Caretaker*, subsequently developed in *The Homecoming*, was accompanied by Pinter's use of personal experiences. Debate around *The Homecoming*, too, has centred on the degree to which the playwright drew on events from his own life, especially in the context of the family's suggested ethnic background. As Francis Gillen's investigation of the early drafts reveals,[33] Pinter began with a typically oblique exchange between an unnamed Man and Woman, but by the first full draft is far more overt in his identification of the patriarch's Jewishness. The father's memories of roisterous nights with an old friend recall how he 'used to knock about with a man called Berkowitz. I called him Berki'; in the margin, the name 'MacGregor' is written, softening the Jewish context. In his biography, Michael Billington associates the veiled references to the north London Jewish community with particular childhood memories of the authoritarian father of a friend who was 'a dead-ringer' for Max.[34] Billington quotes Pinter's grudging admission that his friend's father 'may have been a kind of source', but goes further in his own investigations. Billington discovers through contacting the childhood friend that the latter had himself returned to his Jewish family from Canada in 1964, where he had married a Gentile girl and kept it secret from his family.[35] Further correspondences between the friend's story and *The Homecoming* are detailed by Billington, who without denying the work's universal appeal, felt its specifically Jewish roots are important to understand the way Pinter's 'creative imagination is shaped by his own experience . . . and vivid memory'.[36]

If the degree to which Billington rooted out personal experiences from *The Homecoming* in his biography has been an area of critical debate (Martin Esslin identified nothing more than 'idle gossip'[37]), the importance of memory validated through recollection is a trope that can be increasingly associated with Pinter's work during the 1960s, and would be especially evident in his next two major plays, *Landscape* and *Silence*.

Pinter beyond Britain; or looking for Beckett

By the time that *Landscape* and *Silence* premiered in 1968, Pinter's status as a major contemporary writer was assured. However, if the reception of his work in the 1960s has usually been considered through the prism of the British (i.e. London) theatre scene, Pinter's growing reputation can equally be considered through his early exposure in the two other great theatrical capitals of the 1960s – Paris and New York City – an examination that allows assumptions inherent in the traditional 'London chronology' to be opened up to different, more contingent, narratives. In considering Pinter's overseas reception, it is interesting, therefore, to note the disruption of the well-established London production chronology. In Paris, Pinter's first full-length play (*The Birthday Party*) was his fourth to be produced, and this caused confusion: one critic, apparently accusing Pinter of borrowing from himself in the future with *The Birthday Party*, wrote that from a new author: 'I would say: here's a man looking for something, who hasn't found it yet, but who will go places, here's an author to follow. But coming from Pinter, the same text seems to me to be just his usual tricks.'[38]

Pinter's first play to be produced in Paris had been *The Caretaker* (*Le Gardien*) in January 1961, a production whose evisceration at the hands of what Samuel Beckett termed in a letter to Pinter of 30

January 1961 'the daily bastards' led to it occupying the same role in Pinter's Parisian mythology as had the London failure of *The Birthday Party*.[39] The lead-up had referenced Samuel Beckett to an extraordinary degree, and the presence of Roger Blin as Davies alongside Jean Martin as Aston reunited Beckett's original Pozzo–Lucky (*Godot*) and Hamm–Clov (*Endgame*) pairing. Pre-opening expectation having led critics to assume that Pinter was consciously intending to ape Beckett, first-night reviews either dismissed the author for falling short, or the production for trying too hard. One critic described characters 'still looking like they're waiting for Godot',[40] while Paul Morelle's complaint was typical: 'the clock has stopped at Beckett. But Harold Pinter is not Beckett.'[41] Whether Pinter was trying to be Beckett was generally not considered, and this collective confusion and distrust ensured Pinter's failure to find an audience in Paris for another four years.

When the double-bill of *The Collection* and *The Lover* (*La Collection* and *L'Amant*) was announced in summer 1965, it was therefore widely assumed to be Pinter's Paris debut. The still unknown Pinter again fitted neatly into critical expectations through the pairing of his leading actors, but this time in the context of the star system. Delphine Seyrig and Jean Rochefort had just completed an acclaimed seven-month run of Gabriel Arout's *Cet Animal étrange*, whose director, Claude Régy, had discovered Pinter's texts while looking for opportunities to renew his collaboration with the two leading actors. News of the revival of the Seyrig–Rochefort star billing dominated pre-opening reporting, often accompanied by breathless photo-stories. Reviewers subsequently praised the stars more than the plays, often blurring the characters with the actors' star profiles; referencing Seyrig's role in Alain Resnais's 1961 film *L'Année dernière à Marienbad*, *La Croix* mused on her character, Stella: 'So you never went to Leeds? Or to Marienbad?'[42] The critical response also foregrounded what *Le Soir* termed 'the age-old theme of adultery' in both plays,[43] an underpinning that reassured Parisian audiences and reviewers: an earlier critic of *Le Gardien* writing in *La Croix* was therefore able to reassure his readers 'it's boulevard theatre'. Such narrative and ontological surprises as were evident in the plays were thus reclaimed by the critics within easily understood generic boulevard conventions, and the double-bill's triumphant commercial and critical consensus established Pinter in Paris as 'the man who has shaken up the dying Parisian theatre'.[44]

Meanwhile Pinter's first production in the United States was in July 1960, when Professor Glyn Wickham of the University of Bristol directed *The Birthday Party* in San Francisco. At a time of escalating military presence in South Vietnam, the play's theme of defiance to authority resonated particularly among critics (more explicit references would later be made to Vietnam among leftist critical responses to *The Homecoming*). However, it was not until October 1961 that *The Caretaker* arrived with its London cast at the Lyceum Theatre on Broadway (where *Look Back in Anger* had premiered in 1957). After desultory try-outs in New Haven and Boston, the play enjoyed broadly enthusiastic reviews, and its run (and subsequent tour) was only curtailed by diminishing support from the producers (Alexander Davion, who replaced Alan Bates as Mick after the latter's contracted four weeks, wrote to Pinter from New York in March 1962 blaming the 'soulless bodies' of 'the money men').

The casting attracted the greatest critical attention, with Donald Pleasence's interpretation of Davies privileged in most reviews, although few were as laudatory as the *Morning Telegraph*'s description of 'a performance as golden as a sunburst, as detailed as the construction of a pomegranate'. The spectre of Beckett that had dominated the Parisian reception earlier the same year was also evident ('as talky and meandering as an evening with Godot', according to the *New York Journal American*), but dissenting voices objected more to the physical and moral squalor than to any linguistic disorientation. The tramp trope familiar to British and French audiences put off a number of reviewers – 'Not our dish [*sic*] of tea . . . we like our slices of life cut from the top and not the lowest strata of humanity', the *New York Mirror* complained – while Walter Kerr of the *New York Herald Tribune* regretted the 'abysmal despair' of 'a world turned to stone'.

The attention afforded *The Caretaker* at the Lyceum opened up smaller off-Broadway productions, including the pairing of *The Lover* and Beckett's *Play* in November 1964, but Pinter had to wait until

1967, and the premiere of *The Homecoming* at the Music Box Theatre, for his first real Broadway triumph. New York critics emphasised the unity of the play's structure, making the same allusions to the tautness of classical Greek tragedy as had their Parisian counterparts the previous year. *The Nation's* reviewer called the production 'one of the most complete I have seen on the English or American stage in some years', finding it less striking but 'more organic' than Peter Brook's *Marat/Sade*,[45] and this perfection of construction obviated the kind of criticism of a moral decrepitude that had been levelled at *The Caretaker* in 1961. Perhaps not surprisingly, the US-based philosophy professor, Teddy, received more critical attention in New York than in London or Paris, and his indifference to violence and non-involvement was seen by the more strident leftist critics in the context of the urgency for intellectuals to 'protest against the debasement of their country and all humanity in Vietnam'.[46] Although Walter Kerr in the *New York Times* thought *The Homecoming* unable to justify its length ('the play comes to seem afflicted by an arthritic mind and tongue'), the mostly undisputed approbation ensured the Best Play Tony Award, and established Pinter as a major writer in New York; for the critic of *Newsweek*, Pinter was 'the most significant playwright now writing in English', and *The Homecoming* 'an extraordinarily impressive play, one whose equal we are not likely to see at all soon'.[47]

Censorship

Pinter's Broadway and Parisian successes were closely followed in England,[48] and expectations were high for his next major work, broadcast on BBC Radio 3 on 25 April 1968. The formal simplicity of *Landscape's* partially overlapping, elliptical monologues seemed designed for the medium of radio; in fact, as most reviewers of the radio production noted, the play had been written for the RSC, but would only be licensed by the official censor of the British stage, the Lord Chamberlain, subject to the implementation of a number of cuts. When Pinter refused to implement these cuts, the immediate possibility of a public stage performance was denied, and the play was quickly claimed by the Head of BBC Radio Drama, Martin Esslin.

This stand-off between censor and playwright regarding *Landscape* was not their first confrontation, and the archives of the Lord Chamberlain make clear the degree of subjectivity and personal animus that the Chamberlain's Readers brought to their assessment of Pinter's work throughout the 1960s.[49] The censors' first opportunity to engage with Pinter had been in 1958, when they saw in *The Birthday Party* 'an insane, pointless play',[50] a conclusion perfectly aligned with the verdicts of the majority of critics. Nonetheless, despite some minor changes, the play was licensed for performance; indeed, for all Pinter's anti-establishment impulses, none of his plays in the 1960s was ever refused a licence outright (as will be seen below, *Landscape* was in effect left in limbo until the voting of the Theatres Act in 1968 confirmed the abolition of the system of pre-licensing).

The submission of *The Caretaker* in 1960 followed its successful run at the Arts Theatre Club – it was only when the play transferred to the Duchess for full public performance that a licence was required – and so the play, and its reception, were known to the Reader. The Beckett allusions were again highlighted, despite their irrelevance to the (albeit equivocal) criteria for licensing. Having identified 'a piece of incoherence in the manner of Samuel Beckett', the Reader's anti-intellectual sympathies are evidenced through a barbed reference to *The Caretaker* having been 'received with enthusiasm by the high-brow critics' at the Arts, a not uncommon positioning on behalf of an institution that often understood its role as protecting the public from itself. However, despite a half-reference to the Reader's own boredom, the report confines itself to a two-paragraph summary of the narrative; and subject to seven minor alterations (two of which concerned the phrase 'piss off'), the play was licensed with very little difficulty. An insight into the Chamberlain's attempt to navigate the increasing social permissiveness of the 1960s is evident in a note attached to the file for a 1965 revival of the play in Nottingham. The producers had argued successfully for the reinstatement of 'piss off', which by then had been included in the film adaptation of the play; the Assistant Comptroller confirming in a note to the Lord Chamberlain 'our policy of keeping in step with the Film Board'.[51]

If *The Caretaker* barely troubled the Lord Chamberlain, Pinter's

The Homecoming might have been expected to engender far greater debate. The play was to be staged by the RSC, which aimed to programme adventurous new work alongside the Shakespearean canon. Hall had recently presented David Rudkin's *Afore Night Come* (set on a Worcestershire fruit farm) and Peter Brook's Theatre of Cruelty season, two transgressive works that prompted accusations of inappropriateness for a company whose patron was the Queen. Following this so-called 'Dirty Plays' scandal, the Lord Chamberlain's Office, itself part of the Royal Household, was alive to the potential dangers of new work submitted by the RSC. Nonetheless, the report is conciliatory, and despite some reservation about the final scene, the Reader was minded to recommend the play should be licensed.

However, two phrases caused the Reader concern, and Pinter, Peter Hall and Michael Hallifax of the RSC came to see the Assistant Comptroller specifically to discuss 'Christ' and 'Stuff this mangle up your arse'. The assistant secretary's memo reports that Pinter 'was most reasonable in his approach', but that 'after searching his mind diligently he just cannot find an effective substitute [for "Stuff this mangle . . ."]'. The writer's case was further bolstered by the acknowledged physical impossibility of the assumed insult, and 'since the whole remark is a fantastic one, it can have no really obscene connotation'. As for 'Christ', Pinter clearly knew his way around the system, and argued for its inclusion on the grounds that it had previously been allowed in *The Caretaker* five years earlier. The Chamberlain's conclusions following the meeting are noted in an appendix to the memo, and make every effort to maintain the conciliatory relationship with both Pinter and the RSC: 'I think we shall have to allow "Christ"; but despite the force of Pinter's argument and the physical impossibility of stuffing a mangle up an arse I'm not too happy about this one. However in a play of this sort, you might have to let it go.'[52] During the three-year gap between The *Homecoming* and *Landscape*, the position of the Lord Chamberlain in the theatre became increasingly untenable. Plays such as Edward Bond's *Saved* and John Osborne's *A Patriot for Me* (1965) pushed the idea of members-only club theatre to its limits, the Chamberlain going so far as to initiate proceedings against the English Stage Company at the Royal Court over the staging of *Saved*. However, this only served to demonstrate the anachronistic nature of the Chamberlain's role, and to encourage the campaign opposing it; in 1967 a parliamentary joint Select Committee recommended the abolition of stage censorship, which came wholly into force on 26 September 1968. *Landscape*, therefore, was submitted at a time when the institution of stage censorship had been placed on notice of its own abolition.

The relatively short report, dated 15 December 1967, reprised the usual Beckett comparison ('the nearer to Beckett, the more portentous Pinter gets'), but while criticising the shapelessness and absence of plot, the play was nonetheless recommended for licence, subject to seven short alterations relating to Pinter's 'ornamental indecencies'. In fact, a visit from RSC Chairman Sir George Farmer reduced the disallowances down to three ('bugger', 'bugger all' and 'fuck all'), a decision gratefully acknowledged by the former in a letter to Lord Cobbold of 28 February 1968. The Chamberlain's memo of the meeting makes clear that both sides were keen to avoid conflict, and illustrates the growing significance of Pinter's reputation: 'The RSC are most anxious to keep Pinter and I said I was always most anxious not to prevent productions, especially of distinguished playwrights.' Nonetheless, 'bugger' and 'fuck' were non-negotiable, and an addendum to the memo reports that Peter Hall 'will try to persuade Pinter'.[53]

Landscape and *Silence*

If the Lord Chamberlain did make an ultimately doomed stand against a number of anti-establishment new writers in the 1960s, Pinter's work was not significantly challenged, and even in the case of *Landscape*, it is evident that every effort was made to allow its performance. Similarly, if the playwright's own attitude towards the state's official censor hardened towards the end of the 1960s, for much of the decade the relationship was relatively benign, certainly in comparison to his contemporaries such as John Osborne, or Edward Bond. In fact, Pinter often seemed curiously ambivalent about the

Chamberlain's position, and was not at the forefront of the campaign for abolition. It may be that this can be understood on aesthetic rather than on political grounds, for the exceptionally controlled nature of Pinter's writing demanded a carefully measured linguistic continence; in the *Paris Review* interview of 1966, Pinter discussed some of the excisions forced upon him by the censor, but concluded that 'the pure publicity of freedom of language fatigues me, because it's a demonstration rather than something said'.[54]

Pinter's refusal, therefore, to entertain the Chamberlain's cuts to *Landscape* must be seen in the context of the writer's awareness that the latter's powers to censor the theatre were in the process of being withdrawn; in fact Pinter had to wait just over a year until the Theatres Act (1968) was granted assent, and *Landscape* was able to be staged in a RSC double-bill with a new one-act play, *Silence*, in July 1969.

Both plays (along with the little-known sketch *Night*[55]) are typically seen to signal a move by Pinter to a cycle of so-called memory plays, in which the clash between characters over a defined territory is replaced by the struggle between past and present within a single consciousness. Pinter himself declared that he was bored with the structural formulae of his early plays, with their entrances and exits ('Something else was necessary for me. I couldn't go on with those damn doors'[56]), and his work in the late 1960s adapting L. P. Hartley's *The Go-Between* and Marcel Proust's *À la recherche du temps perdu* for the cinema is evident in the exploration of the way the past acts upon and in the present in these new plays.

Although written later, *Silence* was the first play on the double-bill, and arguably the more challenging for audiences, lacking the (marginally) more definite narrative outlines of *Landscape*. Pinter's spare stage directions established 'three areas' with 'a chair in each area', behind which John Bury's much-praised design proposed a sloping mirrored floor that reflected and refracted the three actors on to the back wall 'as in moving water'.[57] Through short, fragmentary phrases, the situation becomes slowly apparent: two men – Rumsey, and the younger Bates – have both at one time loved the same woman, Ellen, and been subsequently rejected by her. The present merges with several different pasts when Rumsey recalls Ellen as both a young girl, and later as his lover. Whereas Rumsey's memories of Ellen are suffused with descriptions of the natural world – 'on good evenings we walk through the hills to the top of the hill past the dogs the clouds racing just before dark or as dark is falling when the moon' (p. 33)[58] – Bates's coarser language involves more roughly recollected urban nights: 'caught a bus to the town . . . Showed her the bumping lights' (p. 34). The reliability or interrelatedness of the past is questioned early on by Ellen, who recalls telling her drinking companion, in a line that recalls *The Go-Between*: 'I'm old, I tell her, my youth was somewhere else' (p. 36). This line also subverts the reliability of the performed present, as the stage directions indicate that Ellen is 'a girl in her twenties', thus seemingly locating these (non-)memories of the past in some future time.

Landscape, meanwhile, draws from a similarly elegiac melding of past and presents, although it is set in the less de-localised environment of 'the kitchen of a country house', complete with reassuringly naturalistic objects. The play's two characters, Duff and his wife Beth (the play was written in Stratford-upon-Avon when Vivien Merchant was playing in *Macbeth*), sit on either end of a long kitchen table, and trade memories of their life together working for the house's former owner, Mr Sykes. It is unclear if either character can hear the other, and yet the two monologues operate in counterpoint, at times seemingly even prompted by the other's thoughts. As in *Silence*, the two voices are easily distinguished: Beth's dreams are elemental – of water, light, shadow and birth – while Duff is more grounded in the concrete trivia of ducks, dogs and bread, and in common with Bates in *Silence*, his language is often earthier, and more aggressive. An uncertain narrative emerges from the monologues, with two key events established: the moment that Duff confessed an infidelity to Beth, and her passionate response; and a paradisial moment on a beach recalled by Beth, during which she asked her (unidentified) lover if he would have a child with her. The play concludes with a delicate curtain line, as Beth recalls:

My hand on his rib.

(*Pause.*)

So sweetly the sand over me. Tiny the sand on my skin.

(*Pause.*)

Silent the sky in my eyes. Gently the sound of the tide.

(*Pause.*)

Oh my true love I said. (p. 30)

The two plays, and *Night* (in which a husband's and wife's differing memories of their first meeting circle around each other), are typically seen to draw deliberately from the pared-down simplicity of Beckett's short stage works; the economy of language is clearly comparable, and the dislocated staging of *Silence* is instantly reminiscent of the three urns of Beckett's *Play* (1964). For the Lord Chamberlain's Reader, Pinter was getting 'nearer to Beckett', while the *Observer* identified 'a homage to Beckett', referencing not only *Play* but also *Happy Days* (1962) in relation to *Landscape*.[59] Later academic criticism followed in the same vein (e.g. Ronald Knowles's comment that *Silence* 'is the most Beckettian of all of Pinter's plays', or Billington's comparison to *Ohio Impromptu*[60]), and this emphasis has tended to entomb the reception of the plays within a Beckettian astringency. In his biography, Billington cautions against accepting the beauty of Beth's final line in *Landscape* (quoted above) on its own terms, underlining the fact that it concludes a dialogue of the deaf in which recollections of a past happiness serve only to underline the characters' present isolation: 'the final image . . . was as chilling as anything in Beckett'.[61] For Billington, this 'petrified non-communication' parallels the fractured state of Pinter's own marriage at the time of composition,[62] and yet the images that are recalled in all three works are of a powerful iridescence and salty sensuousness. It can in fact be argued that the works present a less pessimistic vision than often understood, a vision that draws as much from a Joycean as a Beckettian aesthetic in the way that it loops back to a crucial image from Pinter's own formative reading of Joyce's *A Portrait of the Artist as a Young Man*.

In his review, titled 'Paradise Lost', Harold Hobson noted that 'in each case what is important is not the past, but the continuing influence that this past exercises on the present which is before our eyes on the stage'.[63] This ever-present past was to be explored by Pinter in a number of works from the late 1960s onwards, and Clive Barnes noted how this concern with memory and time marked not so much a Beckettian homage as 'Pinter's debt to James Joyce'.[64] Particular connections between Joyce and Pinter have been explored by Knowles, who acknowledges the importance of Pinter's acclaimed revival of Joyce's 1915 play *Exiles* in 1970, and its direct influence on not only Pinter's next original work *Old Times* (1971), but also the clear correspondences of verbal detail and structure with *Betrayal* (1978).[65] We may, however, equally perceive a crucial Joycean borrowing in the striking image that dominates and underpins *Landscape*: Beth's memory of standing alone in the water's edge on a beach. In one of the key epiphanic moments in *A Portrait of the Artist as a Young Man*, Stephen Daedalus observes:

> A girl stood before him in midstream, alone and still, gazing out to sea. She seemed like one whom magic had changed into the likeness of a strange and beautiful seabird . . . her skateblue skirts were kilted boldly about her waist and dovetailed behind her . . . she was alone and still, gazing out to sea.[66]

The transcendent warmth of Beth's memory – almost a vision – is entirely absent from the bleaker urban settings of *The Homecoming* and *The Caretaker*, but its multiple recollections dominate *Landscape*, and from the drafts in the Pinter archive, it appears that this image was among the first that prompted the play: on the first of three loose pages of dialogue that preceded the first draft of *Landscape*, Pinter has written the line that he retained verbatim for the final performed version: 'I walked from the dune to the shore.'[67]

Admiration for Joyce was, of course, nothing new for Pinter; the Irishman was regularly cited by the playwright as a formative influence,[68] and Pinter's first published work was an appreciation of the writer for the Hackney Downs school magazine in 1946, in which he called *A Portrait* 'a work of great lyrical beauty'. Nor was this very specific image new to Pinter's work. *Landscape/Silence* can be considered alongside not only *Night*, but also a much earlier radio sketch, *Dialogue for Three*. Broadcast on the BBC in early 1964, in this sketch two unnamed men recall an unnamed woman. In contrast to the men's sharper and more demotically expressed memories, the core of the short piece is the woman's memory of the first time she met her lover/husband:

> Do you remember the first time we met? On the beach? . . . and the waves? . . . and you – standing silent, staring at a sand-castle in your sheer white trunks. The moon was behind you, in front of you, all over you, suffusing you, consuming you, you were transparent, translucent, a beacon. (pp. 233–4)[69]

Intriguingly, the woman in *Dialogue* is described as 'the woman in the blue dress' (p. 233), the same colour as Beth's 'nice blue dress' that is described in *Landscape* (p. 20), which Beth later wears to the beach (p. 26).[70] The girl glimpsed in *A Portrait* wears 'skateblue skirts', and linking Pinter's repetition of this seaside scene to Joyce places it in the context not of a lost past, but of the Joycean epiphany, a moment that removes the observer from time, allowing it to be in some way transcended. In *Stephen Hero*, an epiphany is defined as 'a sudden spiritual manifestation . . . it was for the man of letters to record these epiphanies with extreme care, seeing that they themselves are the most delicate and evanescent of moments'.[71] Joyce himself had recorded such epiphanies from childhood, dividing them into overheard verbal trivia ('little errors and gestures . . . by which people betrayed the very things they were most careful to conceal'[72]) and more personal, lyrical memories or dreams. It is apparent that both definitions apply usefully to Pinter's project; the reclamation of the 'triviality' of the street in earlier plays such as *The Caretaker*, and in *Landscape/Silence*, the valorising of the beauty of the past moment through its recognition and, crucially, recording by the writer.

If many critics and friends picked up on the longing for a lost paradise in *Landscape/Silence*, only fellow playwright – and partner with Pinter in a joint production company, Shield Productions – David Mercer appears to have grasped this more affirmative reading of the plays' imagery. In a letter of 8 July 1969, he wrote:

I think there is a lot of balls written and said about 'non-communication' in your work . . . Whereas what I felt last Wednesday [the opening of *Landscape/Silence*] was the huge reparative meaning of what you do. You restore and reify . . . there's an extraordinary sense of what was lost or forgotten or fragmented . . . being drawn together. When life has passed . . . *Silence* (for me) showed the moving struggle to retain – to grasp and hold whatever it was. For even a moment. But at least once more.

Employing the Joycean-sounding term 'ragbag of trivia', Mercer reveals that these small gestures in the two plays made him weep for the way that Pinter is able to 'give back each thing its full weight'.[73] Rather than lonely plays of 'separation and solitude',[74] *Landscape/Silence* are richly moving affirmations of the way the past can be reclaimed for and in the present; plays – as Mercer described them – of 'plenitude'. Pinter himself, in a letter published in the programme for the German premieres of *Schweigen/Landschaft* in Hamburg, reminded the play's director that 'the fragments [of dialogue] are not necessarily filled with despair', giving the example of Ellen's speech 'all the blue changes, I'm dizzy sometimes' that 'should express her great natural joy'.[75]

'Silence, exile, and cunning';[76] Pinter's re-exploration of Joyce in *Exiles* is paralleled in his remembering of the writer in *Landscape/Silence*, and through a Joycean image of a seaside landscape, Pinter looks back to his own childhood literary influences as much as he borrows from the more recent stage work of Joyce's one-time secretary, Beckett.

Afterword

On the final page of the final scene of Harold Pinter's final play, *Celebration* (2000), the Waiter in the stylish London restaurant of the type that Pinter both frequented and parodied, delivers his closing monologue (or 'interjection'), remembering that:

> When I was a boy my grandfather used to take me to the edge of the cliffs and we'd look out to sea. He bought me a telescope. I don't think they have telescopes any more. I used to look through this telescope and sometimes I'd see a boat . . . The sea glistened.[77]

The old man whose memories are telescoped into a single image of a young boy looking far into the distance is an appropriate way to conclude the oeuvre of one of the greatest theatre writers of the twentieth century. His early plays famously chart a struggle for territory that becomes increasingly complex as it extends from the perspective of an isolated individual consciousness towards more fully realised social groupings, and as part of this power play, characters begin increasingly to lay claim to the past as an affirmation of strength, or a weapon.

These two currents are developed by Pinter during his writing throughout the four decades after the 1960s: local struggles between two consciousnesses will form the root of Pinter's later, more overtly political work during the 1980s and 1990s (e.g. *Mountain Language*, 1988, or *One for the Road*, 1984), while memory – the power its command can bring, and sometimes even its absence (*A Kind of Alaska*, 1982) – becomes ever more vital. These two themes will circle around each other throughout much of Pinter's later work, and are most notably fused in what is often considered to be his late-period masterpiece, *Ashes to Ashes* (1996).

Returning to the decade under review, after leaving the early symbolism of *The Room* and *The Birthday Party*, Pinter's work showed a growing awareness of the past, a shift apparent before the commonly acknowledged memory-cycle plays began with the broadcast of *Landscape* in 1967. This shift is apparent in Pinter's own revival of *The Birthday Party* in 1964, in which he steered the play away from its earlier strained symbolism towards a more realistic (and comic) domestic environment, in which he 'tried to make very detail as ordinary as possible', according to Bamber Gascoigne in an undated review for the *Observer*.[78] Pinter's former teacher and lifelong mentor Joseph Brearley interpreted this production as bringing the play closer to Pinter's own childhood, observing in a letter of 20 June 1964 that while all other productions of the play had started off 'hovering over that fabulous Pinterland which newspaper critics have made their own', this new production 'started off firmly (where it belongs) in Clapton-on-Sea. Down to the ground . . . It was here, now, today, tomorrow. In Clapton . . . I thought of all the Stanleys in Clapton. I thought of another McCann and Goldberg.'[79]

Clapton-on-Sea is a play on words of the Essex seaside resort Clacton-on-Sea that acknowledges the play's coastal setting, but more significantly points to the play's rootedness in the London district of Clapton in which Pinter grew up, and later recalled tramping across in Brearley's company ('I'm at your side,/ Walking with you from Clapton Pond to Finsbury Park,/ And on, and on'[80]).

However, the degree to which Pinter's plays are based on his own lived experience, a subject of periodic debate from the time of *The Caretaker* onwards, is moot. Certainly, behind many of the defining images of Pinter's plays of the 1960s – two men standing in a room, while a tramp roots in a bag; the return of a prodigal son – real-life correspondences may be identified. Even the nautical image that concludes Pinter's oeuvre in the theatre, and which had earlier occurred in *Landscape* and *Dialogue for Three*, might be seen to point to Pinter's memories of wartime evacuation to a cliff-side Cornish castle that gave on to the English Channel.[81] Yet the truth or otherwise of the images that run through Pinter's work is less important than the power of their recollection. As Clive Barnes observed of the nameless couple in *Night* who succeed in merging separate memories to transcend pasts that may or may not have been their own: 'our memory may lie, but its images are always relevant'.[82] The challenge for Pinter's characters – as much as for the playwright – is to successfully incorporate these images into a lived present; through the introduction of this challenge, and the introduction of a vertical axis of time into the previously ahistorical situations of his early plays, Pinter adds layers of complexity and richness into his writing that will endure throughout his career in the theatre.

ALAN AYCKBOURN
by Frances Babbage

> The death of all plays is scholastic analysis. Academics are
> always finding meanings in my plays that don't exist.[1]

It is a little unnerving for an academic to approach the work of Alan
Ayckbourn, given the scepticism with which this writer regards such
analysis. Ayckbourn has represented himself as first and foremost an
entertainer, insisting that 'Significant Theatre, Serious Theatre, are
deadly words'.[2] In the course of a career that now spans more than
half a century, he has certainly provided entertainment on an extraordinary scale: to date he has written seventy-six full-length plays, as
well as working consistently and to acclaim as a director. His oeuvre is
enormously and enduringly popular – he is regularly termed the most
frequently performed playwright in the English language (not
excluding Shakespeare) – and he has received numerous awards and
honours, including a knighthood. But while Ayckbourn has always
maintained that going to the theatre should above all 'be fun', he has
never implied that pleasure is bought at the expense of serious
content.[3] His own plays are manifestly serious on this level (even if
their author resists the attempt to impose 'significance' upon them),
but with themes and social commentary conveyed with great wit and
a strong sense of the ridiculous, and regularly filtered through ingenious formal means.

When his plays first drew critical attention, in the mid-1960s,
Ayckbourn was widely regarded as a promising farceur but not much
more. Reviewing *Relatively Speaking*, Hilary Spurling commented in
the *Spectator* – in a mode characteristic of Ayckbourn's early reception
– that here was a writer with 'no message, nothing to peddle except an
infectious delight in the absurdities of English manners. [. . .] His
amusement at these foibles has a certain timelessness, and his plot
might have been lifted from the eighteenth century.'[4] A few plays
later, a very different assessment had emerged of Ayckbourn the
dramatist: writing on his 1972 comedy *Absurd Person Singular*,
Ronald Bryden described its author as 'a political propagandist who

works on people's minds without letting them know he's doing it'.[5] Such a view was by no means universally shared (and was very likely unwelcomed by Ayckbourn, who has always maintained that he is an apolitical writer); for some time his theatre continued to attract seemingly contradictory descriptions, with those keen to defend its social significance set against others, both supportive and more critical, who regarded him ultimately as an exponent of amusingly reworked comedy in a classical and ultimately conservative tradition. To an extent, both perceptions are true. Like a great many writers, Ayckbourn has avoided stating baldly what his plays are 'about', but he has been perfectly forthcoming in interviews and willing to talk about real-life observations and experiences that have inspired or informed them. At the same time, Ayckbourn's work provides neither simple reflection nor overt critique of his contemporary society. In his early plays, form sometimes dominates over content: this is not necessarily a weakness – although at the time it put him at odds with leftist, Brecht-influenced fellow authors like Edward Bond or John Arden – but rather reflects the conscious attention to dramatic structure which, as I discuss, was for him fundamental in developing a profound understanding of craft.

Part of the larger difficulty facing critics seeking to assess Ayckbourn's contribution has been, somewhat paradoxically, his extreme popularity. Once any work of art has thoroughly demonstrated mass appeal, it becomes by definition part of the 'establishment'; and once embedded there, it is generally no longer considered to be truly critical or challenging. The director Peter Hall commented in the mid-1980s on this 'problem' in Ayckbourn's case, emphatic in his own conviction that Ayckbourn's plays have been, and will continue to be, significant: 'In 100 years' time, when he's been forgiven for being successful, people will read his plays as an accurate reflection of English life in the 1960s, '70s and '80s. They represent a very important document.'[6] In what follows I examine Ayckbourn's plays of the 1960s, showing how these stand both as social 'document', in Hall's terms, but also as the fascinating and sometimes flawed experiments of an emerging writer, obsessed by the possibilities of form and distinguished by an exceptional comic talent.

1960–64: taking (first) steps

At the beginning of the decade, Ayckbourn's playwriting career was still very much in its infancy. The popularity of *The Square Cat* in 1959 had surprised no one more than himself, and *Love After All* the same year was likewise a very solid hit. Yet despite the success of both works, Ayckbourn has refused to allow either to be published or performed subsequently, taking the view that in this early period he had not fully mastered the art of writing for the stage. His facility as a playwright would naturally grow through practice, and be further informed by the responses of actors, critics and the general public, but there would never be for him a leisurely period of exploration and reflection where that skill might otherwise develop: the time pressure under which Ayckbourn wrote and directed *The Square Cat* and *Love After All* established a pattern that persisted throughout his career. In conversation with the academic Ian Watson, in 1981, Ayckbourn explained that typically he set aside four weeks in total and wrote for two of them: for the first ten days or so of this period he might 'wander around and read and sharpen pencils (and) watch telly', eventually getting the script down in the last fortnight. He would already have an idea and maybe even a title in his head, but nothing more formed than this. As a writer, Ayckbourn has continued to be as efficient, or pragmatic, as these relatively early examples suggest.[7] That he is able to complete scripts so quickly is explained in part by his emphasis on play creation as *craft* (highlighted in the title of his 2002 manual *The Crafty Art of Playmaking*).[8] A 'playwright', as the spelling of the word suggests, may be understood – and in Ayckbourn's case, *should* be understood – as someone who makes or fashions a play, rather than simply one who looks for inspiration when putting pen to paper. To connect the playwright with professions such as that of the wheelwright or cartwright in turn implies that knowledge of materials, structure and technique is as important to the creative process as authorial 'vision'. Undoubtedly, Ayckbourn's involvement, from the beginning of his career, in virtually every aspect of theatre making – acting, stage management, direction, sound and lighting, scene painting, prop making – contributed to this sense that the playwright's art is importantly one of construction, and thus a skill that can be acquired and honed: providing, of course, that the ideas are there also. On one level, it seems self-evident that playwriting should require a profound understanding of mechanics; after all, plays are written in order to be put on their feet. Yet there is tension – and certainly, a degree of snobbery – attached to this perception of the dramatist's task, given that 'art' and 'craft' are terms that have histori- cally been held distinct. An artist will have some knowledge of craft, but a craftsman or craftswoman is not automatically considered an artist. Recognition of this helps to explain why Ayckbourn, as a dram- atist both brisk and prolific, has not always been regarded seriously by critics. Yet as director Peter Hall once told him: 'If you didn't write so much they'd realise you were quite good.'[9]

Ayckbourn's first two truly successful plays of the 1960s were *Standing Room Only* and *Mr Whatnot*. This phase of his playwriting also included two shows for children, *Dad's Tale* (1960) and *Christmas v Mastermind* (1962), neither of which proved very popular with audiences (or in the end with their author). *Standing Room Only* was produced at the Library Theatre in 1961 but is set 'futuristically' in 2010. Unusually in Ayckbourn's writing, this play makes a more or less direct social comment, albeit taking this in a thoroughly farcical direction. The play predicts a phenomenal traffic jam that hits London in 1985 – on a day known as 'Saturation Saturday' – as the consequence of overpopulation and a corresponding upsurge of car buying. The play is set on a double-decker bus that is still stuck in the gridlock twenty-five years later; its principal characters are the Cockney bus driver and his extended family and the action hinges on the imminent arrival of the daughter's baby (illegal, the government having since outlawed childbirth unless the woman has passed an 'Advanced Maternity and Housewife's Exam'). *Standing Room Only* was well received and was subsequently considered for transfer to the West End, in part prompted by an inspired line in *The Stage*'s review which demanded: 'Is there a manager to drive this bus to Shaftesbury Avenue?'[10] The play was widely taken up by producers looking to exploit potentially lucrative connections with the popular *Carry On* films, dating from the late 1950s, which – although far more 'saucy' than Ayckbourn's play – were similarly based on comic stereotypes of Britishness and parodies of the country's cultural institutions: indeed, two of that series's main stars, Sid James and Hattie Jacques, were discussed as possible cast members. Despite such conversations, as well as a number of rewritings that Ayckbourn carried out on request, the London production never happened; his archivist Simon Murgatroyd notes that the experience left the playwright justifiably wary of the West End and its ways of working.[11]

Ayckbourn's next really notable achievement as a writer was *Mr Whatnot* (1963). This was also his first play to make it to London (in 1964, in a production that was largely disastrous and critically slated, despite having a cast that included popular comedian Ronnie Barker); the first of his own works that he directed; the first to be made available for future commercial production; and his earliest work to be published.[12] He did not perform in it: and it was at this point that Ayckbourn retired permanently from acting, with no apparent regret. His performances had received largely positive reviews, but he later acknowledged he was the kind of actor that, as a director, he personally 'would hate to work with':[13] impatient, quickly bored and, as a fellow actor remarked, at times 'cutting and very witty' at others' expense.[14] *Mr Whatnot* had its premiere at another theatre that has been important to Ayckbourn's career, the newly opened Victoria Theatre at Stoke-on-Trent, jointly founded in 1962 by Stephen Joseph and Peter Cheeseman. Like the Scarborough space, it was in the round (or more precisely, in the square); its first season featured five new plays, including Ayckbourn's, alongside work by Beckett, Pinter, Anouilh and Bolt.[15] *Mr Whatnot* is an extraordinary piece of theatre that built on Ayckbourn's now proven skills as a farceur, but took the physical aspects of the comedy much further than hitherto and in a direction influenced by silent film actors such as Buster Keaton, Harold Lloyd and Jacques Tati. The play's central character, a piano tuner named Mint, never speaks: more than half of the published text is made up of stage directions. Mint is the 'Mr Whatnot' of the title, so referred to by an aristocratic couple who have employed him to work on their piano but are never sufficiently interested to learn his real name. The Slingsby-Craddocks are ludicrous 'toffs', their dialogue more braying noise than communicated sense. Here Cecil, their daughter's fiancé, is trying out the new piano:

Cecil   Oh, I say . . .

Lord Slingsby-Craddock   What the devil's the matter?

Cecil   It's flat. Piano's flat. Flat as a pancake.

Amanda   Pancake! (*She screams with laughter.*) Pancake – flat as a pancake. (*She goes into hysterics.*)

Lord Slingsby-Craddock   Bally thing can't be flat. Bally thing's brand new. Send the bally thing back if the bally thing's flat.[16]

The arrival of the seemingly innocent Mint throws the stately home and its inhabitants into increasingly surreal chaos. He is drawn into a tennis match, afternoon tea, billiards, dinner (mimed throughout) – in short, the rituals of a 'weekend in the country' – and by the end of it succeeds both in thoroughly exposing the absurdities of everyone present and abducting Amanda, daughter of the house. The end of the play initially appears to show this last action thwarted, as the last scene opens with the weedy Cecil bringing Amanda, now his wife, back to his flat. To her disappointment he suggests she head up to her own room and just 'bang on the floor' if she wants anything. But once in bed, two pairs of feet are visible sticking out of the end: she dives under the covers, uttering the play's final line: '(*Ecstatic*) Oh, Mr Whatnot!!'[17]

Mr Whatnot is manifestly a play about snobbery and social class. Although equally clearly parodic of this, it is not wholly removed from reality; Ayckbourn remarked in a programme note for an amateur production of the work at Leeds Civic Theatre, a few years later, that the 'people in it really do exist. Just buy a copy of the *Tatler* and you'll see where I pinched what dialogue there is.' At the same time he emphasised that he had no point to make with the play, 'no message': it was 'written purely for laughter'. Of his aristocratic characters, he added: '[t]hey're narrow, stuffy, unimaginative, boring and I'm very fond of them.'[18] Ayckbourn's words are in tension with the

insistence of the reviewer in *The Times* that the play had social principles and demonstrated the belief that 'plebeian vigour, sincerity and
enterprise will conquer a decadent aristocracy'.[19] Cordelia Oliver for
the *Guardian* (here referring to a 1976 production) seems closer to the
spirit of its author's intentions in describing *Mr Whatnot* as 'a
good-natured dig at the ineffably self-centred world of the stately
home set'.[20] At this stage of his career, as in future years, Ayckbourn
represented himself more as humorous commentator upon society
than active critic, and in so doing distinguished himself implicitly
from the more overtly politically engaged of his contemporaries, for
example John Arden or Joan Littlewood, or indeed Mike Leigh, with
whose work Ayckbourn's has occasionally been compared. *Mr
Whatnot* illustrates Ayckbourn's particular slant perfectly, dramatising
– with great wit, verve and theatrical inventiveness – his ambition 'not
[to] destroy' but to 'confuse a little, upset *status quos*'.[21] How he
achieves this and the nature of the 'order' he upends will be examined
in detail in the next section of this chapter, in which I consider three
of Ayckbourn's major and diversely ambitious plays: *Relatively
Speaking*, *How the Other Half Loves* and *Family Circles*.

1965–70: comedies of sex and class

> (T)he theatre is predominantly a middle-class woman's occupa-
> tion. The men in Scarborough that I meet say, 'I don't go, but
> the wife does' – it's the famous phrase. You say, 'Why don't you
> go?' 'Well, it's a bit highbrow for me,' they say. And you say,
> 'Oh, so you think your wife is more highbrow than you; I
> mean, that your wife is more intelligent than you?' 'No, of
> course she isn't.' I say, 'Well, what makes it so that she can
> understand it . . .?' 'Well, she's into art, you know.' Art is such a
> dirty word in England, it really is. It's like it's poofy, it's female,
> it's élite, it's exclusive [. . .].[22]

While from the beginning of his career Ayckbourn wrote for a popular
audience, 'popular' here implied diversity – of class, interest, age

– such as one might expect to find in a seaside town like Scarborough, rather than the working-class audience that some of his more politically minded contemporaries aimed to reach. He expressed frustration, whether real or mock, with 'hairy bugger[s] from the Left' (he did not name names) who seemed more interested in theatre's potential to instruct than in meeting its fundamental duty, to entertain.[23] In Ayckbourn's view, illustrated above, such attitudes contributed to a distinctively English embarrassment around the arts that made too many believe the theatre was somehow 'not for them'. Yet as Ayckbourn notes, women were typically more willing to attend, more 'at home' in the theatre than men. While this was and to an extent remains broadly true, at least in Britain, it also begs the question of the kind of experience Ayckbourn's own drama offered to this female majority of spectators. His early plays, as well as almost all later ones, focus strongly on the relations between the sexes; moreover he tends, atypically among dramatists, to include a roughly equal ratio of male to female roles. As already shown, he is in some ways a conservative writer, his stated intention – beyond, first of all, giving pleasure – only to 'confuse' the status quo; despite this, critic Michael Billington considers that his work is marked by an 'instinctive feminism', a claim that might be supported not only by drawing attention to empathetic character portrayals but through the observation that in Ayckbourn's comedies women more than men display the potential for rebellion against, or at the very least stubborn resistance to, the forces that constrain them.[24] Without affiliating himself with feminism per se, Ayckbourn acknowledged in a 2002 interview:

I realised when I was quite young that girls were getting less of a shout than men [. . .]. In many ways things have got better for women over the past 40 years. The progress for women has meant correspondingly increased confusion for men. That's what I have chronicled in my plays.[25]

My discussion of his next three major plays, produced in the second half of the decade, focuses in particular on their depiction of women, and situates this in context of the stirrings of women's liberation and with wider reference to female-orientated popular culture of the period.

Relatively Speaking

Relatively Speaking was initially titled *Meet My Father* and first staged at the Library Theatre in 1965.[26] It was a great success and soon transferred to London, where it established Ayckbourn's reputation almost overnight. The comedy in this play is carefully built through a series of complications derived from a single misunderstanding. Naive Greg is persuaded by his girlfriend Ginny that she is going away for the weekend to visit her parents, when in reality she plans to meet Philip, her married ex-lover, to put a stop to the gifts with which he continues to bombard her. Greg decides to surprise Ginny by going too, in fact beating her to the address – 'The Willows, Lower Pendon, Bucks' – that is scribbled on a cigarette packet he finds in her London flat and taking with him the pair of men's slippers that she has eventually convinced him are her father's. On his arrival in the country, Greg proceeds on the assumption that Philip and his wife Sheila are Ginny's parents. Sheila, unshakably polite, does her best to accommodate this unknown but seemingly harmless young man, hospitably plying him with drinks suited to the hour whenever the conversation turns especially confusing; Philip, for his part, is sufficiently muddled by what Greg says (when the latter is actually talking about Ginny) to imagine him to be his own wife's 'bit on the side', now convinced that Sheila really does have the secret life she has always faked for her husband's benefit in retaliation against his *actual* infidelities. When Ginny arrives, she in turn is obliged to maintain her fiction by posing for Greg as the couple's daughter and for Sheila as Greg's girlfriend, while Philip pretends to Greg that he is Ginny's father and to his wife that the young woman is his secretary. Towards the end of the play Philip reluctantly consents to give his 'daughter' in marriage to Greg, yet draws from him, and a furious Ginny, the agreement that she will first accompany Philip on a 'long business trip' (p. 57), thus '[making] a father very happy'.[27] Just in time, Sheila grasps the real relationships between all those present and puts a stop to the plan. Deftly, she converts Philip's planned break with Ginny all to himself into a six-week honeymoon for Ginny and Greg; furthermore, as it also transpires that the pair of men's slippers returned to their house by Greg are *not* in fact Philip's, a final twist sees Sheila reigniting her husband's old suspicion that she herself is having an affair. Vague as she is, and throughout the most put upon, Sheila is nevertheless at the end the only one fully in the picture.

Relatively Speaking opened at the Duke of York's Theatre in 1967, directed by Nigel Patrick and with an impressive cast: Richard Briers as Greg, Michael Hordern as Philip, Celia Johnson as Sheila and Jennifer Hilary as Ginny.[28] The title of the play was changed after the West End impresario Peter Bridge had described the original as 'very vulgar and seaside': the new choice of *Relatively Speaking* was a self-conscious nod towards the plays of Noël Coward, perhaps most obviously his 1951 comedy *Relative Values*.[29] Patrick had also produced (and starred in) Coward's *Present Laughter* (1942) in 1965, a highly successful revival which had prompted *The Times* reviewer to observe with regret that 'plays as funny as this [were] no longer being written in England'.[30] The validity of that assessment must remain a matter of opinion, but if there was any truth in it then it is fitting that Coward himself should have endorsed this new play's contribution towards reversing the decline. After the London opening, Ayckbourn received a telegram at the BBC, where he was then working, that he initially assumed to be a joke: 'DEAR ALAN AYCKBOURN ALL MY CONGRATULATIONS ON A BEAUTIFULLY CONSTRUCTED AND VERY FUNNY PLAY I ENJOYED EVERY MINUTE OF IT. NOEL COWARD.'[31] *Relatively Speaking* had yet another link to Coward: Celia Johnson, playing Sheila, was well known for her starring role in the romantic film *Brief Encounter* (1945), written by Coward and directed by David Lean. This concentration of connections no doubt furthered a trend that quickly spread among reviewers to represent Ayckbourn as Coward's 'natural successor'.[32] Certainly, the younger man acknowledged his influence – although equally that of Rattigan and, casting further back, of Chekhov, Pinero, Wilde and Congreve[33] – and the two dramatists shared an appreciation of well-crafted plot, humour derived through dialogue (in contrast with the polished aphorisms of Wilde) and a distinctive and to a degree nostalgic notion of 'Englishness'. But the comparison largely ends there: Ayckbourn took classical comedy in a direction that was both more broadly popular and at the same time embraced darker territory through his often profoundly disturbing depictions of middle-class relationships 'falling inexorably apart'.[34]

This bleaker turn is more overt in Ayckbourn's later work and while *Relatively Speaking* draws on such themes it is, as its author recently remarked, 'a French window play [written] at a period when most plays were set around kitchen sinks'. The fact that his style of theatre felt so removed from the prevalent dramatic mood served him well, it seemed: 'I think the critics breathed a collective sigh of relief: instead of dirty dishes and angry northerners they had shiny south-erners having breakfast in the sunshine.'[35] *Relatively Speaking* is highly playful, extracting maximum laughter from its central contrivance. Through the elaborately faked identities and increasingly implausible explanations, as well as the gracious Home Counties setting in which the majority of the action takes place, Ayckbourn seems to mimic the deceptions and confused courtships of Wilde's dazzling, flippant comedy *The Importance of being Earnest*. In Wilde's play, the feckless Algernon has invented a fictional friend called Bunbury, a permanent invalid who must frequently be visited. 'Bunburying' is thus in reality a means of evading unwelcome social obligations of all kinds; it is also, Algernon insists, a resource still more invaluable to a man once he is married.[36] In *Relatively Speaking*, a broadly similar device is employed to explore the comic ramifications of an adulterous affair: but given that here the characters are not Wilde's larger-than-life creations but broadly realistic and recognisable, then reading or viewing the play – despite its jokes – becomes at times distinctly unsettling.

Relatively Speaking remains one of the most regularly revived of Ayckbourn's plays, from which we might infer that it 'travels' well; at the same time, recent UK productions have played up its original 1960s context to the point where a modern audience would seem strongly encouraged to view the work – setting, characters and values all – as a period piece. Orla O'Loughlin's 2011 version for the Newbury Watermill, for example, opened to display a London bedsit, in a design by Anthony Lamble, complete with psychedelic *Sgt. Pepper* record cover, poster on the wall for *Dr Zhivago*, cuddly gonk on a chair and Consulate cigarette packet on the table.[37] Even the critics contributed to the period feel, with Holly Berry remarking in (one hopes self-consciously) retro-sexist terms on the performance of a 'beautifully curvy Ellie Bevan [. . .] as Ginny, the mini-dress wearing eye candy of the show'.[38] Evidence suggests that Ginny had similar status in the London premiere: first-night reviews in several national newspapers featured Jennifer Hilary's legs, despite a last-minute decision by the director to lower the hemline of her dressing gown, prompted by concern that the audience might otherwise be too distracted to concentrate on the play.[39] This anecdote is revealing (no pun intended) as it illustrates how Ayckbourn's comedy occupied a borderland between the relatively 'safe' territory of commercial theatre and something rather more risqué, because if this is a 'French window' play (to use the author's term), for the period it is remarkably open-minded. The scene in Ginny's bedsit is set at seven in the morning, with Greg naked but for a sheet: spectators are left in no doubt that he and she have spent the night together, a realisation underlined by Ginny's reassurance to her boyfriend, in the same scene, that he is 'a fantastic lover' (p. 7). While the boundaries defining what could be represented or implied onstage had been firmly pushed during the preceding decade, above all at the Royal Court – in defiance of the continuing operation of theatre censorship – such tolerance by no means existed in the West End.

Despite what Spurling called 'a certain timelessness', Ayckbourn's play nonetheless demonstrates shifting perceptions of gender relations characteristic of the social moment when it was written. Ginny and Greg are evidently having pre-marital sex, thus the assumption must be that the couple are taking precautions of some sort against pregnancy. Ginny is the more experienced of the pair – she 'chatted [him] up' rather than the other way around, has had relationships before and is in no hurry to marry, she says – so spectators might further infer that she is the one taking the initiative on contraception (p. 11).

The Pill was introduced to Britain in 1961, originally for the use of married women only, but by 1967 (the same year as the London premiere) that restriction had been lifted. Its use was integrally tied up with women's liberation, not necessarily because it enabled women to 'sleep around' but because it brought with it a new level of independence: uncoupling sex from the anxiety of pregnancy allowed a woman to a far greater extent to plan when to have children, rather than find herself economically dependent on her partner (if they married), or alternatively faced with the stigma of single motherhood or the risks of abortion, the latter at this time still illegal in Britain.[40] *Honey*, a popular monthly magazine of the period aimed at young women and older teens, variously reflects this change in gender identities and relationships. Its August 1969 issue published a letter from a reader that announced: 'I've recently been told by a man that I'm unique! Because, at the ripe old age of twenty, I'm still a virgin. Should this revelation be emblazoned across the national newspapers?'[41] Gillian Cooke's editorial for the issue addressed the same phenomenon from a different angle, observing: 'It may be some subtle balancing mechanism at work as girls, enjoying their acquired social and sexual freedoms, become more casual and resilient in their relationships, but nowadays men seem to be the real romantics.'[42] The relationship of Greg and Ginny illustrates Cooke's point precisely. When pushed, Greg admits he has not 'really known' any girl before Ginny: far worldlier than he, she considers him rash indeed to propose with no basis for comparison (p. 13).

While Ginny seems to epitomise the liberated 'Sixties girl' the play nevertheless ultimately shows her options to be limited, her desires manipulated. While Greg tries to charm her into line, Philip's approach is directly predatory to a point that sits at times uneasily within the genre of comedy:

Ginny   All those flowers, the chocolates, the phone calls – it's not fair on me, Philip. Can't you see that? (*She turns to face him.*) Please leave me alone.

Philip   Is that why you came all the way down here – to tell me that?

Ginny   Yes. That is it.

Philip   Right.

Pause.

Ginny   And I want those letters back.

Philip   Ah. That's more like it.

Ginny (*firmly*)   Please – Philip –

Philip   I think they might be safer where they are. (p. 38)

Ayckbourn emphasised in a note on the play that Philip should not be 'a suave moustache-twirling seducer', more 'a sympathetic bumbler'.[43] All the same, Philip is willing to put his threat of blackmail into practice: when Ginny later balks at his insistence that she go abroad with him, he meaningfully tells Greg he is sure Ginny will keep in touch when she's away as she has always been a 'good letter writer' (p. 58). Philip gets his comeuppance in the end, but in bringing this about Ginny too finds decisions made for her, driven by the dramaturgical imperative to bring about a fitting conclusion. At last wise to the situation, as noted Sheila manages to convert the sordid so-called 'business trip' into a honeymoon, and funded by her husband into the bargain:

Sheila   That's plenty of time to get married. A month? That's ample time.

Greg   I don't know if that was quite the idea –

Sheila   It seems obvious. (*Sweetly.*) Don't you agree, Philip?

Philip   Uh?

Sheila   They get married as soon as possible.

Philip   Oh – yes, yes.

Sheila   I should take advantage of the offer while he's in the mood, Greg. You won't get the chance of a honeymoon like this again in a hurry. [. . .] Will they – Daddy? (p. 59)

For spectators this is a gratifying turn of the plot, but decidedly high-handed in its consequences for Ginny; after all, she made it clear at the start of the play that she was in no hurry to get married. Moreover, once Sheila has waved goodbye to the rather surprised pair, she remarks to Philip that Greg and Ginny are '[q]uite wrong for each other of course. It'll be a disastrous marriage but great fun for them while it lasts' (p. 60). If her prediction is accurate, the young couple will if nothing else be a contrast to the older one, whose life together seems very little fun and set to continue that way. Thoroughly mistreated by her duplicitous husband, routinely mocked and patronised, Sheila is described by the crass Philip in the same terms he would use of a car: 'She costs me thirty quid a week to run and that doesn't include overheads' (p. 29). Sheila is the first in a long line of Ayckbourn's 'downtrodden wives', female figures equally unsatisfactorily defined within middle-class marriage but varied in their response to its frustrations: thus Sheila is quietly, and in the end quite effectively, subversive; while Eva in *Absurd Person Singular* (1972) repeatedly attempts suicide (but has her efforts consistently misinterpreted by witnesses); Vera is driven to a nervous breakdown by her wholly uncomprehending husband in *Just Between Ourselves* (1976); *Woman in Mind* (1985) takes this theme still further, filtering the entirety of the dramatic action through the unstable consciousness of the emotionally neglected vicar's wife, Susan. The lives of these characters appear to go on much as they always did, it seems, as if somehow sealed off from forces of change in society at large; at the same time, the manifest tensions bubbling beneath the surface of Ayckbourn's Middle England permanently threaten to explode it. In *Relatively Speaking*, such instabilities are embedded in characters and plot, but in the two plays I discuss next Ayckbourn makes fragmentation a defining feature of dramatic structure and in so doing displays, still early in his career, the readiness to experiment that has marked his work in subsequent decades.

How the Other Half Loves and *Family Circles*

Ayckbourn's next popular success was *How the Other Half Loves*. Between this and *Relatively Speaking* he wrote another play, *The Sparrow* (1967), a comedy set in Cockney London; this was well enough received on its premiere at Scarborough but not taken up elsewhere, dwarfed perhaps by the attention paid to those either side. As had now become the pattern for Ayckbourn, *How the Other Half Loves* was first staged at Scarborough and directed by the playwright himself; this dual involvement allowed him to joke in the programme note that for any confusion experienced watching the show, spectators should 'blame the director and not the author'.[44] In contrast with the still more structurally ambitious plays he came to write later, *How the Other Half Loves* is reasonably straightforward, but at the time its central premise was strikingly original. Where *Relatively Speaking*'s meanings are produced in part through the contrast of Ginny's messy metropolitan bedsit with the chilly bourgeois domesticity of The Willows, Lower Pendon – 'I think you can safely allow me to arrange my own morning . . .' (p. 17) – *How the Other Half Loves* juxtaposes two socially contrasting locations in a single theatrical space: the set consists of the living rooms of Frank and Fiona Foster *and* that of Bob and Teresa Philips, 'smart period reproduction' furniture alternating with 'modern, trendy and badly looked after' respectively. The actors inhabit this composite set throughout, while the focus regularly switches between one house and the other: as the stage directions explain, '[t]he characters in their different rooms will often pass extremely close but without ever actually touching'.[45]

The comic potential of this innovative use of stage space is exploited throughout the play, but above all in Act 1, scene 2, when a third couple, William and Mary Featherstone, are shown attending two dinner parties at once: we see them at the Fosters' home on Thursday night and simultaneously at the Philipses' home on Friday night. Ayckbourn has said that the inspiration behind the central concept came from a period when he was living in a 'soulless' block of flats, 'identical boxes piled one on top of the other':

Each day, each of us occupied more or less identical areas, trod the same well worn paths from kitchen to dining table, table to chair, chair to bed. It was a small step mentally, to superimpose one flat on another, emphasise the differences in the couples as they wove in and out of each other, pursuing their separate pleasures and traumas.[46]

The play's mixed-up set is no mere gimmick, but a means of revealing the characters' fundamentally mixed-up lives. It quickly emerges that Fiona Foster is having a secret affair with Bob Philips, one of Frank's employees: by coincidence, both Fiona and Bob attempt to disguise their adultery to their partners by means of an invented alibi that implicates the innocent and socially awkward Featherstones, Fiona claiming to have been consoling Mary, Bob supporting William, in what each pretends is this third couple's own 'failing' relationship. The punning title of Ayckbourn's play refers to 'the other half' within marriage but equally in terms of class. Frank and Fiona are childless, upper-middle-class and comfortably off, he more immediately thrown by the domestic 'crisis' of running out of 'bathroom stationery' than by his wife coming home in the early hours of the morning (p. 13). Bob and Teresa are solidly middle-class, she harried by the effort to cope at home with Benjamin, their baby who wreaks havoc offstage but is never seen by the audience; Teresa – very possibly suffering from a form of post-natal depression – sits at home 'like a – cow, or something', cutting out articles on matters of social concern from the newspaper and sending letters to the editor that are never published (p. 11). Where Frank tries an elaborately casual 'Where did you get to then?' with his own wife, Teresa and Bob are openly rancorous:

Teresa I mean considering the fact that you rolled in here at two o'clock this morning stinking drunk and I haven't said a word about it . . .

Bob Till now . . .

Teresa Haven't said a word about it, I think it's really a bit of a nerve to sit there complaining there isn't any breakfast.

Bob I'm not complaining.

Teresa Good.

Bob *crosses* L *and pauses* L *of the* C *chair.* **Fiona** *enters from the kitchen* R *with egg and toast on a tray. She crosses to the table* L.

Bob (*going out* L) What on earth have I to complain about? (p. 5)

As in *Relatively Speaking*, Ayckbourn explores the machinations and wider consequences of extra-marital affairs, but in this later play we are invited to consider two adulterers, two deceived partners. Teresa is rendered helpless amid the physical and emotional chaos that is her marriage to Bob, violence barely contained on each side; the elegant and polished Fiona manages her own infidelity with consummate assurance, able calmly to present Frank the next morning with a 'perfectly fresh' egg (p. 6).

In further contrast, Mary and William Featherstone are represented as the social inferiors of both other couples, at all times manipulated by them, whether unable to say no to a glass of sherry (Mary) or somehow ending up tying their host's shoelaces (William). As overawed by the elegance of the Fosters' place as they are shocked by the chaotic home of Bob and Teresa, the Featherstones put themselves automatically or inadvertently in a position of service. William tries, ineptly, to fix the Fosters' plumbing; Mary finds herself vacuuming and making coffee for Bob Philips. Although thoroughly 'used' by the other characters and in a sense by Ayckbourn himself – in that these two are at the very centre of the play as farce and have the most complex physical performance task to sustain – the Featherstones are a pairing that demands equally close scrutiny. Ironically, given the stories spread about them, this marriage seems initially to be the only one *not* in trouble. Yet as the action develops, the wholly false 'revelation' by Frank that Bob has been having an affair with the gentle and put-upon Mary elicits a speech from William that chillingly exposes the assumption that she is, in the end, little more than his personal 'project': 'Do you realise, Mrs Foster, the hours I've put into that woman? When I met her, you know, she was nothing. Nothing at all

. . .' (p. 64). In the hierarchy of the play's characters, Mary, lower-class and female, is evidently at the very bottom. But mirroring the twist at the close of *Relatively Speaking* when the seemingly weak Sheila subverts her husband's somewhat distasteful plans, Mary is likewise given her moment of rebellion against William's bullying. When, realising that he has misread the situation, William abases himself to everyone present apart from his wife, Mary refuses to leave without an apology. Through bluster, he manages no more than: 'In that case I'm – I'm – I'm . . . (*He can't say it.*)' Mary accepts it, excusing him to the others as they leave: 'It's difficult for him. He's never been wrong before, you see.' (p. 73) In fact, 'I'm – I'm – I'm –' is as close as anyone gets to saying sorry for the damage wrought within these relationships. Teresa realises that Bob has been having an affair with Fiona, but – after a very physical confrontation in which sex and violence are disturbingly intertwined – they patch things up, at least for the time being. Fiona for her part admits to a 'fling' but without revealing the identity of her lover; understanding finally dawns even for the obtuse Frank, but when he telephones the Philipses' house to confront Bob, he finds himself caught, when Teresa picks up, in yet another misunderstanding where he is the butt of the joke.

Michael Billington comments in his 2007 history of modern British theatre that class was 'a recurrent theme of Sixties drama: a reminder that, even in a decade that saw the rise of youthocracy and a much greater social mobility, the old structures hadn't greatly changed'.[47] Alongside a play like Edward Bond's *Saved* (1965), *How the Other Half Loves* may seem ultimately a merely light-hearted treatment of the theme. But when biographer Paul Allen once asked Ayckbourn why there were no politics in his plays, '[t]he reply was patient [. . .] but a little terse: "There are politics in every line."'[48] For Allen, the wit and invention in Ayckbourn's drama so dazzled that it risked masking the acuteness of the commentary. The example of *How the Other Half Loves* offers an illustration of this, judging by accounts of what happened when the popular actor Robert Morley was cast as Frank Foster for the London premiere. Morley had star status and a powerful stage presence, but he exerted steady pressure, as rehearsals continued, to make the piece above all a comic vehicle to display his own particular talents. As he was the principal 'draw' for spectators, he was allowed to have his way; but as a result, the production that resulted – although hugely successful in commercial terms – grew ever more unbalanced.[49] There may be 'politics in every line' as Ayckbourn wrote it, but if six strong roles, socially diverse and carefully interbalanced to expose the vanities and vulnerabilities of each, are allowed to become five supporting parts that are foils for one pompous pillar of the establishment, the play as commentary loses much of its bite and becomes nothing more substantial than 'good farcical, slapstick fun'.[50]

Like *Relatively Speaking*, *How the Other Half Loves* has maintained its popularity over time but is now regularly regarded as a period piece. This was evident in Peter Hall's 2007 production for Bath Theatre Royal, which incorporated a set by Paul Farnsworth that was a 'masterpiece of retro design: with the Phillipses' vibrant orange, brown and purple colour scheme, "Kerplunk" and Paul Newman posters, spliced with the neat chintz, the fine bone china and the many costume changes of the Foster household'.[51] But design features aside, it is above all the play's representation of the female 'half' of each couple that dates it. Ayckbourn acknowledged this, explaining that for his own 2009 revival of the work at Scarborough the decision had been made to leave the play in the 1960s, given that '[o]bviously the whole social scene has shifted somewhat. Men and women's attitudes have changed quite a lot. It's interesting that in that period when I was writing, none of the women worked. They were all so-called housewives. [. . .] Audiences today sit and say, "Gosh, I would never take that".'[52]

How the Other Half Loves implicitly says much about what women were and were not prepared to 'take' at the end of the 1960s. At one end of the class scale, Fiona, bored and dissatisfied, passes the time with affairs and 'an awful lot of dashing around': the phrase perfectly captures the effort required to sustain the conspicuous leisure that defines the fashionable woman about town (p. 2). At the other end, the timid Mary has been pushed – 'perhaps bullied [. . .], some might say' – by her socially aspirant husband into dressing differently, cooking differently, thinking differently (p. 64). Caught in the middle, Teresa exemplifies most starkly the frustration at her own situation: sometimes inspired, sometime angered by what she reads, veering between apathy and explosive energy, she is a figure positioned, it seems, on the brink of feminist self-consciousness.

The unique constraints placed on women's lives are critically exposed in *How the Other Half Loves*, more overtly so than in *Relatively Speaking*. This insight is achieved in part by character contrasts made all the more speaking by the layered staging device employed. Ayckbourn's next play expanded still further the versions of femininity set out for audience contemplation, here through a sometimes bewildering multiplicity that recalls the terms in which he once described growing up with his (single) mother: 'When I looked up as a child all I saw was skirts.'[53] *The Story So Far . . .* was Ayckbourn's first offer for the new decade, opening at Scarborough in August 1970; it was retitled *Me Times Me Times Me* (for tours in 1971–72) and came to rest as *Family Circles*, so called from 1978 onwards. *Family Circles* has been staged twice at Richmond's Orange Tree and was revived in Scarborough in the mid-1980s but, unlike the two earlier comedies, has not proved one of Ayckbourn's enduring successes. Its cast of eight, brought together for a none too happy family reunion, consists of Emma and Edward Gray, their three daughters, Polly, Jenny and Deirdre, and the daughters' men folk, Oliver, David and James. *How the Other Half Loves* is structurally bold in its staging, and *Family Circles* is equally so in terms of character and narrative. In the opening scene, the three daughters are coupled one way with the three men, but in the following scene, the partners are swapped; at the start of Act 2, they are exchanged yet another way; in the final scene, all three permutations are played out against one another (and here stage directions identify the entrances of 'Polly 1', 'James 2' and so on). Individual figures are sharply drawn (as they must be for so complex a composition to be decipherable by spectators), as 'types' more than rounded characters; and, in by now characteristic 'Ayckbourn mode', each pair seems to varying degrees incompatible. Polly, the eldest, is a domineering career woman in a permanent state of anger, partnered to the weak and neurotic David. Jenny is a domestic martyr, always close to hysterics and married to smug Oliver: 'Met her, have you, my wife? [. . .] Speak slowly to her or she misses the point.'[54] The youngest daughter, Deirdre, is the family 'rebel', bringing her new boyfriend – the more or less passive James – to the party uninvited and dressed in shorts, later having 'banging and caterwauling' sex with him in the Grays' spare room as if with the express intent of shocking her conservative parents. The subsequent rotation of partners brings no improvement but only variously pessimistic predictions of what each alternative arrangement might bring. In writing the play, Ayckbourn said he wanted to explore a question that most people will have asked themselves: what life would have been like, what kind of person he or she might have become, if married to someone else.[55] The response of the play seems summed up in Edward's remark to Emma, made at the very start: 'Whoever you decide on to share your life with invariably turns out to be the worst possible choice you could have made.' He adds, hastily: 'present company excepted, of course' (p. 2). Yet the marriage of Edward and Emma may be no less precarious. The daughters have suspicions – well founded or not we are never sure – that their father is trying to kill their mother, having learned that a neighbour recently found Emma on her knees 'gasping' in the greenhouse, its thermostat 'set by someone at a dangerously high level' (pp. 20–1). Murderous intent may be directed the other way too: a plate of sandwiches prepared by Emma is discovered to be full of broken glass; David chokes after drinking hot milk previously identified by Emma, rather pointedly, as 'Father's' (pp. 38, 46).

The title ultimately settled on, *Family Circles*, is more usefully suggestive than those Ayckbourn previously gave to the play. Most obviously, the phrase conjures mental images of intimacy and 'togetherness', against which the drama, as it unfolds, produces a pointed and painful contrast. Formally, the title gestures towards the play's complex partner-swapping, reminiscent of some kind of deadly dance; we might find echoes here of the German playwright Arthur Schnitzler's *La Ronde* (1900), which employed the metaphor of a round dance to explore sexual transgression and inter-class tension (and which provoked outrage among Schnitzler's contemporary audiences). In suggesting motion without progress, *Family Circles* as a title also recalls Emma's account of past hiking trips with Edward: 'He was hopeless with maps, you see. We usually went in huge circles. Round and round. I could barely keep up with him. He refused to stop and ask, you see' (p. 35). Beyond this, and given the bleakness of the overall picture, the play's title might evoke the circles that shape Dante's vision of Hell, here suggesting that suburban marriage is regularly if not invariably doomed. Indeed, if the 'marriage in difficulties' was an emergent theme in Ayckbourn's plays of the 1960s, it became a central motif for him in the 1970s. While autobiographical analyses should always be undertaken cautiously, it is worth noting that this period at the end of one decade and the beginning of another was marked by considerable domestic and emotional upheaval: Ayckbourn separated from Christine Roland in 1971 and moved in with the actress Heather Stoney the same year (the two eventually married in 1997). Yet knowledge of Ayckbourn's personal situation should be put in a wider context: official government statistics show that the number of remarriages in the UK rose from 57,000 in 1960 to 82,000 in 1970, with the divorce rate correspondingly climbing from 26,000 to 63,000 in the same period; these trends were reflected and to an extent encouraged by legislative reform between 1969 and 1971 that introduced a 'no fault' divorce law, which, among other effects, lessened the guilt associated with divorce and thus made the process considerably easier.

Finally, Ayckbourn's title, *Family Circles*, has still a further resonance, as it plays linguistically upon *Family Circle*, the name of a then-bestselling magazine in Britain aimed at 'the modern family woman'.[56] Where *Honey*, like its American elder sister *Cosmopolitan*, spoke to a female readership that was 'young, gay and get-ahead',[57] *Family Circle* sat more comfortably on newsagent shelves beside *Woman* and *Woman's Weekly*, directed towards those already married, or otherwise 'settled', typically with the added responsibility of children. At the end of the 1960s, such magazines generally reflected a tranquil, warm and whimsical image of family life, with the woman – of course, the mainstay of this picture – preoccupied alternately with keeping the house spotless ('Letters on cleaning problems form a large part of our postbag . . .'), knitting from currently fashionable patterns, producing 'delicious and economical' meals, or – ironically, given the dubious beverage prepared in Ayckbourn's play for Edward – deciding 'which hot drink for your family'.[58] They also provided quantities of escapist romantic fiction, like Flora Kidd's novel *My Heart Remembers* ('he was taunting and sarcastic – and made her so angry she forgot her fears . . .'), originally published as a serial in *Woman's Weekly* in 1970.[59] At the same time, tensions were regularly apparent and jarringly at odds with the serene surface. The 'Agony Aunt' page in a 1969 issue of *Woman* included accounts of a mother made 'ill with nerves' by her daughter's serial affairs ('we're respectable people'); of misery over infertility; and, most disturbingly, a letter titled 'Lost weekends':

> During the week he is a perfect husband but at weekends he always drinks too much, and when he arrives home, he hits me. I tried locking myself in the bathroom away from him, but he broke the door and attacked me. My mother advises me to leave him, but our three children adore their daddy and would be so upset if they were separated from him.

Evelyn Home's reply treats this reader's problem with startling pragmatism: 'During the week, when he's a model spouse, can't you make your man see reason about his alarming weekend behaviour?' If the reader were to go out *with* her husband, Home adds, this would probably '[restrain] him from drunkenness, but of course this would mean finding baby-sitters'. Her sign-off strikes a less optimistic note: 'When a man's violence is really dangerous to his wife's life, separation is inevitable. Tell your husband this, and it may make him change his habits.'[60]

In a way, perhaps *Family Circle* and *Family Circles* are not so far apart. Magazine and stage comedy both offer the blandly, soothingly bourgeois as their surface, but reveal this disrupted by an undercurrent of gender frustration, whether intellectual, emotional or sexual, and by the reality of violence, threatened or immediate. Such indications of anxiety are subdued, buried even, within *Family Circle*, and where they do come through they are met with compassion. In Ayckbourn's play, by contrast, bitterness is the dominant mood. It is perhaps the most brittle and bleak of his early comedies: just about everyone is unhappy and, as partners swap and confusion mounts, the misery is farcically increased. The play's central structural device is comic but simultaneously alienating, and in a way that *How the Other Half Loves*'s ingenious setting is not. The impossible dream of swapping one's partner for another model is here translated by Ayckbourn into a surreal stage nightmare: this quality is evident above all in the final scene, where each daughter comes down the stairs to say goodbye but keeps rematerialising on the landing above, as yet another version of herself. Where Emma rises somewhat vaguely above the chaos of whirling femininity, Edward is baffled and outraged; but as Emma remarked of him earlier in the play: 'He was never very fond of women, for some reason. [. . .] It wasn't that he didn't like them. He was perfectly healthy. He just didn't want them around' (p. 34). As we have seen, Ayckbourn's post-1965 drama twists the form of middle-class comedy – in this last example, with a new viciousness – and in so doing offers a complex theatricalisation of gender identities and sexual politics, an arena in which steadily mounting pressure would fuel the force of feminism's second wave.

Afterword

In 2010 Ayckbourn's seventy-fourth play, *Life of Riley*, opened at the Stephen Joseph Theatre under the author's direction. It featured a number of what have now become 'trademark' features of Ayckbourn's drama, such as a challenging stage set – this one requires a farmyard and three suburban gardens that variously reveal distinctions in the class and temperament of their owners – as well as a character we never see, but whose influence casts a shadow over the onstage action. Ayckbourn has employed this latter device extensively, from the early example of the destructive Benjamin in *How the Other Half Loves*: but in *Life of Riley* for the first time the unseen figure – Riley himself – is also the protagonist. The action centres on a 'typical' cluster of Ayckbourn's couples, brought together to rehearse a play for their local amateur dramatic society. When they learn the news that Riley has terminal cancer and six months to live, his friends decide to cast him in the play to keep him occupied and demonstrate their support. But as rehearsals progress, secrets emerge about past relations the three women have had with Riley, and fractures widen in their current partnerships: it appears increasingly that Riley is manipulating his friends' lives still, although perhaps ultimately for their benefit and by way of a parting gift he hopes to make before he dies.

The play being rehearsed in *Life of Riley* is Ayckbourn's first hit as a young writer, *Relatively Speaking*. The dialogue of Philip and Sheila ('I can't say I'm very taken with this marmalade' – 'They didn't have our sort'), which then comically exposed a relationship in stagnation, is here embedded metatheatrically to a very similar end, at the same time permitting Ayckbourn a nostalgic and gently mocking glance at his own developing style. The inclusion of the early play within the mature one is lightly self-referential, rather than a feature rooted deep in the work, yet it remains a vivid illustration of the contrasting shades of mood that have characterised Ayckbourn's theatre over the decades. *Relatively Speaking* is one of his brightest, most sparkling comedies; *Life of Riley* is far from the most bleak – perhaps *Just Between Ourselves* (1976) or the futuristic piece *Henceforward* (1987) might draw that description – but in exploring the ripples that surround an imminent death, we see Ayckbourn's willingness, in evidence from the beginning, to tackle the darkest of subjects.

CHAPTER 4
DOCUMENTS

John Arden

What follows is an edited version of a telephone interview with John Arden and Margaretta D'Arcy, which was carried out by Bill McDonnell on 5 January 2012.

Bill McDonnell   You wrote of Lindsay Anderson that he had helped to turn *Serjeant Musgrave's Dance* 'into the shape the play was demanding for itself'. I wonder, even at this distance, if you could talk a little about how the rehearsal process worked, and about how the script was reshaped or sections redrafted in response to rehearsal?

John Arden   Well, he read the play, and then read it again I suppose, and then read it a third time . . . and then said to me that the problem was that . . . I can't remember exactly what changes had to be made, but it began with the scene in the churchyard, where Musgrave says something like 'Oh God, have you delivered this town into my hands'. And I remember Lindsay saying, 'He's being too mysterious here. You have to have some notion of what it's all about, and at the end it has to be much more clarified.' It was really about clarification all the way through. And the relationship of the striking coal miners to the soldiers wasn't very clear . . . there were a whole load of things like that . . . but it was all in the nature of 'The plot is going to puzzle the audience unless we give them some clues. Reading it isn't the same as seeing it in the theatre. If people don't understand where it's going they're going to turn off and turn themselves out.' And that was basically it. We worked on it together and then I redrafted some bits of the play and gave them to him. And I remember one night he rang me up . . . I was living in London at the time. He rang me up, and said 'This still isn't satisfactory you know . . . you still haven't solved x' . . . whatever problem it was . . . I can't remember now . . . and I said, 'Oh for God's sake Lindsay, I think it's as good, as clear, as it can be.' And so he said very sharpishly, 'Ah, I see, so I am now holding the definitive text am I?' And I said, 'I don't think so. Because I don't think there is such a thing as a definitive text.' And he said, 'Good! I'm glad to hear you say that. Some authors would have thought there was.' We messed about with it, and in rehearsal we cut bits and so on. It's a process that goes on really with any play. But Lindsay was particularly sharp-eyed about it. His view of the director was that a playwright requires a second eye. If you just write a play and serve it up to the actors as it is, there's nearly always something wrong with it.

BM   Did you ever revisit the *Musgrave* text after that first production? Did that become the definitive text?

JA   Well, I did revisit the text because there was a television production by Granada a year or two later, produced by Stuart Burge. And he was in difficulty because the play in the theatre with intervals lasted two and a half hours, which is pretty long for a stage play. Granada would only give him ninety minutes. And so something like forty-five minutes of text had to be cut out. We worked on very much the same lines as before – how much do we need to know, how much detail do we need to have? . . . this speech, will the play be wrecked if it's not said, and so on and so forth.

BM   Did the cuts sharpen the text?

JA   No. In fact I saw the television version last year when the Town Hall Theatre in Galway offered me the stage for an eightieth birthday little show . . . And we had some bits of film as well, including a piece of the Granada production. Of course they sent me all of it, and I looked at all of it, and I thought, well, it's all very well but really it's a bit too peremptory. It suddenly came to a conclusion. It was clear enough but it was kind of coarsened. They had done a good job on shortening it but it was something I

217

thought didn't need to be done. And then there was another play by the 7:84 theatre company in the early 1970s, shortly after Bloody Sunday. John McGrath had the notion that *Serjeant Musgrave's Dance*, what had gone on in the back-story of that play, sounded like Bloody Sunday. And could we rewrite it to suit the Northern Ireland situation, in modern dress? And they did a version. John McGrath did it, not me. It was done pretty well, but it wasn't what you might call a great artistic success, simply because I don't think you can do this with plays. For temporary immediate effects you can do it, but once the topicality has faded, you're left with something that is neither one thing nor the other. It was a legitimate point of view to be adopted at the time, but reading it now it doesn't necessarily reverberate.

BM　In relation to that, John, the fact that *Musgrave* has been revived during the Vietnam War, the Troubles, Iraq and so on, points to its continuing relevance: *Armstrong's Last Goodnight* would have spoken powerfully to the Irish peace process, and to the current attempts to disengage from Afghanistan and Iraq. They go to the heart of certain historical continuities. Do you think the same holds true of the *Non-Stop Connolly Show* or *Vandaleur's Folly*?

Margaretta D'Arcy　Well, we did a version of *Vandaleur's Folly* which actually was a version of the *Manchester Enthusiasts*[1] a couple of years ago, and we did parts of the *Non-Stop Connolly Show* in Galway. And of course they are very relevant still. The one we haven't done is the *Ballygombeen* or *Little Grey Home in the West*, which would not be so relevant today . . . But I think that to make plays relevant it needs other dimensions. When we did the *Non-Stop Connolly Show* in Galway we were able to bring in contemporary issues, and people came and spoke about what was happening, and so it meant that the audience then had the choice of becoming part of a struggle that was ongoing.

BM　How do you see the Royal Court 'revolution' from the vantage of fifty years? Was it really as significant in reshaping British theatre as orthodoxy suggests it was?

JA   Well the first thing is everyone talks about it as if you were always there all the time. As if it was a sort of club, in which writers and directors and so on used to sit around all day discussing the need for good work and committed plays and everything. I mean I didn't go to the Court a great deal . . . I used to go once a week and pick up a script, because I was paid for reading scripts that people had sent in you see, it's how I earned my living at that time. And I'd pick up some scripts to take home and read, and while I was there I'd talk to George Devine if he wasn't too busy, or Bill Gaskill or John Dexter or Lindsay if they were around the place. And we had cards to allow us to sit in at rehearsals, which was always interesting, it's always very interesting watching actors rehearse – so long as you don't have to spend too long doing it! But that [being a writer] is a solitary pursuit: one didn't sit in a sort of club. There were the meetings of playwrights, with Anthony Page and his group of actors who all met in Ann Piper's house where one did have a certain amount of confabbing . . . but by and large you know the Court was a kind of individual thing. I mean you were fine if your play was in rehearsal and everyone thought it was going to be a success. If it wasn't a success you were ostracised almost. People didn't want to have anything to do with you. You were dead. Until you were able to come back with another script a year later. Otherwise you didn't want to go to the Court. But with all its faults George Devine was endeavouring to establish a theatre for new playwrights . . . or rather for new plays, not necessarily new playwrights . . . a theatre in which the script and the meaning of the play would be the essential quality, rather than its value as a vehicle for a star. West End theatre at the time was always presented as if, you know, we must go and see Ralph Richardson at such and such a theatre, go and see Rex Harrison at such another theatre . . . and to begin with this was not what was happening at the Court. And then of course they needed the money, so they had to put on plays which would transfer to the West End as kind of star vehicles. Some of them were successful and others weren't. The thing about the Court was the tension between George Devine and Tony Richardson. Tony

Richardson was anxious all the time for more commercial success, and I think he got a bit fed up with George's almost educational policy there.

BM   There must have been a great tension between being lauded as Britain's Brecht and a writer of Shakespearean quality on the one hand, and then being rejected by the Court on the other? Was the rejection a matter of politics?

MD   I think you've got to understand that in that time neither of us was aware of all the wonderful things that people were saying. Because we did not live in London. After *Musgrave's Dance* we lived down in Bristol, and then we moved up to Kirbymoorside. So we were never really aware of the stuff people were talking about. And the feeling of rejection was many years later after *Musgrave*. The first indication we had about this cooling off towards us was when we put the *Non-Stop Connolly* show on at the Almost Free. And Pauline Melville was in *Live Like Pigs*, and she was in the *Non-Stop Connolly Show*, and she asked Bill [Gaskill] if he was coming along to one of the episodes, and he said, 'Oh, no, that'll be one of the boring ones!' . . . At the beginning they were all madly excited about *Live Like Pigs* . . . and then, when the reviews came out and there was nobody sitting in the theatre, literally then, you were out [. . .] It wasn't as if the Court was writing you a letter saying 'please write us another play'. They did ask to do *The Workhouse Donkey* but that got very messed up, and Lindsay wasn't interested. But the directors were not interested in John. I think part of the reason he became isolated was that he didn't have one director who was pushing him. Arnold Wesker had John Dexter. And John Dexter was very faithful to Arnold Wesker and was associated with everything. If you're not associated with a single director then you're just another playwright.

BM   Was there a director who you would have liked to have worked with consistently?

JA   I enjoyed working with Bill Gaskill, I enjoyed working with Lindsay Anderson, and I very much enjoyed working with Stuart

Burge, who did *The Workhouse Donkey*. I did not have quarrels with these people. But none of them was committed to me as such, in the way that Dexter was to Wesker. One doesn't complain, but it was a fact. I'm not quite sure even now what happened with *The Workhouse Donkey*. I wrote it, George Devine said he liked it, and would put it on, and Lindsay would do it. Lindsay then communicated with me for quite a while about improving the script, which I accordingly did, and then I never heard anything more from him. Until I got a letter from George saying that if I was in London would I come and see him. And I went to see him and he said that they were going to do the play but not as a Court production: it was going to be passed on to Larry Olivier to do at the Chichester Festival by what was the early nucleus of the National Theatre. And a man came in and said, 'Hello George', and George asked if he wanted a drink. I didn't know who he was. He looked as if he'd come to read the gas meter . . . he had a moustache anyway. I suddenly realised when George called him 'Larry' who he was. There was a play on in the West End at the time about a middle-class man, an insurance clerk or something of the sort, living in Birmingham, and Olivier was carrying his character in appearance around with him.[2]

MD   Of course all John's plays were different. And the director would only really take the play up if the subject matter of the play interested them. If you take Arnold Wesker, all his plays have a continuity of theme and interest [. . .] so the directors themselves were on the lookout for areas or themes which would satisfy them. George's dream I think was to have a permanent group of playwrights and directors and actors, and there would be this kind of family feeling. But when George died that was the end of it really.

BM   The one consistent feature of these three plays is their rich dramaturgy. I am struck by the potent use of popular forms and conventions, for example the 'mansions' in *Armstrong's Last Goodnight*. But I get the impression you didn't see a vast amount of theatre as a child. What was the source of your knowledge of these forms?

JA   My techniques are traditional. People asked me how far was I influenced by Brecht, and I would say I was; on the other hand I was possibly more influenced by exactly the sort of theatre forms that Brecht himself was influenced by. A lot of it I read from books, and why not? Illustrated books setting out the sets and costumes from different periods of history, and discussions as to the how the plays were done. This began shortly after I left school. I bought a book by Walter Hodges about the Elizabethan theatre in London, full of drawings, and this was something I had never really thought about before – I mean I had an idea of what the Globe Theatre looked like – but I hadn't got any notion as to how it would have worked in terms of production. And the question of the 'mansions' in *Armstrong's Last Goodnight*, I studied that when I was working as a resident playwright at Bristol University. There was a series of lectures on the early English theatre . . . and I thought this was very interesting. And they had this new theatre at Bristol which could be shaped in various ways – proscenium or amphitheatre or Elizabethan style. So when I was asked to write a new play – the *Happy Haven* resulted – it was specially written for that theatre in the Elizabethan mode. I wanted to see what it looked like, and it looked very well. But it didn't look very well when it was done at the Royal Court by the same director and most of the same cast, because the theatre was not sufficiently appropriate.

BM   Fintan O'Toole has called you 'the last of the sixteenth-century playwrights'. I wonder if you could talk a little about your fascination with the art and writers of the late-medieval and early-modern period? It has been the source of significant works.

JA   Well, he wrote a review some time ago of a novel I wrote called *Books of Bale*, and that was an attempt to examine the shift between medieval Catholic theatre, and the secular theatre of the Elizabethan period . . . the theatre was strongly political in what you might call those gap years . . . and controversial in connection either with the Reformation or with the anti-Reformationists, the Catholic conservatives. And then suddenly Queen Elizabeth put a stop to it: no more religion in plays or else you'll have your company banned. And they had to find other ways of doing it. I was very interested in the way that developed. What came out of it, of course, were Shakespeare and Ben Jonson and a very exciting period of theatre. So I suppose in that way my mind has been for a long time formed in theatre terms by that period.

BM   Gaskill says you worked with the actors on the 'Babylonian' dialect you created for *Armstrong's Last Goodnight*. Could you talk about that?

JA   The language for *Armstrong* came from my seeing Tyrone Guthrie's production of the *Three Estates* in Edinburgh when I was a soldier there in 1949. That was a tremendous occasion because not only was it a wonderful production on an approximation of an Elizabethan-style stage, but it was also in the Scots dialect in which Lyndsay had written it.[3] And I thought that this was the most powerful theatre language that I had ever heard. And then a few years later John Barton produced *Julius Caesar* with the Marlowe Society in Cambridge in what he was persuaded was the popular Elizabethan pronunciation of English, which was nearly as remote to the modern era as the Scots of the *Three Estates*, and also very strong. I would love someone else to do it, and try and make a regular thing of it, because it does something to the English language. And of course the *Three Estates* production, as Margaretta has just been saying to me, was developed in the context of Scottish independence . . . the political movement was beginning to gain strength in those days.

BM   I wonder if we could turn to *The Workhouse Donkey* now. You talk here of corruption as a Dionysian value. When the MP expenses scandal broke in Britain (or indeed in Ireland) did you feel sympathy for their imperfections?

JA   Well, corruption makes for comedy to start with. I had been brought up in the town of Barnsley, in a Conservative household mind you, where the corruption of the local Labour Party was a common theme for conversation, and among people who, when they were not professedly shocked by it, were amused. Because it really was very funny sometimes, the things that happened. And of course it didn't stop the Conservatives being as corrupt in their own way. And I thought that there was good corruption and bad corruption. That if a politician breaks the rules in order to build a housing estate for the workers, which otherwise wouldn't get built, then that's a great thing. There was a man in Tyneside at the time I wrote the play, T. Dan Smith [. . .] I was very much aware of him . . . his architect was a man called Poulson, who got I think sent to prison for getting involved in corruption and he had done a job for the factory which my father managed, so there was a certain connection there. I thought then, and I still think this, that T. Dan Smith was a pretty good example of well-intentioned corruption [. . .] In my play Charlie Butterthwaite is contrasted with Barney Boocock, the mayor, who is puritanically honest, and very much disapproves of his friend's behaviour. You know, I think living in a corrupt state is sometimes better than living in a strictly puritanical one. You have to weigh these things up. We're an imperfect race.

BM Indeed we are. Well, look, thank you both again very very much for talking to me. I very much appreciate it.

MD Well, thank you for a stimulating time. It's been very interesting.

Edward Bond

In April 2011 I made contact with Edward Bond and asked if he would be willing to respond to some questions about his early plays. He agreed, and we engaged in email correspondence over several weeks. I suggested at the start that he should feel free to choose which of my questions to answer, but he replied to them all, always promptly and often in surprising detail. He also went out of his way to be helpful – not least by sending me copies of other unpublished material relevant to issues I had raised.

What follows is an edited selection of my questions and his answers.

Steve Nicholson   When I've 'taught' *Saved* to undergraduate students they sometimes see the play as an attack on young people, and perhaps on the working class. Does that surprise you?

Edward Bond   You should explain to your students that I am concerned (as they should be) with humanity in general, with the relation between self and society which is the foundation of all drama. I would not attack a particular section such as young people. It should be clear to students that the play is concerned with a general cultural negativity. (Parents could say the play was an attack on parents.) The student attitude you describe seems to be part of a cultural collapse in which particular groups judge things from their own point of view . . . The play raises the questions of moral society. In fact the young men kill the baby as a means of gaining their moral self-respect. This question is more interesting – and fruitful – than whether the play attacks young people. It says something about the society of which the students are members – and that ought to be what interests them. This should be true of when the play was written and also of now. It seems pretty certain that the students you mention are particularising the problem in this way in order to avoid it – what it says about the present situation of humanness. It's more useful to speak about the purpose of drama. (*Hamlet* isn't of use only to heirs apparent.) And even if it were an attack on these youths it is just silly and thoughtless to regard that as an attack on all youth – the attitude shows the destructive sectionalisation of our society.

SN   About the sound at the end of scene six in *Saved* – the 'curious buzzing'. I've never been able to imagine quite what the sound should actually be, or how it would be created.

EB   When the scene is staged properly it itself makes the sound. It's as if the air tremors. It is a fore-shock not an after-shock. When the scene works (I repeat this because it is usually badly staged and then it can't work) it is as if the sound comes not even from the audience but from the air where they are – it is the premonitory silence before a storm turned into sound. If the scene is staged properly . . . the sound will be there. That is of course the antithesis of modern theatrical trickery – which is to be identified with the lie hiding from itself behind the blatant effrontery of consumerism.

SN   I wonder how you view these early plays of yours now – you're probably as well known for *Saved* and *Lear* as for anything you've written since. Are you happy for these to be the plays that people like me put on courses for students to see as representative of your best work?

EB   My plays sequentially explore certain problems. They should be understood as a whole. Some plays deal with particular aspects of the problems. They do this in order to show the nature of the whole problem. There has to be some basic, enduring concern that demands to be dramatised. In this sense each play leads to the next. About plays representative of my best work: in the UK this may be true of the plays you quote. But it varies in different countries. My feeling is that because theatre is now moribund in this country students are not encouraged to study texts which more directly deal with their immediate contemporary world. They could then better understand the relation of *Saved* to their own lives. It would be mistaken to deal with *Lear* or *Saved* and not *The Crime of the Twenty-first Century* or *Coffee*.

SN   I always assumed that the starting point for your plays would be something specific you wanted to say – a 'political message', I suppose. But I was struck when I was looking through your published notebooks that this seemed not necessarily to be the case. For instance with *Early Morning*, it looks as though you had an image of Siamese twins before you knew what the play was going to be about. Is that so? Is that how other plays have started – from an image, rather than an idea or concept?

EB   Plays stretch from the kitchen table to the edge of the universe – or they are not dramas. If I have an image of Siamese twins why does it interest me? It would be absurd to say I would want to write an interesting play about Siamese twins. You need to relate to politics, economics, history, society and then perhaps to one shoe abandoned on the seashore or to say the crumbs lying on the edge of the universe. The play must enact the interrelation between self and society – and if it's ignited by an object, then it's because you are day-and-night concerned with the total problem. You are interested in the shoe because you are interested in the shore – and the other way round. But objects, even in my early plays, have had a particular dramatic function. The best director of my plays in France said: 'In Bond's plays you have to get the small things right or the big things will not be there.'

SN   When you wrote *Early Morning*, was there any part of you that was motivated by a deliberate wish to provoke and antagonise the censors? You must have known that being offensive about the monarchy – perhaps especially about Queen Victoria – was the most insulting thing you could have done?

EB   I intended *Early Morning* to be a simple and lucid record of history. It would be absurd to worry that anyone might find history insulting. I don't understand this – would the Queen be insulted because her great-great-grandmother was a lesbian or because she was a cannibal?

SN   The Lord Chamberlain said that he might allow *Early Morning* if it was ruritanianised – i.e. if you had removed the names of real people and made it more obviously a fantasy and fiction. If censorship had remained, would you have considered doing that with this play – or with others?

EB   The question of whether I would set a play in Ruritania is hypothetical. It was either the censor or me – and it was going to be the censor. The Court wanted me to compromise because everyone always had – and I said no. And so the censor had to go.

SN   Could you say anything about how the titles of *Saved* and *Early Morning* came about or what they refer to?

EB   My first three plays (*The Pope's Wedding*, *Saved* and *Early Morning*) were difficult because although I knew them thoroughly when I wrote them I didn't – in an analytical sense – know what they were about. I was taken with Russian double titles: *War and Peace, Crime and Punishment*. So I wanted *Saved* and ***. But I couldn't think what. The Court wanted to advertise the play and gave me an urgent deadline. During my work lunch-break I went to a park. I walked up and down thinking. I must have come up with some ideas. I remember none of them. When I settled for *Saved* I had a slightly surprised feeling of having entered the modern world. Now when I am asked to explain the title I say, 'It's what goal-keepers do.' If in future I am pressed I shall say, 'You should enter the modern world.'

SN Do you still have any notes or first drafts of the 1960s plays which it might be possible to look at?

EB My notes for a play are many times longer than the finished play (I have over eighty large notebooks filled with minute scribble) and I make many drafts of each play – sometimes ten or fifteen. And there are as many theoretical notes and unpublished poems. When the harvest is cut and in the winter cold mice leave the fields and come into the house and eat some of them. But unfortunately they are still far too many for me to ever search through to find anything – so I have to be disobliging when I am asked to do that. I'm sorry.

SN I noticed when I read the text of the 'Teach-In' that the Royal Court held on *Saved* in 1965 that you said, 'I think the play is open to several interpretations.' And David Hare says somewhere that however much you think as a playwright that you're saying one thing, there will always be people in the audience who think you're saying the opposite. Do you think your plays have explicit and specific meanings which it is the duty of a production to communicate?

EB This is a misunderstanding. Texts are written in accordance with certain techniques. These have to be understood and used if the play is to confront its problems – and this means saying what a solution would be. But that doesn't say how a play is to be acted – every performance has to be different. The aim of directing should be to reveal the 'invisible object' and only the actors (individually and together) can create this. This would have been obvious to any generation other than ours – because that is the absolute purpose of drama: to see the humanness of the actor (revealed in the extreme situation) and to be confronted by it in our own humanness. This is why I talk about the logic of humanness and the logic of imagination. The question isn't as simple as Hare supposes – a text can confront the audience with a moral value which cannot be reduced to a moral, optional, fact. Would it have been possible for drama (not theatre) to allow a German audience in 1944 to be of the opinion that Auschwitz was a good thing – and doesn't drama always deal with fundamental problems of this sort, because as one of the Karamazov brothers says: if one child is brutalised there is no God. Drama is not a consumer product – it needs the humanness of the audience. That's why I wouldn't write a play criticising young men (though the hooligan-critics wanted me to). Years later a director at the Court said his method was to split the actors into groups. They went away and then came back and showed what they'd arrived at – and he could see if it worked. That's phoney democracy – anything can be 'made to work'. The point is, should it?

SN   I know you tend to be dismissive of the screenplays you wrote, but I wanted to ask about *Walkabout*. For instance, I presume it would have been your idea to replace the plane crash with the father deliberately setting fire to himself (and shooting at the children)?

EB   I'm not interested in films that I'm alleged to have contributed to. All English-language films are in the service of Lollywood. I acknowledge only two film scripts and I'm pretty sure they are masterpieces. The potential director (an Oscar winner) of one said that it was the most imaginative script he'd ever read. But the accountants in Lollywood wanted me to rewrite it with a professional 'screenist'. I wouldn't. Fifty years after my death (when Lollywood loses the copyright) they will be published – and be my gift to a public I will never know. Really, I remember very little about writing the scripts that were filmed, but now you have mentioned it I do remember writing the plane crash and the shooting at the start of *Walkabout*. My wife asked me not to write film scripts because when I did I grated my teeth in my sleep and it kept her awake.

SN   A few years ago *Lear* was staged at the Crucible Theatre and one of my colleagues told me she was shocked by the sexism (or anti-female) tone of the play. She cited in particular the speech where Lear looks at the body parts of his dead daughter and says that he would never have behaved as he did if he had known how beautiful she was. Now I thought this was an unfair charge by my colleague; Lear isn't looking at her face or the exterior of her body, but at the organs. But she did make me wonder whether the play could be seen as anti-women. It could be argued, perhaps, that the most vicious and cruel characters in the play are actually women, and I wondered why?

EB   If your colleague thought that Lear suddenly saw his daughter was, in the conventional sense, beautiful, or noticed the beauty of her external body now it was being cut up – then her judgement is weird. Lear is having a Blake-ian vision of the orderliness and structure of nature. Is it more pro-woman to make Cordelia an ideal heroine because she never does anything, never has to make any political decision – I thought it was more positive to face her with the dilemmas of reality, of men politicians, and I gave her a case which is reasonable. Shakespeare's Cordelia seems to have read Kant, but Kant never met Stalin – so I thought Cordelia should. I suppose I could have made Goneril nice, in the interest of all-round fairness – but then I would be escaping from, and not trying to face, the problems Shakespeare sets.

SN   I am aware that you had some bad experiences with the National Theatre and the Royal Shakespeare Company and that you now prefer your new plays to be staged in very different contexts. But if either of them asked to perform *Lear* (or another of your 'older' plays) today would you give them permission?

EB   The RSC and the NT would be unable to stage my plays – they have lost the skills of dealing with the problems that concern me and the way that they have to be embodied in drama. This is just a fact – they cannot deal with the problems of our time. They gift-wrap plays. If I sent *Saved* or *Lear* to the Royal Court now they would reject them.

SN   Do you think things – society, the world – are getting better or worse? By comparison with the 1960s, do you think it's easier or harder now for a young playwright starting out to write plays about society?

EB   Are things getting better or worse? In many ways worse, commodification seeps into everything. And certainly theatre has deteriorated alarmingly. I think the Royal Court actually now destroys young writers. It has become a trade-counter for the West End – and the NT doesn't exist. The RSC was strangely persistent in trying to get me to take part in their anniversary celebrations this year. I refused because I think it's pointless. The most important younger dramatist was Sarah Kane and the theatre certainly contributed to her suicide. Young writers have nowhere to learn the craft of the stage – when they write for the stage they use the techniques of film and television and these are the opposite of those that enact reality on the stage. I think other writers of the 1960s – such as Arden – ceased to write because they were working in ways created in the 1930s but which had been kept out of the UK by the censors. I know this is a simplification but it's true. You can see that my first play [*The Pope's Wedding*] was a sort of homage to drama – but the next two [*Saved* and *Early Morning*] seem from different worlds, but they are one world and they have to be integrated if we are to see our world and also – because drama is innate in our psyche – if human reality is to be released to create itself and not regress to revenge. Drama is important and young writers should not commit suicide or be corrupted by Lollywood and TV. But you are dealing with the tragedy of our times. Here, drama is becoming a silent dead language – and theatre is now the spoken language of the dead. But drama has always renewed itself.

SN From your essays and letter you appear to have been very consistent in terms of your ideas and beliefs right through your career. I always warn students not to quote something Brecht said in 1929 and assume he still believed the same thing in 1955, because people's views can change. But I don't think I really do perceive contradictions or changes of direction in your views. Would you agree?

EB The origin of my understanding of human beings? It occurred when I was four or perhaps three. I was evacuated when I was five and it was certainly before then. In the Depression my mother had moved to London from the Fens. Fen people went to nonconformist chapel – it was serious, dissenting (which it combined with conformity) and entertainment (in the way drama should be). My mother wasn't devout but in London it was natural for her to seek out the comfort of the local Baptist church – just as later West Indian immigrants sought out churches from their own home culture. She and I were walking along a road in Holloway. I was holding her hand. I was puzzled by what I'd heard in the sermon. I said: 'Why did God kill his son?' She said: 'Because he loved him – and us.' I was a son. God the Father had killed his son because he loved us? I had a sensation of dumb horror. I can still feel it. (I think 'physically' as a dramatist must.) And it was like a patch of thick brown fog in the road before us. There was already what I would understand as an irreconcilable contradiction between the psyche – the self and its psychology – and the situation, the reality of the world. Later, when I was caught in the Blitz, the contradiction was reinforced. The violence came from the sky (God's des-res) and it was as if the sky were breaking. Much later I found a quote from Himmler: 'I gas the Jews out of love.' It was obvious even to a child that ideological explanations are false. Later I asked why the false explanations were needed. It is obviously to maintain a distorted relation between the psyche – the self and its psychology – and natural reality: the community is always at this crossroads. The self is taught to lie to itself. It has always been the purpose of drama – it is in fact its species function – to inhabit that contradiction, to be at the crossroads, and by describing the situation to turn the compulsion to assent into the compulsion to dissent – remember that the lie is (obviously) seeking truth and so it is seeking itself or (because it is strangely objective) the lie – when under the extreme of drama – is seeking to understand its need to lie and so it must resort to its need for truth, which is our radical innocence: that is all the paradoxes of drama, the corruption of justice into revenge, the ontology of the neonate. Hitler said you 'must always make the lie big enough'. History shows that it is never big enough. So it has been necessary for me only to consistently analyse the situation of the lie-truth and the truth-lie. Everything follows from this. You say that Brecht contradicts himself. This is because he is a liar who believes the lie and must keep changing it so that he can never see through it.

I think I have given some sort of answer to most of your questions.

Harold Pinter

In 2007, for the fiftieth anniversary of the first production of The Room, *the Theatre Archive Project[1] undertook a series of interviews concentrating on the background to the first performance of Harold Pinter's first play. What follows are edited extracts of the previously unpublished interviews generated by the Theatre Archive Project in relation to Pinter's early work.[2]*

The Room *(1957/1960)*
Creating The Room *at the University of Bristol*

Q Can you remember the first time that you were told that this copy of a play called *The Room* had arrived?

Susan Engel [played Rose] Yes, I can remember it very, very vividly. I was great friends with Henry Woolf anyway. And one day he comes up to me: 'I've got a friend', he said, 'who's at Bournemouth in rep, and he's trying to put a play together. If you're not doing anything next term . . .' And I said, 'Fine, that would be terrific.' And then I think time passed and Henry kept on saying, 'I can't get him to finish it, to make it into a play.' And then came the day when Henry said, 'Yes, he's written the play.'

Q Now can you remember how much Harold had told you about the play before he actually started to write it?

Henry Woolf [producer, director and played Mr Kidd]   He wrote it in two days, although he says four days.

Q Was it what you were expecting after having had that conversation?

HW Yes and no. The broad outlines yes. The actual bones, blood, veins, arteries, musculature of the play, no. And it's sort of marvellous – what this play had was a terrific structure. And it was a wonderful step forward for playwriting. You should have seen the audience on the first night. They awoke from their polite cultural stupor into a real awareness that something new was happening, that English theatre was never going to be the same again really, because it was terribly funny, and terribly menacing.

Q You knew Harold, you obviously had some understanding of the play before you even saw it because you had discussed it with him. For everyone else in early rehearsals it would have been the first time they'd read it. Can you remember what their reactions were?

HW Yes. They were very, very puzzled, particularly by 'pause' – the word 'pause'. What I was really trying to get out was the fact that Harold's plays in my opinion are tightly constructed, but the pauses are inhabited and populated.

Re-creating The Room *at the Hampstead Theatre Club*

Q Can you remember how the rehearsal process would have differed from back in '57/ '56?

Auriol Smith [played Mrs Sands]   Well, yes it differed quite a lot actually because we were rehearsing in something like a village

hall. That was where the Hampstead Theatre Club was at that
time. And Harold Pinter himself was directing it – which of
course at the time one wasn't aware of how lucky one was to be
being directed by Harold Pinter. Although one knew one was
lucky because it was the author and you know, one assumed that
he could give you all the best direction. I remember being very
impressed by his knowledge and intellect.

Audience's reactions

HW   They were a wonderful audience, and they laughed and
then were hushed – totally hushed – and attentive. One of the
best audiences one could have asked for . . . It would have been so
easy to have an audience for that play who said, 'What on earth is
going on?' They weren't like that; they were generous, interested,
eager to be excited by a new play.

Q   Looking at that first night – there were only two nights – can
you remember anything about the production, both how it went
for the actors who were more comfortable with the play by that
point, and how the audience reacted?

David Davies [played Mr Sands]   Yes. Well my memory of it is
one of being received by gales of laughter at so much of what
Auriol and I were doing. Within the play itself there is farce, there
is tragedy, there is drama.

Impressions of the play

Julia Kellerman [assistant stage manager]   With *The Room*, it
was really this question of starting off in quite an ordinary setting,
and people being quite banal talking about their breakfast and the
cold outside. And then you realised as you went on, that you
learnt all sorts of things about these characters.

  And really, when I mentioned to a fellow student that I'm still
in touch with, that I was going to come and talk to you about *The
Room*, she said, 'Do you remember how we kept saying "What
does it mean? What does it mean?"' And I think we were just quite
fascinated by it, because as I said there was this rather ordinary

setting, and rather ordinary characters, and then there were the undertones, the political undertones of a sort of racism, and women being not marginalised, but being rather dominated by the men.

The Birthday Party *(1957/1966)*
Discovering Pinter

Q How did you discover Harold Pinter? That must be the find of the century.

Michael Codron [producer] It seems to be. Yes. Well, it was getting known amongst literary agents that there was somebody looking for new plays, and willing to take a gamble. And I think Pinter had written a short play, and Harold Hobson gave it a very very good review. A review to make you sit up. So I then said to the agent, 'Can I meet him, and has he got any plays?', and he said, 'Yes, you can meet him.' So we met – Pinter and the agent Jimmy Wax – in the Regent Palace Hotel. A very unlikely place. And I always wondered – one of the most famous Pinter remarks is 'The weasel under the cocktail cabinet'. And I often wonder if he was referring to the cocktail cabinet in the Regent Palace, and if it gave him the idea. And then he handed me *The Birthday Party*. I could see that it was slightly obscure, but not as obscure as the critics thought when they first saw it. But it had a sense of menace about it.

About the play

Q As an actor who has appeared in *The Birthday Party*, what do you think it is that makes the play so innovative and fresh?

Timothy West [actor] I think it caused people to examine their traditional ways of looking at things. It opens in a way which is immediately recognisable. You don't see the kitchen sink. You see the front room of a recognisable boarding house in a recognisable south coast resort. There's a recognisable, if fairly batty, landlady, and a recognisable and kind husband, and then you see Stanley, who is somebody who has obviously had some kind of an emotional breakdown and has been befriended by this motherly person. You don't quite know the extent of the relationship but it is intriguing, and then these two men come in and intimidate him, and destroy him, and cart him off. Why? They seem to be drawn deliberately from people who are traditionally regarded as persecuted sections of the community, the Jews and the Irish, people who are always talking about how they're victimised. They victimise Stanley. And, I think it's a very exciting, a very dramatic play of course, but it has this sense of people feeling that their traditional moral values have all been turned upside down and questioned, and that's what Pinter does all the time doesn't he? As I tried to explain in my book, a conventional playwright tries to tell you more about the characters than they know about themselves. Pinter wants you to know less about them, because you are an eavesdropper on something that you don't understand, in the way that we are as human beings if we suddenly eavesdrop on a conversation between two people that we don't know.

Reaction

Tudor Williams [audience member] In the first year of the Everyman Theatre, they put on Pinter's play *The Birthday Party* and he was in it under his stage name of David Baron. And I went along to it – there wasn't a big crowd there by any means. And I do remember that the lady next to me fell asleep and the gentleman sat on the other side didn't return after the interval. And I don't think it was my influence, I think it was slightly more Mr Pinter. I was very struck with it, but I don't think it was popular, not by any means.

Q Perhaps it was too challenging at that time?

Tudor Williams It was too big a change I suppose . . .

The Caretaker *(1959)*

About the play

Q The debut performance of Harold Pinter's *The Birthday Party* wasn't received well by critics and was superseded by the success of

237

The Caretaker. Why do you think audiences originally preferred *The Caretaker*?

Timothy West   Well, *The Caretaker* was a little later and I think that, although people didn't like *The Birthday Party*, they thought perhaps they'd give him another go.

But, I think there's another reason, which is that the character of Davies in *The Caretaker* was somebody that the audience immediately felt: 'Ooh, I don't really want to know about this man. He's an invader, he's a squatter, he's somebody who worries us, and yet we want to see what happens to him.' Whereas *The Birthday Party* is much more obscure, it makes you feel quite uneasy as we don't really know what's happening or who these people are. We have to do a lot more thinking with *The Birthday Party*. In *The Caretaker*, although the characters' actions are peculiar and wonderfully convoluted in a Pinteresque way, you actually know what they're on about, and I think people related to that a lot more immediately.

Reaction

Richard Foster [audience member]   But we went to see *The Chairs* . . . and *The Caretaker* all in one night at the old Sheffield Playhouse. And I couldn't cope with it at all. It didn't do a thing for me then. It's been on again, *The Caretaker*. Wonderful. I think I've grown up now. I don't know whether or not at that time I was either too young for it or it was too far advanced for me.

Q   What didn't you respond to?

RF   I just couldn't cope with the setting of it or anything. It was very wordy, which didn't mean a lot to me at that time. Now it does but it didn't then.

Beginning to be recognised

Q   *The Birthday Party* wasn't a commercial success, but you kept faith with Pinter, because two years later you had *The Caretaker*. What was your motivation for sticking with him?

Michael Codron   Yes, that makes me sound as if I'm a bit more of a hero than I am. It was a great blow that it came off, and I think by that time I had taken the Arts. Though I became a West End producer, or you think of me as a West End producer, all my beginnings were in the fringe, like the Arts, or Bristol, or the Lyric Hammersmith, the Bush. Doing plays there first, which is the correct way to do it, to protect the writer so that he isn't exposed immediately to the glare of the West End critics. And I think that by the time Harold had written *The Caretaker*, I was running the Arts. And the play came to me and I thought, 'I can't afford to let Harold have another failure, what can I do?', and my partner said, 'You can put it on at the Arts, they'll let you put it on at the Arts, and have a director that he likes.'

Q   What do you think that the difference was in the eyes of the audience between *The Birthday Party* and *The Caretaker*? Do you think they just needed time to adjust?

MC   I think they had to adjust. You know, it was a magical performance, and people could recognise the brother relationship, and the threat of this tramp trying to inveigle himself into a set up.

Q   Critics look at Pinter's work now and say it was new wave, that it was revolutionary, that it changed the face of theatre and so on – was there a sense of that at the time? Did it feel like a new wave?

MC   No, I felt a sense of immense relief that he had been acknowledged as a good writer.

The Homecoming *(1964)*
Creation at the Royal Shakespeare Company

Terence Rigby [actor]   The Royal Shakespeare Company could not put their finger on anyone who was exactly right for the part of Joey. They described the part to me as a boxer, and filled out the details. So I rang up Gillian Diamond, who was the head of the casting department at the RSC. I said to her, 'I hear you are having trouble casting this part, which Peter Hall is going to direct, and I think I could do it. Can I come and see you?'

I did three or even four auditions in all. I thought it was a genuine knock-out competition, but we started off with five or six people, and then it was down to three, and the next time it went up to eight. I said to them, 'Look, I have been here three times, and I am very pleased to have been here, but I would rather not have to come back again.' Harold was very sympathetic and he said, 'Peter Hall is going home to read the play again. We will know by Monday one way or other and let you know.'

By Monday, they'd decided they wanted me in the part. At the time, I did not really know, to be honest, how important a matter it was, how important Pinter was as a writer, how important it was for my career to be involved in a production of this stature.

But although the reviews of *The Homecoming* were not particularly good – a lot of reviewers did not quite understand the piece, but that was par for the course anyway as far as Pinter was concerned, it was judged to be a success and we went to Broadway. We opened there to poor reviews – but we won four Tony Awards, so that brought the punters in and we ran for six months before we were replaced by essentially an American cast.

Reaction

Philip Bramley [audience member]   *The Homecoming* was pretty badly received by a lot of people, they were shouting out 'Animals!' I thought the play was really to do with class – I wasn't particularly surprised by it, because I knew families that acted like that, where people argued and fought for a position in the family, the pecking order.

Recognition

Q   Do you remember much about *The Homecoming*?

Sarah Detmer [audience member]   Well, I can remember it being very different. I hadn't really seen a great deal of theatre before then outside my home town and it was certainly different from plays that we'd read and done at school. It was very striking, it was a bit violent in a way. I was quite bowled over by it.

Q   Can you remember why you went to see it?

SD   I think I chose to go and see it because Pinter was the up-and-coming writer of the period, he was the person to go and see.

Pinter's style
Underlying menace

Q   What are your memories of early Pinter?

Dorien Brook [theatregoer]   What I remember about Pinter particularly was his uncanny genius for picking up casual conversation. The most trivial sort of conversations really, but once again, they're the essence of pithy. I've often been on a bus and heard people behind me, and thought 'My God, that's absolute Pinter!'

Q   You don't think Pinter was naturalistic?

Anne Piper [playwright]   No. His voice is always so full of hidden menace. It's not to do with what's happening every day, is it? It's really heavily stylised.

The silences

David Davies   What I can remember is that I didn't understand the pauses. The play was littered with pauses, and yet I couldn't understand them. But gradually it began to evolve. In fact I'm not even sure in the early stages whether I just didn't run over some of the pauses, instead of pausing, and just carried on. Of course, they're so important: whatever a character said before the pause creates the pause, because of the reaction on the character that the line's been directed to. And it creates this feeling of unease and uncomfortableness, which of course is the heart of Pinter's work.

Terence Rigby   No point analysing Pinter – the text is there. You work out the text, you say the text, there is no point analysing, no benefit from analysing, you play what's there, play the pauses, you've got to play the silences.

Interviews from the Theatre Archive Project used in this article

Susan Engel interviewed by Jamie Andrews, 17 October 2007.

Henry Woolf interviewed by Jamie Andrews, 20 July 2007.

Auriol Smith interviewed by Jamie Andrews, 27 June 2007.

David Davies interviewed by Jamie Andrews, 25 February 2008.

Julia Kellerman interviewed by Alec Patton, 25 February 2008.

Michael Codron interviewed by Adam Smith, 7 April 2009.

Timothy West interviewed by Catherine Jones, 5January 2004.

Tudor Williams interviewed by Ewan Jeffrey, 3 April 2004.

Richard Foster interviewed by Sarah Burbridge, 11 December 2006.

Terence Rigby interviewed by Kate McNiven in 2005.

Philip Bramley interviewed by Alison Louise Parry, 10 November 2006.

Sarah Detmer interviewed by Kate Dorney, 1 February 2005.

Anne Piper interviewed by Kate Dorney, 12 March 2005.

AFTERWORD

John Arden
by Bill McDonnell

'Who wrote John Arden's plays?'

The question is taken from an essay by American director and academic Tish Dace, who argues, correctly, that after 1965 and *Armstrong's Last Good Night* it is not meaningful to talk about an 'Arden play'. The great majority of 'Arden' texts were written with his wife and long-time creative partner, Margaretta D'Arcy. It was a partnership that began with the *Happy Haven* in 1960, and continued throughout the 1960s and 1970s. Between 1959 and 1978 they collaborated on some seventeen plays. These included many which are central to 'Arden's' reputation, and to academic critique of his work: *Ars Longa, Vita Brevis* (1964), *The Royal Pardon* (1966), *The Hero Rises Up* (1968), *The Island of the Mighty* (1972), plus the three plays on the Troubles which are examined below. All these texts provided a tight and immediate historical urgency and focus for Arden's reflexive radicalism.

And yet, as Tish Dace demonstrates through a careful review of major studies of their work, D'Arcy has been effectively eclipsed from their joint history.[1] When she is mentioned it is generally in a derogatory fashion, blamed for the perceived inadequacies of 'his' writing post-1968, a literary Lady Macbeth who has unmanned the great writer. D'Arcy was and is a writer of distinction, a sophisticated political thinker and activist, and a fearless and independent-minded radical, who brought to their writing and theatre practice a praxis in which Irish Republicanism, socialism and feminism intersected. Arrested and imprisoned for her activism in anti-imperial and Republican campaigns during the Troubles, including spells in Armagh Jail during the IRA Dirty Protest, D'Arcy's political commitment nourished Arden's anti-imperialism. Theirs was at once an aesthetic and a political marriage, a historical process through which theatre and cultural activism, aesthetics and politics were brought into unitary alignment. The refusal to accept their partnership is, as noted, made up in equal part of misogyny, anti-Irish racism, and political and cultural censorship. It has persisted despite the evidence, in their separate and joint writings, that theirs was a team of equals. Arden has consistently sought to foreground her role. In an essay on *The Non-Stop Connolly Show* he writes: 'D'Arcy divined a basic image for his character on which we could build the play' and 'it has been D'Arcy who originally conceived the Connolly idea'.[2] Embedded in the plays we find exchanges, such as this from *Vandaleur's Folly*:

> **Thompson**   You are about to say I am a hypocrite. We shared our bed, we shared our book-writing, page between page, we shared everything all these years –
>
> **Anna**   With men, it is a common condition.
>
> **Thompson**   As we have abundantly proven within the argument of our joint works. Our joint works with *my* name on them. (p. 64)

This theme is taken up again in scenes from Part Two of *The Non-Stop Connolly Show*, where Lillie Connolly is shown not only helping shape her husband's prose, but also the clarity of his political thinking.[3] In a fascinating commentary on their very different creative approaches, Arden wrote:

> To begin with I was never concerned with such things [the content of plays]: what they tell and to whom. I found a story which appealed to me, for whatever reason, and began to write it, in dialogue; and that was it . . . [whereas D'Arcy's] instincts as a playwright have tended to operate in the reverse order to mine. She will think of a *subject* that requires to be dramatized: and will relate it to the condition of the time and the potential

audience to be sought for it. Only then will the idea of a story
. . . become uppermost. [4]

The ascription of the plays reflected this dialectic, with one or the
other's name given first. In the 1970s, as the authors' attention
increasingly turned to the crisis in Ireland, it was D'Arcy's name
which took precedence, as texts were developed which addressed the
Troubles, and the larger question of Ireland's colonial history.

Serjeant Musgrave *dances on*

Britain's post-imperial history from 1968 onwards has been dominated by two crises: first Irish irredentism in the northern counties of
Ireland during the period of the Troubles (1968-96), an urban war
fought over the historically intractable and unresolved issue of parti-
tion and Irish unity; second the group of wars post-9/11 which have
involved the British armed forces on active service in Afghanistan,
Iraq and latterly, Libya. All these conflicts find their source and
defining themes in the imperial histories of Britain, France and Italy,
and the post-imperial imperatives of an oil-based global economic
order.Arden and D'Arcy's response was to intervene through three
important plays which dealt directly or indirectly with the crisis in
Ireland, *The Ballygombeen Request* (1972), the *Non-Stop Connolly
Show* (1975) and *Vandaleur's Folly* (1978). In 1972, an adaptation of
Arden's 1959 text, *Sergeant Musgrave Dances On*, was toured by the
7:84 theatre company in Britain and Ireland. Adapted, indeed
rewritten, by John McGrath, the production was part of a double-bill
The Ballygombeen Request – an Irish Melodrama in two acts (later reis-
sued as *The Little Gray Home in the West*, 1978). *The Ballygombeen
Request* was a savage satire, which drew on contemporaneous events in
the couple's home town of Oughterard to explore the continuing
oppression of Ireland's poor tenants by absentee landlords in the
context of the British occupation of the north of Ireland. Its first
performance was a community production, given on 1 May 1972 by
the St Joseph's and St Mary's Colleges of Education Dramatic Societies
at St Mary's College on Belfast's Republican Falls Road. In August of
the same year 7:84 gave it its first professional performance at the

Edinburgh Fringe Festival, where it was eulogised by Michael Anderson in *Plays and Players* as 'a stunning political drama as good as the best of Arden and . . . an equal to most of Brecht'. [5] The tour would end in chaos and bitter recriminations between the principals when a Commander Burges, who was named in the performances (but not the text) as an example of absentee landlordism, sued. The case dragged on for five years before the playwrights issued an apology.

Although the adaptation of Musgrave was Arden's idea, McGrath's rewriting was so extensive that it might be more appropriate to talk of it being 'based on' the original rather than a version of it. Nonetheless, for Arden the historical situation of Britain and Ireland in 1972 offered uncanny parallels with his imagined colonial crisis:

> Years after my plays have been written and performed, events have as it were come full circle. I find my imaginative figments turning out as established fact . . . *Serjeant Musgrave's Dance* (1959) dealt with a massacre of civilians during a British Army 'peace-keeping' operation at the same time as a bitter colliery strike in England. In January 1972 thirteen people were shot dead by the Paras in Derry while industrial trouble raged in the coalfields on a level unknown since the 1920s.[6]

In McGrath's version one of many changes has the skeleton of Billy replaced by a body, that of a soldier shot in the Irish conflict. The industrial conflict is foregrounded and, significantly, Musgrave is now condemned for individualism: his apocryphal revenge is seen as an aberration. Class solidarity, not individual acts of terror, is the solution to oppressions. The text does not explore the complexities of Republican irredentism: indeed, in giving primacy to the industrial struggles, in some ways it domesticates Arden's fable, removing its anti-imperial bite. This would be sharpened in another revival post-9/11.

The illegal invasion of Iraq by the USA, Britain and their allies in 2003 marked a new and problematic escalation of the 'war on terror'. British troops, sent to cement a swift victory and initially hailed as saviours, swiftly became caught up in a sectarian conflict that sucked in Al-Qaeda networks. In direct echoes of *Serjeant Musgrave's Dance*, young soldiers, caught up in a complex situation, resorted to indiscriminate violence and forms of collective punishment. The most notorious case involved hotel manager, Baha Mousa, who died in British custody in Basra after being systematically and horrifically beaten. There were many others. Again as in Ireland, the British state would be obliged to pay compensation for these extra-judicial deaths, and for the torture and abuse of detainees. So when in 2003 the Oxford Stage company staged a new production of *Serjeant Musgrave's Dance*, Arden's Victorian deserters again seemed to speak to and about contemporary experience. In interviews Arden pointed to these parallels, with young panicking soldiers facing situations they do not understand. He lamented the obvious paradox: that his play should be revived was clearly good for a great writer shamefully neglected. However, that it should need to be revived as a counterweight to new imperial and post-colonial adventures was, he says 'depressing'. 'I'd like to think there was no more use for the play', he told critic Michael Billington, and yet 'depressingly ... it's one of those plays that continues to be relevant'. Billington concurred, noting that: 'We may not, as Arden admits, have learned the lessons about military occupation and cyclical murder taught by Serjeant Musgrave – but it is precisely because of our own failings that this remains a great and necessary play.'[7] A view shared by other positive reviews of the production.

'From the same well'

The period after 1978, notwithstanding a number of joint writing projects, is primarily defined by Arden's return to sole authorship. After *Vandaleur's Folly* Arden concentrated all his writing energies into radio dramas, novels and short stories. Most explore that period of English history between 1350 and 1650, the transitional ground between the late-medieval and Jacobean worlds, which he mined so fruitfully and consistently throughout his career. The radio play *Pearl*, for example, a tale of political intrigue and fantastical events set in 1630s London's theatre world, was voted by *Guardian* readers as one of the finest examples of the medium. *Garland for a Hoar Head*, a biographical study of John Skelton, the sixteenth-century poet and satirist, was the fruit of a fascination with the poet dating from Arden's youth. The theatre critic D. A. N. Jones called the latter play a 'dense and broodingly poetic play. Like all Arden's recent major pieces . . . it examines the relationship between the writer and society.'[8] Compared with the reception of the stage plays, reviews of the radio drama are consistently laudatory, commending the powerful interplay in these dramas of politics, historical imagination, and a rich and complex language which moved with facility from verse to prose. Arden had returned to a world which mediated his texts without distorting them, as the theatre apparatus had, and radio drama was felt in some ways as a kind of liberation. In a fascinating article in the *Sunday Times* he celebrated the sheer speed with which a play could move from recording, 'the assemblage in just two or three days . . . of one's entire fictional creation from the written page to the recorded broadcast'. And then, most strikingly: 'For all the physical distance between yourselves and the public, you seem so very much nearer to them than is ever possible in the theatre.'[9] A different kind of intimacy was found in novels, where theatre remained an ever-present focus. The first, *Silence Among the Weapons*, which was shortlisted for the 1982 Booker Prize, recounts the life and times of an actor's agent in Asia Minor as an expansionary Roman Empire ground its way towards the Bosphorus Sea. It was followed by more novels in the same epic vein, including, in 1988, the *Books of Bale* about the Reformation playwright and Bishop of Ossory John Bale, and in 2003 the collection *Cogs Tyrannic*. He continued to write for radio and to produce short stories. His last collection, *Gallows and Other Tales of Suspicion and Obsession*, was published in 2009 and contains illustrations by the author. The book's stories are set in Galway, London and Arden's native Yorkshire, with one, inevitably perhaps, dealing with the Gunpowder Plot and Ben Jonson the playwright, whose comedies were an inspiration for plays like *The Workhouse Donkey*.

Pressed as to whether he missed the theatre, Arden would say that in the end he was a storyteller, and playwriting was just another way of telling stories: 'it's all from the same well'. Perhaps. But it remains one of the more sobering aspects of post-war British theatre that a writer of this tremendous range and power, the heir, some said, of Shakespeare and Brecht, no longer felt he had a place in the British theatre.

Edward Bond

Let us now be serious and for a start change everything . . .[1]

Bond has been a prolific writer for more than fifty years and continues to be so. He remains convinced of the need to create a just society to ensure our survival as a species, and of theatre's potential to contribute to the process. Many of his recent plays have been staged in Britain by youth groups rather than professional theatres, for he has long been disenchanted with what these institutions offer and believes that young people both need and are better equipped to perform them. Elsewhere in Europe it is a different story, and in Germany, Italy and particularly France Bond has long been recognised as a major European playwright and widely performed. But at home he has frequently refused permission for revivals, believing that previous productions have misunderstood his texts or approached them wrongly, and granting it only when confident they will be approached in the correct way. In Bond's view, most directors ask the wrong questions and rely on tricks and devices in order to 'make things work' instead of working out what the text needs. 'Anyone with an elementary knowledge of theatre can make things work on stage', says Bond; it is 'very easy', but also 'very shameful'. Too often 'directors don't ask "what is this?" but "how do I make this work?"'[2] He cites a recent production of one of his plays in which a choreographer was brought in to help devise movement and staging, without even reading the text.[3]

In addition to some fifty plays, Bond also writes extensively about his work, about theatre, about politics and about society. He does so through prefaces and programme notes, but also in theoretical essays – where he has constructed his own performance vocabulary – in notebooks and – above all – in letters, many of which have been published. He is also the author of poetry and songs, television dramas, translations and adaptations, libretti for operas and a text for a ballet. In the 1970s and early 1980s Bond wrote a series of extremely strong and powerful plays, many of them large-scale and for major theatres. Following *Lear* (1971) came *The Sea* (1973), a comedy (in part) set in an English seaside town early in the twentieth century, and exploring more lightly some of the same themes as *Lear*. He described the subject of his next three plays as 'the burden of the past which makes change so difficult'. *Bingo: Scenes of Money and Death*, imagines the last days of Shakespeare, exposing the gap between the humanity evident in his plays and his behaviour as a landlord and owner, and culminating in his suicide. 'Was anything done?', Shakespeare asks himself repeatedly – a question also close to the heart (and brain) of Bond. In 1975 came *The Fool: Scenes of Bread and Love* – an episodic play about the nineteenth-century 'peasant' poet John Clare, who having achieved recognition and patronage from the educated and wealthy classes, then comes into conflict with them over the radical political perspectives of his verse. In 1978, *The Woman: Scenes of War and Freedom* became the first contemporary text to be staged on the National Theatre's Olivier stage, and was directed by Bond himself. It drew on Euripides' *Trojan Women*, but, as ever, Bond invents his own narrative to focus on the attempts to challenge a world obsessed by war and fighting. As Michael Mangan points out, Bond's rewriting of the myth allows us to question debilitating assumptions about the impossibility of changing things, and 'undermines the audience's sense that the logic of tragedy is inevitable'.[4]

In the same year, the RSC staged *The Bundle: New Narrow Road to the Deep North*, returning to the Japan of Basho and the abandoned child from his earlier play. This time round, Bond shows the baby growing up to become a successful revolutionary whose actions create the possibility of a better world. *The Worlds* (1979) was set in the contemporary Britain of industrial conflict, but *Restoration* (1981) returned to the past and its relationship to the present. The first half sees Bond at his most comic, drawing knowingly on conventions of Restoration drama, but the second half makes clear the exploitation practised on the poor by the wealthy as the aristocratic Lord Are allows his servant to be imprisoned and executed for a murder which he himself has committed. The most surprising and provocative element of the play is the servant's willingness to accept the deceit without protest, because it is just another part of his duty. In 1982 came *Summer* for the National and *Derek* for the RSC – both conceived on a reduced theatrical if not political scale, and again raising issues of class and exploitation; the latter – 'a farce' – involves the transplantation of the intelligent brain of a working-class boy into the head of an upper-class but stupid MP. It is a metaphor, of course, for how Bond saw class relationships and exploitation.

In 1984 came three plays, performed by the RSC as *The War Plays* trilogy. It was after this production that things changed for Bond in terms of his relationship with the major subsidised British theatres. His method of directing had already provoked some acrimonious confrontations with actors, and he was forced to withdraw from *The War Plays* part way through rehearsals. He subsequently expressed dissatisfaction with the final productions, declaring that if he had paid for a ticket he would have demanded his money back. Working with the RSC, said Bond, insultingly, had been 'like going back to the nineteenth-century', with actors seeking 'to hide in the characters and produce "actorish" voices', and the emphasis on superficial effects: 'bang an air-filled paper bag and you have a theatrical shock', observes Bond disapprovingly. Crucially, he believed the wrong questions were focused on in rehearsal: 'All the time they ask, does it work – and not, what does it mean.'[5] Bond was equally negative about Royal Court revivals of his early plays in the mid-1980s. He had acquired a reputation of being almost impossible to work with and he now turned his back on the theatrical establishment – as it largely turned its back on him. His next play, *Human Cannon*, might have been staged by either the RSC or the National, but negotiations about collaboration and casting proved impossible to resolve, leaving Bond feeling betrayed. From his perspective, the NT's director, Peter Hall, 'welshed on the undertaking he gave me'.[6]

Central to Bond's contempt for the mainstream cultural establishment was his belief – with which it is hard to disagree – that theatre in Britain had become a commodity like any other, produced to the demands of the market – even where it is subsidised by the Arts Council – full of tricks rather than substance, and turned into entertainment rather than art. By contrast, Bond saw 'raising human consciousness' as theatre's true function: 'Why is it these Greeks two-and-a-half thousand years ago could do that and we can't? It's because our society is devoted to prostitution and exploitation.'[7] Censorship by the Lord Chamberlain is long gone, but in Bond's view it has become harder than ever for playwrights to ask the important questions:

> When I started to write theatre was trivial – middle-class angst and fake poetry. The Royal Court changed that. At that time playwrights had their great disasters behind them, the world war and the death camps. They could not avoid asking urgent questions . . . The problem for new writers now is that the great disasters are ahead of them and theatres will not allow them to be asked. The Royal Court stages the sort of plays it was founded to abolish. And the RNT and RSC don't exist.[8]

In 2006, Bond refused a request from the Royal Court to participate in celebrating its achievements over the last fifty years; he told the press that where that theatre had once been 'an oasis in a desert' it was now 'a graveyard in a desert'.[9]

Bond has little doubt about whom to blame: 'At the moment drama is dead', he wrote, 'for which theatre directors are largely responsible.'[10] In his view, the people running the National, the RSC and the Royal Court are little more than 'high-class embalmers', unable to respond appropriately to a living text: 'If I were desperate I'd send you a play to murder knowing that you'd embalm it beautifully, beautifully, beautifully', he told one of them; 'You'd probably even wire it up with a semblance of life. But of course it isn't what I want.'[11] The National Theatre, says Bond, is 'a nineteenth-century institution' with misplaced priorities; 'If I were running it I wouldn't waste money on cleaning the windows or running the bars', he declared; 'the windows could be black and covered with graffiti – if you wanted food or drink you could bring sandwiches and a flask.'[12] Even the 'new' plays it puts on are really old ones. 'Of course, many contemporary plays are not modern, and for them you will keep your door open', he wrote to Peter Hall in 1984; 'You are closing it down to the new drama.'[13]

Bond is sometimes accused of arrogance, but the truth is more complicated than that. 'I don't know how to write plays and I am still learning', he said in 1983; 'I think that when we write and direct we should keep a very open mind.' And he denies that he is overly dogmatic: 'I don't object to sharing the direction of my plays', he insists; 'On the contrary, I enjoy cooperation.'[14] Nor does he look for quarrels: 'I don't like confrontation (very much the opposite) and I'm sorry if I'm abrasive', he wrote to one director following a disagreement. 'I sometimes forget to bring olive branches. But I clutch the seeds of olive trees in my hands.'[15] Bond's quarrel with directors is not that he sees himself as an authority, or the actors as mere puppets: 'I wrote the play but that doesn't mean that I know how it should work on stage. We have to create that together.'[16] What he does claim to know is the right questions to ask of a text.

Bond has been no less prolific since the mid-1980s. *In the Company of Men* was staged by the RSC in 1996 under Bond's direction, though it had premiered four years earlier in France, and several other plays had their first performances outside Britain. 'At present UK theatre is dead – and has no useful purpose or intelligent responsibility', he writes; 'no doubt [it] will find its role again but it doesn't need me to help it do this.'[17]

If there is hope, then it is with the young, and Big Brum youth theatre in Birmingham have so far staged the premieres of seven of his texts. Bond maintains that he is liberated rather than confined by writing for the group, since he is producing work for those who recognise the relevance of his ideas.

When I write for children I always write about the most profound questions because I think they're interested in the most profound questions. Now those children gave a performance, an interpretation of that play that was better than the National Theatre could do, because they needed the play. They needed that play because it was showing something about their future.[18]

Throughout his career, Bond's subject – it is, he says, 'the only subject of theatre' – has been 'the relation between people and society'. In his view, our institutions and our morality are designed to suppress and control us, and the pattern of shaping the individual to fit society. It is no good, says Bond, accepting the 'moonshine' that 'we must all love one another more, be nicer, kinder, cleaner, more tolerant etc!'[19] The only solution is to create a just society: 'The starving will be fed only when the causes of starvation are removed, and the world will be at peace only when the causes of war are removed . . . you will escape nuclear destruction, only if you change society.'[20] Survival is far from guaranteed: 'History does not have humanness sealed into it – it must be created.' It requires us to act (in both senses of the word), and the demise of theatre is 'dangerous because drama is one of the only two sources of human truth available to us . . . on which the survival of our species depends'.[21] Bond longs for his plays to be of use in encouraging us to believe in the possibility of change. 'None of us are creatures of fate', he insists; 'Each individual is a possibility of the world being different.'[22] Presumably that is why he is still writing.

Harold Pinter

When Harold Pinter died in 2008, he had written around thirty plays and nearly as many screenplays during a career lasting half a century. He was also a poet, an uncompromising speaker and polemical essayist, an accomplished director and a genuinely powerful performer who in his last stage appearance acted Samuel Beckett's *Krapp's Last Tape* 'with an unsentimental rigour that was poleaxing'.[1] His many awards included France's highest civil honour, the Légion d'honneur, the European Theatre Prize and the Nobel Prize for Literature. In the last quarter of his life, he was heavily and publicly engaged in campaigning against torture, dictatorship and injustice, and opposing the military actions carried out in the names of the British and American peoples by their respective governments.

Pinter's death provoked a stream of tributes. He was described as 'the most influential, provocative and poetic dramatist of his generation';[2] 'the last great playwright';[3] and 'the most inspirational playwright of the twentieth century'.[4] Some even compared him to Shakespeare. 'Yesterday when you talked about Britain's greatest living playwright, everyone knew who you meant', wrote David Hare; 'today they don't.'[5] Actors paid homage: 'He was our God', said Michael Gambon; 'the man who wrote the plays you wanted to be in.'[6] His abilities in the rehearsal room were similarly lauded; 'the best director I've ever known ... all actors who've worked with him would say that.' Not that Pinter had always been an easy person to work with; 'he was very quick to lose his temper', said Kenneth Cranham; 'he could be quite frightening'.[7] And Douglas Hodge recalled that while 'there were constant jokes', there was also 'always the possibility of a good fight'. Hodge summed up what made Pinter so distinctive: 'It was very rare to meet someone who might very quickly get into a punch-up but also has the greatest vocabulary you'd ever come across.' Pinter, he said, was 'the most violent pacifist I ever met'.[8]

Pinter's texts were perfectly nuanced and shaped for performance: 'If you said the lines exactly as he wrote them – observing the pauses, the commas and semi-colons – the rhythm would speak for itself.'[9] But he always maintained that he wrote for himself. 'I don't give a damn what other people think', he said; 'I'm not writing for other people.'[10] Certainly not for audiences: 'I tend to regard the audience as my enemy', he declared; 'they're guilty until they're proved innocent.'[11] And he once claimed that his final note to actors before they went on stage was always 'fuck the audience'; in a market-based culture which increasingly sees the artist's duty as being to please customers, Pinter's view becomes radical: 'If you want the audience to love you, you're finished', he insisted; 'you've got to take a very strong view, saying you're going to get what we're giving you, you're not going to get what you want.'[12]

Though not embarrassed about describing himself as an intellectual ('I'm part of a tradition which includes Joyce and Eliot . . . I read

Ulysses every night when I go to bed'[13]) Pinter distrusted theoretical approaches to making theatre. In one of his last interviews, he recalls standing in the wings with John Gielgud and Ralph Richardson – two of the finest actors of their generation – in the moments before they went on stage to perform *No Man's Land*, and listening as they compared the exquisite restaurant dishes and wines they had enjoyed that lunchtime, until the moment they entered the stage, and switched without preparation or hesitation into script and character.[14] As a playwright, he worked instinctively. The trigger for a play was never an idea, but always something specific and solid; a line, a word, an image, which would arrive 'out of the blue into my head' with no further information attached. 'What follows is fitful, uncertain, even hallucinatory, although sometimes it can be an unstoppable avalanche.' The trick was to trust where his characters led him, without asking too many questions or imposing limits of rationality.

> You certainly can't dictate to them. To a certain extent you play a never-ending game with them, cat and mouse, blind man's bluff, hide and seek ... The characters must be allowed to breathe their own air. The author cannot confine and constrict them to satisfy his own taste or disposition or prejudice. He must be prepared to approach them from a variety of angles, from a full and uninhibited range of perspectives, take them by surprise, perhaps, occasionally, but nevertheless give them the freedom to go which way they will.[15]

While Pinter's plays are not, in a conventional sense, autobiographical, fragments and observed images are woven into the text, or made use of as points of departure; he also acknowledged that there must be connections on a more profound level. In a 1979 interview, he was asked the question: 'Do your plays have more to do with your life than we know?' Pinter's reply is telling: 'They have more to do with my life than I know.'[16]

From around 1970 until the mid-1980s, Pinter's focus moved more into the interior rather than the exterior world. 'What interests me a great deal is the mistiness of the past', he stated in 1971; 'So much is imagined and that imagining is as true as real.'[17] In the early 1970s, Pinter spent three months reading Proust ('I would do nothing else but read Proust all day, and I emerged, to say the least, dizzy'[18]), as preparation for adapting *A la Recherche du Temps Perdu* for cinema. That film would never be made, but issues of time and ageing and contested memory are at the heart of *Old Times* (1970), *No Man's Land* (1974) and *Betrayal* (1978), Pinter's three great plays of this period. By the mid-1970s too, Pinter had separated from his first wife and was living more easily with Antonia Fraser, whom he married in 1980. Yet it is important not to exaggerate the shift of focus; domestic power struggles, the need to control and dominate, and the will to impose subjective perceptions as objective truths – all these carry through from earlier work. 'I cannot say that every work I've written is political', said Pinter in 1988; 'But I feel the question of how power is used and how violence is used, how you terrorize some-body, how you subjugate somebody, has always been alive in my work.'[19]

While it might not always have been transparent in his plays, Pinter's political position had always been well to the left. Yet at the start of the 1980s, he found himself in a confrontation with Edward Bond, a committed Marxist, concerning the function of artists. Bond had published a newspaper article in which he had strongly criticised the 'obsolete' approach of Samuel Beckett and other writers who chose not to confront political issues directly in their work. Pinter wrote to the newspaper defending Beckett ('[who] knows as much about the monster in man as Bond does') and Bond responded with a personal letter which demanded that 'Writers should concern them-selves with describing and understanding the political and human horrors of our time.' Pinter was an admirer of Beckett, as well as a friend, and Bond's diktats were anathema:

Dear Edward Bond,

I regard your views . . . as singularly complacent and arro-gant; the self-esteem which shines through them sickening.

Don't lecture me about fascism. I am a Jew and grew up in the war. After the war I fought against English fascists in

London – physically. I can smell fascism a mile off, including your own brand . . .

Don't bother to answer.[20]

From the mid-1980s onwards Pinter did begin to produce work which – while never doctrinal or explicit – was much more overtly political. In *One for the Road* (1984) the suave and articulate head of a secret police service interrogates and tortures a family, including a child. By not tying it to a specific situation, the setting becomes anywhere and any time – including Britain. 'I see Pinter's discovered politics', wrote Bond, disparagingly; 'It doesn't say why people torture other people – what the biological, social and political causes are.'[21] That had never been Pinter's way: 'Sermonising has to be avoided at all costs.'[22] *Mountain Language* (1988), a short but intense play, was inspired by the brutal silencing and persecution of the Kurdish population in Turkey, prevented from speaking their language and systematically victimised, tortured and abused. Pinter had visited Turkey with Arthur Miller a few years earlier and been more or less thrown out of the American Embassy for speaking against the Turkish dictatorship and Western collusion. Even so, Pinter was clear that 'I am not writing a play simply about Turkey.' Indeed he claimed that the repression also 'reflects a great deal that's happening in this country' where, under Margaret Thatcher's right-wing government, 'the dissenting voice and the minority are in great danger'.[23]

If that seems like an exaggerated claim, then the world of *Party Time* (1991) – described by Pinter as being about 'a bunch of shits and a victim'[24] – seemed somewhat less remote. The play concentrates on the banal and arrogant conversations of a successful and wealthy elite, celebrating themselves and their lifestyle, while disturbances and unrest outside are suppressed. It was not a million miles away from home. But arguably the most unsettling of Pinter's later texts is *Ashes to Ashes* (1996), 'a hauntingly elusive play that starts with a man's nagging enquiries about a woman's lover but that almost imperceptibly opens up to admit Auschwitz, Bosnia and the whole landscape of 20th-century atrocity'.[25] According to one critic: 'No play of our time more profoundly marries the personal and the political.'[26]

From the mid-1980s onwards, Pinter himself began to use his writing and his public profile to draw attention to abuses of power committed by governments and authorities. He was heavily involved with both Amnesty International and the writers' organisation PEN, and he wrote and spoke forcefully and without equivocation against American and British involvement in the wars in Kosovo and Iraq. Much of the speech he gave in accepting the Nobel Prize for Literature in 2005 was devoted to an attack on American foreign policy of the previous fifty years: 'The crimes of the United States have been systematic, constant, vicious, remorseless', he insisted. But he was equally scathing about the failure of others to draw attention to what was going on – the self-imposed silence and the turning away:

> The United States supported and in many cases engendered every right wing military dictatorship in the world after the end of the Second World War. I refer to Indonesia, Greece, Uruguay, Brazil, Paraguay, Haiti, Turkey, the Philippines, Guatemala, El Salvador, and, of course, Chile . . .
>
> Hundreds of thousands of deaths took place throughout these countries . . . But you wouldn't know it.
>
> It never happened. Nothing ever happened. Even while it was happening it wasn't happening. It didn't matter. It was of no interest.[27]

The Nobel Literature Prize was awarded to Pinter on the grounds that his work exposes 'the precipice under everyday prattle and forces entry into oppression's closed rooms'.[28] Yet there remained for Pinter a conflict between the demands of Art and those of Politics. He began his Nobel lecture by quoting a statement he had made in 1958: 'There are no hard distinctions between what is real and what is unreal, nor between what is true and what is false. A thing is not necessarily either true or false; it can be both true and false.' Now, nearly fifty years later, he offered an important rider: 'I believe that these assertions still make sense and do still apply to the exploration of reality through art', he declared; then came the qualification: 'As a writer I stand by them but as a citizen I cannot. As a citizen I must ask: What is true? What is false?'[29] It is a tension which has no resolution.

Alan Ayckbourn

Claims that Ayckbourn is the most successful, the most performed or the most popular playwright are regularly advanced, and although they might be impossible to justify without defining the criteria for judgement, there is no doubting his achievements or the status he has acquired over the last forty years. In the 1980s, the Arts Council identified him not only as 'the most watched and performed playwright in regional repertory theatres in the UK' but as 'more popular than Shakespeare'.[1] He is now the author of well over seventy full-length plays, most of which he has himself directed for premieres at the Library/Stephen Joseph Theatre in Scarborough, where he was Artistic Director from 1972 until 2009, or, occasionally, in London, where for several years he ran a company at the National Theatre. In 1973 Ayckbourn established a record of five plays running simultaneously in London's West End, and a couple of years later he had four plays running on Broadway. He has won a long list of awards – 'best play', 'best comedy', 'best revival', 'best musical' – from a variety of bodies, while Ayckbourn himself has been honoured with decorations including Critics' Circle Award for Services to the Arts and Special Tony Award for Lifetime Achievement in the Theatre, as well as a CBE and a knighthood. His plays are said to have been enjoyed by the Queen and the Queen Mother, and, unusually, he has been embraced by the major subsidised as well as commercial theatres. On the one hand he is a pillar of the cultural mainstream. On the other his work has been compared (often favourably) with dramatists including not only Chekhov, but such scourges of the establishment as Congreve, Molière and Ben Jonson.[2]

While Ayckbourn's work has never been avant-garde, he has carried out remarkable experiments with form and structure, and it is hard to argue with his biographer's claim that 'in almost every play he does something he has never done before'.[3] *The Norman Conquests* (1973) consists of three separate two-hour plays, performed on different nights and each showing the same events from the perspectives of different characters. While the interweaving and layers emerge only through viewing all three plays, it was also part of Ayckbourn's aim that each should work if seen in isolation, and that they could be viewed in any order.

In *Sisterly Feelings* (1979) the script of the opening scene is fixed, but the two succeeding scenes can be played in alternative versions which take the narrative and relationships along different routes. Decisions about which versions are played on each night are reached actually during the performances, partly through the toss of a coin and partly through choices made by the actors in the moment. It is as perhaps as close as Ayckbourn – as a playwright – could go to the dreams of his early mentor, Stephen Joseph, of improvising the script in front of the audience. In this case, the script of the final scene is fixed, but will carry different meanings and effects, depending which versions of the middle scenes have been played. By contrast – and yet building on this – *Intimate Exchanges* (1982) has sixteen different possible endings.

In the case of *Way Upstream* (1981) it was the ambitious requirements of the staging which took the attention. The play is set on board a boat, and the stage has to be filled with water. (When it was performed at the National Theatre, parts of the building were accidentally and seriously flooded.) In *Woman in Mind* (1985) the narrative is told from inside the head of a woman gradually losing her sanity, so that the borders between what is real and what is fantasy become unclear. Perhaps most remarkably, *House and Garden* (1999) consists of two plays staged at the same time in different auditoria (and to different audiences) about the same characters, played by the same actors who leave a scene in one theatre to enter the other one almost immediately.

Though some of his plays have been adapted for radio, television and film versions, Ayckbourn writes almost exclusively for the stage, and, with a few exceptions, for performance in the round. He has returned occasionally to producing texts for children (notably *Mr A's Amazing Maze Plays* in 1988), and has also 'collaborated' with dead playwrights, including Chekhov (an adaptation of *Uncle Vanya* in 2011), Sheridan (*A Trip to Scarborough*, 1982) and Ostrovsky (*The Forest*, 1999). In 1975 he created (with Andrew Lloyd Webber) an unsuccessful musical based on P. G. Wodehouse stories (*Jeeves*), which he reworked twenty years later into an award-winning triumph, and directed on Broadway. While Ayckbourn himself has suggested that roughly one in every five or six of his plays is 'a dud', he appears never to have gone through a barren period, and has never failed to produce an annual script for Scarborough. Perhaps one of the most remarkable things is the speed with which he works. He typically spends only four weeks a year writing, with productions regularly being advertised and cast long before there is a script. In fact, he devotes most of his working time to directing. His production for the National Theatre in the 1980s of Arthur Miller's *A View from the Bridge* was described by Miller himself as the best production of that play he had seen, while Michael Gambon, who has frequently acted for him, describes Ayckbourn as 'a great director'.[4]

In 1992, Ayckbourn was appointed Visiting Professor of Contemporary Theatre, at Oxford University. Yet despite – or possibly because of – his widespread acclaim, theatre academics have often been more sceptical, and it is rare to find him featured on syllabuses for study. 'Alan Ayckbourn is popular. He is prolific. And he writes comedies', observes Michael Billington; 'For all those reasons he is . . . seriously underrated.'[5] Ayckbourn's success in appealing to West End theatregoers is anathema to many, and the distrust is mutual. 'Often we quite wrongly suspect simplicity. We go digging around in the creative sand trying to make our art more meaningful, somehow "deeper"', argues Ayckbourn; 'Generally all we do is end up with our heads entirely buried, presenting the audience with our rear end.'[6] He is happy to acknowledge connections between his writing and that of Noël Coward, J. B. Priestley and Terence Rattigan – all of whom had been supposedly drowned in the new waves crashing through British theatre in the 1950s and 1960s. 'Thank God for the well-made play.'[7] On the other hand, Ayckbourn also acknowledges Pirandello, Ionesco and especially Harold Pinter – theatrical innovators all – as important influences on his writing.

It can be argued that Ayckbourn's own inventions are tricks and exercises, rather than ways of raising more profound questions. Indeed, the playwright seems to encourage this: 'What I want to say is relatively simple', he suggests; 'In order to throw any fresh light – or at least fresh slants – it's necessary to find new ways to tell the stories.'[8] Yet there is surely more to it than that. To show the 'same' situation or narrative from different perspectives – without privileging one of them – does raise questions about the possibility of objectivity, and whether there can ever be a 'true' account of anything. And a script containing alternative scenes and narratives selected through chance and live choices invites us to consider the arbitrariness of what 'really' happens, and reminds us of the fact that at any given moment there are multiple alternatives available to us.

One reason for Ayckbourn's popularity is that his plays are genuinely funny, and he argues that comedy is too often looked down on: 'I suspect we don't really believe we're seeing anything worthwhile unless we've had a really miserable time.' He suggests – probably only half-jokingly – 'that to be genuinely respectable as a so-called comic writer, on a par with an equivalent "serious" writer, you need to have been dead preferably for a century. By which time, of course, most of the comedy is incomprehensible and can only be laughed at by scholars.'[9] But important though it is, comedy is far from the only engine driving his plays. Michael Billington argues persuasively that Ayckbourn 'is not a reassuring writer' but is adept at 'using comedy to say harsh, true things about our society'.[10] Another critic, John Peter, agrees: 'when [he] is safely dead, things will change. He'll be seen for the domestic political dramatist he really is.'[11]

In fact, there is often a darkness within the comedy of Ayckbourn's plays which is more than satire. Much of his best work exposes the cruelty people inflict on each other within supposedly close relationships. 'I don't think people were meant to live with each other for too long', he has observed, and one of the recurring themes is the demonstration of 'how we destroy ourselves and others through small daily acts of indifference and casual cruelty'.[12] This is more than comedy. 'What I always try to do is to write a very serious play', says Ayckbourn; 'Hopefully it has this veneer of fun on top of it, but it's only a veneer.'[13] Even in 1972, one of the characters in *Absurd Person Singular* is a woman who repeatedly tries to kill herself. Her failures (and the failures of the other characters to realise – let alone understand – what is going on) may become comic, but alongside it is tragedy. Similarly, while the confusions in *Woman in Mind* may allow laughter, the play is about a woman driven mad by the repression and suffering she endures through her marriage to a clergyman. Most often the damage is particularly done by men, with women as the victims.

Sir Peter Hall, who brought Ayckbourn to the National Theatre during the 1980s, describes his work as 'a document of our age'.[14] The 1981 text *Way Upstream* was, in its way, a 'state of the nation play'. While its apparent focus is the power struggles between two couples, it has also been widely read in metaphorical terms as representing a battle between political extremists.[15] Generally, Ayckbourn is suspicious of theatre which is overtly political in intent. 'Political theatre is usually too much politics and too little theatre', he suggests.[16] John Osborne declared him 'a right-wing boulevardier'; Michael Billington, on the other hand, views him as 'a left-wing dramatist using a right-wing form'.[17] *A Small Family Business*, written in the mid-1980s at the height of Thatcherism, and which pursues an almost Brechtian exploration of the difficulty of remaining honest within a corrupt society, was described by Mark Ravenhill as '*the* political play of its time'.[18] Yet when he expresses them directly, Ayckbourn's own political views tend – as he himself realises – to come across as naive: 'It sounds awful, but I really like things to be fair. I think people should treat each other well.'[19]

The audience for Ayckbourn's work in Britain is surely much larger than for any other playwright of his generation, but it can be argued that it is largely defined by class. Ayckbourn himself refers to 'the world I usually visit' within the plays as being sited 'four or five miles outside Reading'.[20] Primarily, it is the world of an actual or aspiring middle class, and for all that the focus is often on the appalling damage that characters (especially men) perpetrate, their victims are usually other members of their own class rather than the economically downtrodden or society as a whole. For some of his detractors, Ayckbourn wastes too much time and sympathy on characters who hardly need or deserve it. Whether his plays can escape their specificity and represent a broader spectrum of humanity is debatable. But certainly, their considerable success outside Britain suggests that they can resonate powerfully within other cultures and societies.

In 2009, Ayckbourn ceased to be Artistic Director of the Stephen Joseph Theatre, following a stroke three years earlier and after thirty-seven years in charge. He continues to write new plays for Scarborough.

NOTES

Introduction to the 1960s

1. Much of the information included in this chapter is derived from two key works about the decade, both written by Dominic Sandbrook: *Never Had It So Good: A History of Britain from Suez to the Beatles* (London: Abacus, 2006); and *White Heat: A History of Britain in the Swinging Sixties* (London: Abacus, 2007). I have also drawn on other books listed in the first section of the Select Bibliography, and on various newspapers and magazines of the period. And a bit on memory . . .
2. 'Annus Mirabilus' in Philip Larkin, *Collected Poems* (London, Faber and Faber, 2003), p. 146.
3. *Observer*, 1 April 1962, p. 13.
4. See, for example, *Guardian*, 9 April 1963, p. 6.
5. Leary seems to have coined the phrase in 1966 or 1967 and used it frequently – including as the title of a record he released.
6. This was how the newspaper advertised its new section.
7. From 'The Blood Donor', first broadcast 23 June 1961.
8. For more details see Peter Oborne, *Basil D'Oliveira. Cricket and Conspiracy: The Untold Story* (London: Time Warner Books, 2005), pp. 186–95.
9. See, for example, Mike Marqusee, *Redemption Song: Muhammad Ali and the Spirit of the Sixties* (London: Verso, 1999), pp. 162 and 214.
10. Marqusee, p. 244; and www.historylearningsite.co.uk/Mexico_1968.htm.
11. See *Radio Times*, 1 January 1960.
12. Roger Coleman, Introduction to Catalogue to the 'Situation' exhibition at RBA Galleries, August 1960. See www.artcornwall.org/features/situation_roger_coleman.htm. Also quoted in Chris Stephens and Katharine Stout (eds), *Art & the 60s: This Was Tomorrow* (London: Tate Publishing, 2004).
13. See, for example, Sandbrook, *Never Had It So Good*, pp. 373–77.
14. King made his speech as part of a Civil Rights rally at the Lincoln Memorial in Washington, DC on 28 August 1963.

1 Theatre in the 1960s

1. *Observer*, 1 October 1961, p. 27.
2. 'A View from the Gods', *Encore*, March/April 1960, pp. 4–5.
3. Ian Bannen, 'Contracts, Not Cash', *The Twentieth Century*, vol. 169, no. 1008, February 1961, pp. 135–40.

4. 'A View from the Gods', *Encore*, March/April 1960, op. cit.
5. *Guardian*, 28 December 1961, p. 5.
6. 'Goodbye Note from Joan', *Encore*, September/October 1961, pp. 15–16.
7. 'A View from the Gods', *Encore*, September/October 1961, pp. 6–9.
8. Albert Hunt, 'Roots in Norfolk', *Encore*, May/June 1960, pp. 30–31.
9. 'A View from the Gods', *Encore*, September/October 1961, op. cit.
10. *Guardian*, 29 July 1961, p. 5.
11. 'An Interview with Arnold Wesker: Centre 42', *Encore*, May/June 1962, pp. 39–44.
12. Geoffrey Reeves, 'The Biggest Aunt Sally of Them All: Some Notes on the Centre 42 Fesivals', *Encore*, January/February 1963, pp. 8–16.
13. See www.artscouncil.org.uk/who-we-are/history-arts-council/1960s/.
14. Peter Brook, 'Search for a Hunger', *Encore*, July/August 1961, pp. 8–21.
15. J.W. Lambert, 'Theatre for Kicks', *Sunday Times*, 28 June, 1964, p. 33.
16. Martin Esslin, 'Violence', *Encore*, May/June 1964, pp. 6–15.
17. *Encore*, January/February 1960, pp. 14–20.
18. 'The Theatre of Cruelty', *The Times*, 30 December 1961, p. 5.
19. Laurence Kitchin, *Drama in the Sixties* (London: Faber and Faber, 1965), pp. 23–6.
20. *Encore*, May/June 1961, pp. 31–32.
21. 'Why Does Romeo Wear a Juliet Cap?', *News Chronicle*, 4 October 1960.
22. See *Daily Express*, 5 October 1960, p. 4; Kenneth Tynan, *Observer*, 9 October 1960, p. 24; *Star*, 5 October 1960, p. 17.
23. Jan Kott, *Shakespeare Our Contemporary* (London: Methuen, 1964).
24. *Encore*, January/February 1965, pp. 8–12.
25. *The Times*, 15 December 1964, p. 6.
26. Kitchin, op. cit., p. 21.
27. Ibid., pp. 151–2.
28. *Daily Mail*, 12 September 1960, p. 3.
29. *Daily Mail*, 17 February, 1961, p. 3.
30. *Daily Herald* and *Daily Mail*, both 23 February 1961.
31. Peter Brook, 'From Zero to the Infinite', *Encore*, November/December 1960, pp. 6–11.
32. *The Times*, 23 February 1961, p. 8, and *Daily Herald*, 23 February 1961.
33. *Daily Mail*, 23 February 1961, pp. 1 and 3.
34. *Daily Mail*, 24 February 1961, p. 3.
35. *Queen*, 15 March 1961.
36. Martin Esslin, *Theatre of the Absurd* (London: Eyre & Spottiswoode, 1962).
37. *The Times*, 27 August 1960, p. 9.
38. Alan Bennett, Peter Cook, Jonathan Miller and Dudley Moore, 'Aftermyth of War', *Beyond the Fringe* (London: Souvenir Press, 1963), pp. 50–7.
39. Ibid., pp. 58–64.
40. 11 May 1961, p. 18.
41. *Illustrated London News*, 10 September, p. 446 and 27 May 1961, p. 900.

42. *Daily Telegraph*, 14 May 1961.

43. *Queen*, 10 May 1961, p. 100.

44. *Tatler*, 31 May 1961.

45. Michael Frayn, 'Introduction' to Bennett, Cook, Miller and Moore, op. cit., pp. 7–11.

46. Theatre Workshop, *Oh, What a Lovely War!* (London: Methuen, 1984).

47. *Daily Mail*, 20 March 1963, p. 3.

48. See Lord Chamberlain's Correspondence Archive: *Oh, What a Lovely War!*

49. *The Times*, 31 May 1963, p. 8.

50. Sally Beauman, *The Royal Shakespeare Company: A History of Ten Decades* (Oxford: Oxford University Press, 1982), p. 270.

51. *Daily Sketch*, 3 September 1964.

52. See, for example, *The Times*, p. 14; *Daily Mail*, *Daily Sketch* and *Evening Standard*, all 3 September 1964.

53. See Lord Chamberlain's Correspondence Files: *Dingo*.

54. All quotations from the published text: Charles Wood, *Dingo* in *Two Plays by Charles Wood* (London: Methuen, 1978).

55. Op. cit., n. 53.

56. *The Times*, 9 May 1964, p. 9.

57. David Rudkin, *Afore Night Come*, published in *New English Dramatists: 7* (Harmondsworth: Penguin, 1963), pp. 73–139.

58. *Evening Standard*, 13 December 1962.

59. 28 March 1962.

60. 1 April 1962, p. 27.

61. 28 March 1962.

62. See *Daily Telegraph* and *Evening Standard*, both 20 July 1962.

63. See Lord Chamberlain's Correspondence Files: *The Representative*.

64. Peter Shaffer, *The Royal Hunt of the Sun* in *Plays of the Sixties: Volume One* (London: Pan Books), pp. 119–208.

65. 'A View from the Gods', *Encore*, January/February 1963, pp. 6–7.

66. 'A View from the Gods', *Encore*, September/October 1963, pp. 6–8.

67. *The Times*, 3 September 1963, p. 14.

68. *Encore*, November/December 1963, pp. 8–11.

69. Ibid., pp. 12–16.

70. Ibid., pp. 8–11.

71. *Daily Express* headline, 14 September 1963, p. 4.

72. See *Guardian*, 9 September 1963, p. 3.

73. '1964 Awards', *Plays and Players*, February 1965, p. 8.

74. See Lord Chamberlain's Correspondence Files: *Afore Night Come*.

75. *Queen*, 20 August 1964; *Guardian*, 21 August 1964, p. 9.

76. *The Times*, p. 11; *Guardian*, p. 9; and the *Daily Mail*, all 21 August 1964.

77. See Lord Chamberlain's Correspondence Files: *Victor*.

78. Cited by the theatre manager John Counsell in the programme for a production of Frederick Lonsdale's 1920s comedy *On Approval* at the Windsor Theatre Royal, June 1964.

79. 'Dare you take your daughter to the theatre?', *Evening News*, 2 July 1964, p. 8.

80. See *The Times*, 22 August 1964, p. 7.

81. *The Times*, 25 August 1964, p. 11.

82. See *Daily Telegraph*, 25 August 1964.

83. *The Times*, 26 August 1964, p. 9.

84. *Daily Mail*, 26 August 1964.

85. *The Times*, 28 August 1964, p. 11.

86. Op. cit., n. 80.

87. *The Times*, 27 August 1964, p. 11.

88. 'A View from the Gods', *Encore*, March/April 1965, pp. 6–7.

89. *The Times*, 22 December 1965, p. 11.

90. 'A View from the Gods', *Encore*, March/April 1965, pp. 6–7, op. cit.

91. *Plays and Players*, February 1966, pp. 46–7.

92. See Lord Chamberlain's Correspondence Files: *Loot*.

93. Joe Orton, *Loot*, in Orton, *The Complete Plays* (London: Methuen, 1980), pp. 193–275.

94. Op. cit., n. 92.

95. *The Times*, 28 September 1966, p. 14.

96. Lord Chamberlain's Correspondence Files: *Spring Awakening*.

97. *The Times*, 18 August 1965, p. 11.

98. *Observer*, 15 August 1965, p. 17.

99. *Sunday Times*, 15 August 1965, p. 31.

100. *Daily* Mail, 11 August 1965, p. 12; *Evening Standard*, 13 August 1965.

101. *Daily Mail*, 10 August, 1965, p. 12.

102. www.artscouncil.org.uk/about-us/history-arts-council/1960s/.

103. *Encore*, July/August 1965, p. 47.

104. See www.belgrade.co.uk/take-part/theatre-in-education/.

105. 'View from the Gods', *Plays and Players*. December 1966, p. 74.

106. David Wright, 'Documentary Theatre', *Plays and Players*, December 1966, pp. 60–1.

107. See, for example, *The Times*, 7 September 1959, p. 3 and the *Daily Telegraph*, 8 July 1964, p. 16.

108. Wright, op. cit.

109. Lord Chamberlain's Correspondence Files: *Hang Down Your Head and Die*.

110. Lord Chamberlain's Correspondence Files: *In the Matter of J. Robert Oppenheimer*.

111. *Punch*, 7 December 1966.

112. *Daily Mail*, 29 November 1966.

113. Quotations from published text: Peter Brook/RSC, *US* (London: Calder and Boyars, 1968).

114. *Evening News*, 14 October 1966.

115. *The Times*, 14 October 1966, p. 7; *Guardian*, 3 November 1966, p. 6; *Sunday Times*, 16 October 1966, p. 51.

116. 'The Actor and Vietnam: Peter Brook on "US"', *Plays and Players*, January 1967, pp. 56–7.

117. See, for example, *Guardian*, 27 September 1966, p. 1.

118. www.tate.org.uk/collections/glossary/definition.jsp?entryId=36.

119. *Plays and Players*, October 1966, p. 8.

120. See *Guardian*, 29 October 1967, p. 23, and 3 November, p. 5.

121. *Guardian*, 20 December 1967, p. 5.

122. See *Daily Mirror* and *Daily Express*, both 19 May 1967, front pages (p. 1).

123. *The Times*, 27 December 1967, p. 8.

124. *Guardian*, 17 December 1969, p. 6.

125. *Guardian* 25 November, 1969, p. 8.

126. Lord Chamberlain's Correspondence Files: *The Premise*.

127. Unpublished script. See Lord Chamberlain's Collection of Licensed Plays 1900–1968: *Nymphs and Satires*.

128. See Roland Rees, *Pioneers of Fringe Theatre on Record* (London: Oberon Books, 1992), p. 101.

129. Lord Chamberlain's Correspondence Files: *You in Your Small Corner*.

130. Lord Chamberlain's Correspondence Files: *Sit Down Banna*.

131. W. A. Darlington, 'Simple Parable of African Life', *Daily Telegraph*, 13 December 1966, p. 15.

132. 13 December 1966, p. 6.

133. *Daily Mail*, 13 December 1966.

134. *Guardian*, 17 September 1965, p. 13.

135. *The Times* 13 December 1966, p. 6.

136. *Illustrated London News*, 24 December 1966, p. 28; *Sunday Times*, 18 December 1966, p. 24; *Daily Telegraph*, 13 December 1966.

137. *Plays and Players*, January 1967, pp. 60–1.

138. Jonathan Miller, quoted in *Sunday Times*, 19 July 1964, Colour Supplement, p. 54.

139. Andrew Parkin, *File on Nichols* (London: Methuen, 1993), p. 33; *The Times*, 17 October 1969, p. 15, cited in Parkin, op. cit., p. 34.

140. Peter Nichols, *Diaries, 1969–1977* (London: Nick Hern, 2000), p. 22.

141. See Alec Patton, 'Funny Turns: Peter Nichols, The National Theatre, and the Royal Shakespeare Company, 1967–1982', unpublished PhD thesis, University of Sheffield, 2008, p. 117.

142. *New York Times*, 27 November 1966, p. D1.

143. Publicity leaflet – see Royal Court Archive.

144. *Daily Mail*, 3 August 1967, p. 10.

145. *Daily Mail*, 29 November 1966.

146. Lord Chamberlain's Correspondence Files: *Macbird*.

147. Ellen Stewart programme note for London productions of *Tom Paine* and *Futz*.

148. *Observer*, 27 August 1967, p. 16.

149. *The Times*, 6 September 1967, p. 7.

150. 17 September 1967, p. 20.

151. 12 September 1967, p. 6.

152. 18 October 1967, p. 8.

153. Victoria and Albert Museum Theatre and Performance Archives Production File: *Tom Paine*.

154. 18 October 1967.

155. Op. cit., n. 153.

156. 'View from the Gods', *Plays and Players*, August 1966, p. 74.

157. 'A View from the Gods', *Encore*, September/October 1963, pp. 6–8.

158. Michael Billington, *State of the Nation: British Theatre Since 1945* (London: Faber and Faber, 2007), p. 162.

159. *The Times*, 21 July 1967, p. 6.

160. Bernard F. Dukore, *Barnestorm: The Plays of Peter Barnes* (London: Garland Publishing, 1995), pp. 3–28.

161. Peter Barnes, 'The Ruling Class' in Barnes, *Plays: One* (London: Methuen, 1989), pp. 7–118.

162. *The Times*, 22 September 1967, p. 7.

163. John Weightman writing in *Encounter*, July 1967; quoted in Malcolm Page, *File on Stoppard* (London: Methuen, 1986), p. 19.

164. Quotations taken from *Zigger Zagger* in Peter Terson, *'Zigger Zagger' and 'Mooney and His Caravans'* (Harmondsworth: Penguin Books, 1970), pp. 31–134.

165. *Guardian*, 20 March 1968, p. 9.

166. Margaret Croyden, 'Peter Brook's "Tempest"', *Drama Review*, vol. 13, no. 3, Spring 1969, pp. 125–8. Reprinted in David Williams, *Peter Brook: A Theatrical Casebook* (London: Methuen, 1988), pp. 137–41.

167. *Plays and Players*, November 1968, pp. 69–71.

168. *Guardian*, 19 July 1968, p. 6.

169. Croyden, op. cit.

170. Gerome Ragni and James Rado, *Hair: The American Tribal Love-Rock Musical* (New York: Pocket Books, 1969).

171. *The Times*, 28 September 1968, p. 18.

172. Billington, op. cit., pp. 202–3.

173. 'View from the Gods', *Plays and Players*, November 1966, p. 4.

174. *Guardian*, 6 November 1968, p. 6.

175. Judith Malina and Julian Beck, *Paradise Now* (New York: Random Books, 1971).

176. Nicholas de Jongh, *Guardian*, 10 June 1969, p. 6.

177. Ibid.

178. 15 June 1969, p. 49.

179. *Guardian*, 10 June 1969, p. 6.

180. Billington, op. cit., p. 204.
181. *Plays and Players*, January 1969, p. 51.
182. See Lord Chamberlain's Correspondence Files: *Why the Chicken* (John McGrath, 1959); *Serjeant Musgrave's Dance* (John Arden, 1959); *The Lily White Boys* (Harry Cookson, 1959).
183. *Daily Mail*, 16 April 1969.
184. David Benedictus, 'The Theatre of Contempt', *Plays and Players*, March 1967, pp. 24–5.
185. See, for example, C. Marowitz, T. Milne and O. Hale (eds), *The Encore Reader* (London: Methuen, 1965), p. 40.

2 Introducing the playwrights

John Arden

1. All quotations this section from John Arden and Margaretta D'Arcy, *Awkward Corners* (London: Methuen, 1988), pp. 71–2.
2. Ibid., p. 19.
3. Cited in Malcolm Page, *Arden on File* (London: Methuen, 1985), p. 7.
4. Cited in Charles Marowitz, *Theatre at Work: Playwright and Productions* (London: Methuen, 1967), p. 38.
5. Arden and Darcy, op. cit., p. 55.
6. Francis Dillon, 'Fossicking', *The Listener*, 22 July 1971.
7. Simon Trussler, 'The Book of the Play', *Tribune*, 5 February 1965.
8. Albert Hunt, *John Arden* (London: Eyre Methuen, 1974), p. 36.
9. John Arden, 'A Thoroughly Romantic View', *London Magazine*, VII, July 1960, pp. 11–15.
10. Julius Novick, *Beyond Broadway* (New York: Hill and Wang, 1968), p. 52.
11. Simon Trussler, *John Arden* (New York: Columbia University Press, 1973), p. 9.
12. Lord Chamberlain's Correspondence Files: *Live Like Pigs*.
13. Hunt, op. cit., p. 51.
14. John Arden, 'Introductory Note', *Plays Three* (Harmondsworth: Penguin, 1962), p. 101.
15. Kenneth Tynan, 'A World Fit for Eros', *Observer*, 5 October 1958, p. 19.
16. Eric Keown, 'At the Play', *Punch*, 8 November 1958.
17. Ronald Hayman, *John Arden* (London: Heinemann, 1969), p. 15.
18. Robert Hatch, 'Arden', *Nation* (New York), 21 June 1965.
19. Margaretta D'Arcy, *Loose Theatre: In and Out of My Memory* (Manchester: Trafford Publishing, 2006), p. 265.

Edward Bond

1. Quoted in Philip Roberts, *Bond on File* (London: Methuen, 1985), p. 7.
2. Malcolm Hay and Philip Roberts, *Edward Bond: A Companion to the Plays* (London: TQ Publications, 1978), p. 7.
3. Interview with Bill Gaskill, *Gambit*, vol. 5, no. 17, 1970, pp. 38–43.
4. Edward Bond: *Letters Volume I* (Amsterdam: Harwood Academic Publishers, 1994), p. 136.
5. Edward Bond, unpublished letter to Peggy Ramsay.
6. Ian Stuart (ed.), *Selections from the Notebooks of Edward Bond: Volume I: 1959–1980* (London: Methuen, 2000), pp. 38–70.
7. Bond, unpublished letter, 25 November 1982. See Royal Court Archive.
8. *Daily Telegraph*, 10 December 1962.
9. *Daily Mail*, 10 December 1962.
10. *Guardian*, 13 January 1966, p. 6.
11. *Sunday Telegraph*, 16 January 1966.
12. *Sunday Times*, 16 January 1966, p. 43.
13. *The Times*, 19 April 1967, p. 6.
14. *Sunday Times*, 23 April 1967, p. 49.
15. Quotations from *Black Mass* as published in Edward Bond, *Plays: Two* (London: Methuen, 1978), pp. 225–36.
16. Quotation from *Passion* as published in Edward Bond, *Plays: Two*, pp. 237–53.
17. *Guardian*, 29 September 1971, p. 10.

Harold Pinter

1. Harold Pinter, *The Caretaker* (London: Methuen, 1960/1971), p. 73.
2. Henry Woolf, 'My Sixty Years in Harold's Gang', *Guardian*, 12 July 2007.
3. 'Theatrical world applauds life and art of our greatest modern playwright', *Guardian*, 27 December 2008.
4. Woolf, op. cit.
5. *Sunday Times*, January 1958 (n.d.). Cited at www.haroldpinter.org/plays/plays_room.shtml.
6. *Sunday Times*, 25 May 1958.
7. Lord Chamberlain's Correspondence Licensed Plays 1900–1968: *The Dumb Waiter*.
8. Cited in Malcolm Page (ed.), *File on Pinter* (London: Methuen, 1993), p. 13.
9. Mel Gussow, *Conversations with Pinter* (London: Nick Hern Books), 1994, p. 71.
10. *London Daily News*, 19 June 1987. Quoted in Page, op. cit., p. 105.
11. Gussow, op. cit., p. 36.
12. Ian Smith, *Pinter in the Theatre* (London: Nick Hern Books, 2005), p. 45.
13. Ibid., p. 48.
14. Harold Pinter, 'Introduction', *Plays: One* (London: Methuen, 1976), pp. 9–16.
15. Gussow, op. cit., p. 70.

16. *News Chronicle*, 28 July 1960. Quoted in Page, op. cit., p. 101.
17. W. A. Darlington, *Daily Telegraph*, 20 May 1958. Quoted in Page, op. cit., p. 13.
18. Woolf, op. cit.

Alan Ayckbourn

1. http://biography.alanayckbourn.net/BiographyPinter.htm.
2. Michael Coveney, 'Scarborough Fare', *Plays and Players*, September 1975, p. 18.
3. Paul Allen, *Alan Ayckbourn: Grinning at the Edge* (London: Methuen, 2001), pp. 72–4.
4. Ian Watson, *Conversations with Ayckbourn* (London: Faber and Faber, 1981), pp. 40–1.
5. Ibid., pp. 43–4. See also http://christmasvmastermind.alanayckbourn.net/CVM_Quotes.htm.
6. Review by Benedict Nightingale, *Guardian*, 14 November 1963, p. 9. See also http://mrwhatnot.alanayckbourn.net/MW_Reviews.htm.

3 Playwrights and plays: John Arden

1 Albert Hunt, *Arden: A Study of His Plays* (London: Methuen, 1974), p. 143.
2. John Arden, *To Present the Pretence* (London: Eyre Methuen, 1977), p. 158.
3. Ibid., p. 158.
4. *The Times*, 6 October 1959.
5. Hunt, op. cit., p. 58.
6. Ibid., p. 6.
7. Ibid., p. 37.
8. Asked why he reduced the number of injured by a factor of ten, from 250 to twenty-five, Arden replied that he did not want the vengeance to seem excessive.
9. *Serjeant Musgrave's Dance* (London: Methuen, 1960, reprinted 1976), p. 7. All quotations from this edition.
10. Harold Hobson, 'Hardly a Silver Lining', *Sunday Times*, 25 October 1959, p. 25.
11. Phillip Hope-Wallace, 'Something Just Short of a Great Play', *Manchester Guardian*, 24 October 1959.
12. Felix Barker,'A Slow Fuse, but What an Explosion!', *London Evening News*, 23 October 1959.
13. Programme note, Royal Court revival of *Serjeant Musgrave's Dance*, 1965.
14. Margaretta D'Arcy, *Loose Theatre: In and Out of My Memory* (Manchester: Trafford Publishing, 2006), pp. 237 and 239.
15. John Arden and Margaretta D'Arcy, *Awkward Corners: Essays, Papers, Fragments* (London: Methuen, 1988), pp. 80 and 164.
16. John Arden, Introduction to *The Workhouse Donkey* (London: Methuen, 1964);

reprinted in *Plays Two* (London: Methuen, 2002), p. 3. All quotations are from this edition.

17. Cited in Malcolm Page (ed.), *Arden on File* (London: Methuen, 1985), p. 30.

18. Frank Cox, 'Arden of Chichester', *Plays and Players*, August 1963, p. 16.

19. Philip French, 'Led by Donkeys', *New Statesman*, 74, 3 November 1967.

20. Introduction to *The Workhouse Donkey*, p. 4.

21. 'On Comedy: John Arden talks to Albert Hunt', *Encore* 57, vol. 12, no. 5, September–October 1965, pp. 13–19, p. 15.

22. John Arden, 'Correspondence', *Encore*, May–June 1959, p. 42.

23. Hunt, op. cit., p. 89.

24. Unless indicated otherwise, all quotations in this section are from the author's introduction, John Arden, *Armstrong's Last Goodnight* (London: Methuen, 1965); reprinted in *Plays Two* (London: Methuen, 2002), pp. 135–8. All play quotations are also from this edition.

25. John Arden, 'Letters', *Encore* 51, September–October 1964, pp. 51–2; my emphasis.

26. 'Building the play: an interview with the editors', *Encore* 32, vol. 8, no. 4, July–August 1961, pp. 22–41.

27. Cited in Malcolm Page, *John Arden* (Boston, MA: G. K. Hall, 1984), p. 83.

28. Ibid.

29. Penelope Gilliatt, 'Adjusting the Focus of History', *Observer*, 11 July 1965.

30. Harold Hobson, 'One up from the Gorillas', *Sunday Times*, London, 11 July 1965.

31. Tom Milne, 'Armstrong's Last Goodnight', *Encore* 57, September–October 1965, p. 37.

32. All quotations from Gaskill in this section taken from: William Gaskill, 'Producing Arden', *Encore* 57, vol. 12, no. 5, September–October 1965, pp. 20–6.

33. Albert Hunt and Geoffrey Reeves, 'Arden's Stagecraft', *Encore* 57, vol. 12, no. 5, September–October 1965, pp. 9–12.

34. All quotations from Arden in this section taken from John Arden, 'Telling a True Tale', *Encore* 25, vol. 7, no. 3, May–June 1960, pp. 22–6.

35. *Plays One*, p. xi.

36. *To Present the Pretence*, op. cit., p. 83.

37. Trish Dace, 'Who Wrote John Arden's Plays?', in Jonathan Wike (ed.), *John Arden and Margaretta D'Arcy: A Casebook* (London: Garland, 1994), pp. 199–221, p. 211.

3 Playwrights and plays: Edward Bond

1. Bond interviewed in the *Guardian*, 29 September 1971, p. 10.

2. Lord Chamberlain's Correspondence Files: *Saved*.

3. Teach-In on *Saved* (Royal Court Archive).

4. Lord Chamberlain's Correspondence Files: *Saved*.

5. 'Author's Note on Violence', Edward Bond, *Plays One* (London: Methuen, 1977), pp. 9–17.

6. Edward Bond, 'Censor in Mind', *Censorship*, no. 4, August 1965, pp. 9–12.

7. 'A Discussion with Edward Bond', *Gambit*, vol. 5, no. 17, 1970, pp. 5–38.

8. 'Bond in the English Style', *Politika*, 19 September 1969 (Royal Court Archive).

9. Heidi Stephenson and Natasha Langridge, *Rage and Reason: Women Playwrights on Playwriting* (London: Methuen, 1997), p. 131.

10. Edward Bond, *Letters Volume IV* (Amsterdam: Harwood Academic Publishers, 1998), p. 190.

11. All quotations from text of *Saved* as published in Edward Bond, *Plays: One* (London, Methuen, 1977).

12. Bond, quoted in Malcolm Hay and Philip Roberts, *Edward Bond: A Companion to His Plays* (London: TQ Publications, 1978), p. 9.

13. Lord Chamberlain's Correspondence Files: *Saved*, op. cit.

14. Bond, email to author.

15. Lord Chamberlain's Correspondence Files: *Saved*, op. cit.

16. See Victoria and Albert Museum Theatre and Performance Archives Production File: *Saved*; and Teach-In on *Saved*.

17. *Vecernje Novosti*, Belgrade, 17 September 1969. See Royal Court Archive.

18. *The Times*, 8 February 1969, p. 19.

19. Lord Chamberlain's Correspondence Files: *Saved*.

20. *Daily Express*, 4 November 1965, p. 8. Cited in David Davis, 'Commentary' to the student edition of *Saved*. See Edward Bond, *Saved* (London: Methuen, 2009), pp. xviii–lxxxiv.

21. *Guardian*, 29 September 1971.

22. Gaskill in Royal Court programme for *Saved* season (Royal Court Archive).

23. Penelope Gilliat, 'Despair in the Depths', *Observer*, 7 November 1965, p. 24.

24. Edward Bond, unpublished letter to Outrider Films Ltd, November 1982.

25. Edward Bond, *Then, Now and To Be: A New Introduction for Saved*. Written for the programme of production at the Lyric Theatre, London, October 2011, www.edward-bond.org/Comment/comment.html.

26. *Daily Telegraph*, 30 September 2011.

27. Teach-In on *Saved*, op. cit.

28. Leaflet advertising Teach-In on *Saved* (Royal Court Archive).

29. Edward Bond, 'Author's Note to *Saved*', written for publication of text in 1966. Published as appendix to Edward Bond, *Plays One*, pp. 309–12.

30. Bond, 'Censor in Mind', op. cit.

31. Teach-In on *Saved*, op. cit.

32. *Daily Telegraph*, 4 November 1965, p. 18.

33. Review of Royal Court production at Belgrade Festival, published in *Borban*, 18 September 1969. See Royal Court Archive.

34. Note by Gaskill in Royal Court Archive, 5 November 1968, and Edward Bond, *Letters Volume III* (London: Routledge, 1996), p. 122.

35. Edward Bond, letter to theatre critics, 7 November 1965 (Royal Court Archive).
36. *Daily Mail*, 4 November 1965, p. 18.
37. Bond, 'Censor in Mind', op. cit.
38. Note by Gaskill in Royal Court Archive, 5 November 1968.
39. Bond, letter to theatre critics, op. cit.
40. Ian Stuart (ed.), *Selections from the Notebooks of Edward Bond: Volume One: 1959 to 1980* (London: Methuen, 2000), p. 73.
41. Edward Bond, 'Author's Note to *Saved*', op. cit.
42. Edward Bond, letter to *Sunday Times* critic, 7 November 1965 (Royal Court Archive).
43. Bond, 'Author's Note to *Saved*', op. cit.
44. Bond, letter to theatre critics, op. cit.
45. Gilliatt, op. cit., p. 24.
46. Edward Bond, 'Author's Note to *Saved*', op. cit.
47. *Observer*, 21 November 1965, p. 11.
48. Gaskill, speaking at Teach-In on *Saved*.
49. Edward Bond, unpublished letter to the composer Hans Werner Henze, 3 December 1986.
50. Edward Bond, 'My play predicted the riots', *Sunday Telegraph*, 9 October 2011.
51. All quotations from text of *Early Morning* as published in Edward Bond, *Plays: One* (London, Methuen, 1977).
52. *Gambit*, op. cit.
53. In an email to the author.
54. Ian Stuart (ed.), op. cit., p. 92.
55. *The Times*, 8 April 1968, p. 6.
56. *Gambit*, op. cit.
57. Edward Bond, unpublished letter to Peggy Ramsay, 3 December 1985.
58. *Gambit*, op. cit.
59. Edward Bond, letter 8 April 1968; quoted in Philip Roberts, *Bond on File* (London: Methuen, 1985), p. 20.
60. *Daily Telegraph*, 8 April 1968, p. 15; *Daily Mail*, 8 April 1968, p. 10; The *Times*, 8 April 1968; *Sunday Times* 14 April 1968, p. 25; *Financial Times*, 8 April 1968; *Observer*, 14 April 1968, p. 25. See Victoria and Albert Museum Theatre and Performance Archives Production File: *Early Morning*.
61. *Evening Standard*, 14 March 1969; *Sunday Times*, 16 March 1969, p. 57; *Financial Times* (n.d.), Ibid.
62. 'John Bird may play "lesbian" Victoria', *Daily Telegraph*, 4 August 1967.
63. *The Times*, 14 March 1969.
64. Michael Patterson, *Peter Stein: Germany's Leading Theatre Director* (Cambridge: Cambridge University Press, 1981), pp. 31–5.
65. 'Interview with William Gaskill', *Gambit*, vol. 5, no. 17, 1970, pp. 38–43.
66. All quotations from text of *Lear* as published in Edward Bond, *Plays: Two* (London, Methuen, 1978).

67. 'Edward Bond: The Long Road to Lear', *Theatre Quarterly*, January–March 1972, pp. 3–14.
68. Edward Bond, unpublished letter to Peggy Ramsay.
69. Cited in interview with Edward Bond by John Tusa. See: www.bbc.co.uk/radi03/johntusainterview/bond_transcript.shtml.
70. Edward Bond, unpublished letter to Peggy Ramsay.
71. *Gambit*, op. cit.
72. *Guardian*, 29 September 1971.
73. *Plays and Players*, November 1971, pp. 42–6, 53; *Sunday Telegraph* (n.d.). See Victoria and Albert Museum Theatre and Performance Archives Production File: *Lear*.
74. *The Times*, 30 September 1971, p. 11.
75. *Guardian*, 29 September 1971.
76. Ibid.
77. Ibid.
78. Email to author.
79. Edward Bond, unpublished letter, July 1980.
80. Bond, 'My play predicted the riots', op. cit.
81. Email to author.
82. Ibid.
83. Teach-In on *Saved*, op. cit.
84. Email to author.

3 Playwrights and plays: Harold Pinter

1. Ian Smith, 'Harold Pinter's Recollections of His Career in the 1950s: An Interview Conducted by Ian Smith at the British Library, 1997', in Dominic Shellard (ed.), *British Theatre in the 1950s* (Sheffield: Sheffield University Press, 2000), p. 72.
2. *Daily Herald*, 23 March 1960.
3. Richard Eyre, *Talking Theatre: Interviews with Theatre People* (London: Nick Hern, 2011), p. 173.
4. *Observer*, 1 May 1960.
5. Letter from Ted Hughes to Olwyn Hughes from the Olwyn Hughes archive, ADD. 88948, British Library, London.
6. *The Caretaker* (London: Methuen, 1960). All quotations from the play are from this edition.
7. Martin Esslin, *The Theatre of the Absurd*, 3rd edn (New York: Vintage, 2004), p. 237.
8. This version, submitted to the Lord Chamberlain prior to performance, also eschews Petey's plea 'Stan, don't let them tell you what to do', retrospectively one of Pinter's most famous lines. See Lord Chamberlain's Plays: *The Birthday Party*, p. 110.
9. Esslin, op. cit., p. 249.

10. Harold Pinter, *Various Voices: Sixty Years of Prose, Poetry, Politics 1948–2008* (London: Faber and Faber, 2005), p. 177.

11. Larry Bensky, 'Harold Pinter: The Art of Theater No. 3', *Paris Review*, fall, 1966, www.theparisreview.org/interviews/4351/the-art-of-theater-no-3-harold-pinter.

12. Michael Billington, *Harold Pinter* (London: Faber and faber, 2007), p. 115.

13. Harold Pinter and Clive Donner, 'Filming "The Caretaker"', in Lois Gordon (ed.), *Harold Pinter: A Casebook* (London: Garland Science, 1990), p. 130.

14. Bensky, op. cit.

15. Austin Quigley, 'Pinter, Politics, and Post-Modernism', in *The Cambridge Companion to Harold Pinter* (ed. Peter Raby) (Cambridge: Cambridge University Press, 2009), pp. 7–27.

16. Esslin, op. cit., p. 249.

17. Eyre, op. cit., p. 48.

18. *Sunday Times*, 14 August 1960.

19. Ibid., p. 174.

20. 'Scrapbooks: UK and International Productions' (Harold Pinter archive ADD. 88880/8/1–8), British Library, London.

21. Mel Gussow, *Conversations with Pinter* (London: Nick Hern, 1994), pp. 42–3.

22. Mark Batty, *About Pinter: The Playwright and the Work* (London: Faber and Faber, 2005), p. 165.

23. *The Homecoming* (London: Methuen, 1965). All quotations from the play are from this edition.

24. Bensky, op. cit.

25. Peter Hall, 'A Director's Approach', in *Harold Pinter: A Casebook*, op. cit., p. 20.

26. Ibid., p. 13.

27. Ibid., p. 14.

28. *Sunday Times*, 6 June 1965.

29. *Observer*, 6 June 1965.

30. Billington, op. cit., p. 175.

31. 'Plays by Pinter for stage' (Harold Pinter archive ADD. 88880/1/1–69), British Library, London.

32. Gussow, op. cit., p. 23. In 1960, Pinter had also told Charles Marowitz in relation to *The Caretaker* that 'It's about love'. Charles Marowitz, 'A Kind of Masterpiece', in *Harold Pinter: A Casebook*, op. cit., p. 164.

33. Francis Gillen, 'Pinter at Work: An Introduction to the First Draft of *The Homecoming* and Its Relationship to the Completed Drama', *Pinter Review*, vol. 9 (1997–98), pp. 51–66.

34. Billington, op. cit., p. 164.

35. Ibid.

36. Billington, 'An Experience of Pinter: Address to the International Conference on Harold Pinter', *Pinter Review*, vol. 10 (1999–2000), pp. 41–51.

37. Ibid., p. 44.

38. *Réforme*, 1 June 1968.

39. 'Special Personal Correspondence' (ADD. 88880/7/1–13), British Library, London.

40. *Le Parisien Libéré*, 27 January 1961.

41. *Libération*, 30 January.

42. 8 October 1965.

43. 13 October 1965.

44. *L'Aurore*, 3 November 1965.

45. 23 January 1967.

46. *The Worker*; see also *New York World Journal Tribune*, 29 January 1967.

47. 16 January 1967.

48. See, for example, the *Evening Standard* of 5 November 1965: 'Pinter has pulled off the remarkable feat for a non-French playwright of being currently the biggest hit in Paris.'

49. Of the recent literature regarding British censorship, Steve Nicholson, *The Censorship of British Drama 1900–1968* (Exeter: University of Exeter Press, 2003, 2005 and 2011), and Dominic Shellard et al., *The Lord Chamberlain Regrets: A History of British Theatre Censorship* (London: British Library, 2004), are indispensable.

50. Lord Chamberlain's Correspondence Files: *The Birthday Party*, British Library, London.

51. Lord Chamberlain's Correspondence Files: *The Caretaker*, British Library, London.

52. Lord Chamberlain's Correspondence Files: *The Homecoming*, British Library, London.

53. Lord Chamberlain's Correspondence Files: *Landscape*, British Library, London.

54. Bensky, op. cit.

55. *Night* was first presented as part of an evening of short sketches on the subject of marriage, *Mixed Doubles*, on 9 April 1969.

56. Gussow, op. cit., p. 18.

57. Billington, op. cit., p. 199.

58. All quotations from *Landscape* and *Silence* are from the 1969 Methuen edition.

59. 6 July 1969.

60. Ronald Knowles, 'Pinter and Twentieth-century Drama', in *The Cambridge Companion to Harold Pinter*, p. 76; Billington, op. cit., p. 199.

61. Ibid., p. 201.

62. The role of Beth was given to Peggy Ashcroft, to the disappointment of his wife, Merchant – Pinter's usual leading lady – who consequently refused to see the play.

63. *Sunday Times*, 6 July 1969.

64. *New York Times*, 25 July 1969.

65. Ronald Knowles , 'Joyce and Pinter: *Exiles* and *Betrayal*', *Barcelona English Language and Literature Studies*, Vol. 9 (1998), pp. 183–9.

66. James Joyce, *A Portrait of the Artist as a Young Man* (New York: Viking, 1964), p. 171.

67. 'Plays by Pinter for Stage', op. cit.

68. Bensky, op. cit.

69. *Plays Three* (Faber, London: 1991). All quotations are from this edition.

70. The very first image that Pinter noted when beginning to draft *Silence* is of 'my friend

who wears a blue blouse', changed in the published version to 'my girl who wears a grey blouse' (p. 33).

71. James Joyce, *Stephen Hero*, 2nd edn (London: Jonathan Cape, 1956), p. 216.
72. Ellmann et al., 'Epiphanies: Introduction', in James Joyce, *Poems and Shorter Writings*, ed. Richard Ellmann, A. Walton Litz and John Whittier-Ferguson (London: Faber, 1991), p. 157.
73. 'Special Personal Correspondence', op. cit.
74. Billington, op. cit., p. 197.
75. 'Scrapbooks: UK and International Productions', op. cit.
76. Joyce, *A Portrait of the Artist as a Young Man*, op. cit., p. 247.
77. *Celebration* (London: Faber, 2005), p. 100.
78. For the critic of *The Times* (undated), this represented a 'less dangerous Pinter'.
79. 'Special Personal Correspondence', op. cit.
80. Pinter, *Various Voices*, op. cit., p. 177.
81. Billington, op. cit., p. 6.
82. *New York Times*, 25 July 1969.

3 Playwrights and plays: Alan Ayckbourn

1. 'Alan Ayckbourn: You Ask the Questions', *Independent on Sunday*, 1 July 2003.
2. Mel Gussow, 'Ayckbourn, Ex-Actor, Now Plays Singular Writer of Comedies', *New York Times*, 11 October 1974.
3. Ian Watson, *Conversations with Ayckbourn* (London and Boston, MA: Faber and Faber, 1988), p. 86.
4. Hilary Spurling, 'Farewell the Hairy Men', *Spectator*, 7 April 1967.
5. Ronald Bryden, *Plays and Players*, August 1973, p. 39.
6. Michael Church, 'Shakespeare of the South Bank', *Sunday Times*, 1 June 1986.
7. Watson, op. cit., pp. 72–3.
8. Ayckbourn, *The Crafty Art of Playmaking* (London: Faber and Faber, 2002).
9. Sarah Lyall, 'Ayckbourn the Juggler, in Triple Time', *New York Times*, 21 April 2009. Article written in connection with Matthew Warchus's 2009 production on Broadway of Ayckbourn's trilogy *The Norman Conquests*. Hall has directed many of Ayckbourn's plays over the years, the first being *Bedroom Farce* at the National Theatre in 1977.
10. Joan McAlpine, 'Is There a Manager to Drive This Bus to Shaftesbury Avenue?', Review of *Standing Room Only* at the Library Theatre, *The Stage*, July 1961. The force of this very positive response to the play is somewhat undermined, however, by the knowledge that Joan McAlpine was at the time stage manager at the Library Theatre; evidently at this time *The Stage* accepted reviews submitted from various quarters, and McAlpine's name was not credited. Paul Allen, *Alan Ayckbourn: Grinning at the Edge* (London: Methuen, 2001), p. 85.

11. Simon Murgatroyd, 'An In-Depth Background to *Standing Room Only*', 2010, www.alanayckbourn.net, accessed 6 June 2011.

12. *Mr Whatnot* was not the *first* play of Ayckbourn's to make it into print, however; this was *Relatively Speaking*, published by Evans Bros. in 1968.

13. Allen, op. cit., p. 93.

14. The actor Stanley Page, quoted *ibid*.

15. Cheeseman remained director of the Victoria Theatre until 1998, when he quit in frustration at what he considered the persistent underfunding of the arts. During his career, he established a reputation for commitment to theatre in the round, a repertoire that combined new writing with innovative productions of classics, and a preoccupation with regional history and social issues. Jeffrey Wainwright, 'Exit Stage Left: the Big Cheese of People's Theatre', *Independent*, 25 February 1998. Cheeseman died in 2010.

16. Ayckbourn, *Mr Whatnot* (London and New York: Samuel French, 1992), p. 2.

17. *Mr Whatnot*, op. cit., p. 47.

18. Acykbourn, programme note for *Mr Whatnot* at the Leeds Civic Theatre, 1968, www.alanayckbourn.net, accessed 7 June 2011.

19. Anon., 'Theatre of the Ridiculous', *The Times*, 7 October 1964.

20. Cordelia Oliver, review of *Mr Whatnot* at Ochtertyre, Scotland, *Guardian*, October 1976 (n.d.).

21. Malcolm Page (ed.), *File on Ayckbourn* (London: Methuen, 1989), p. 15.

22. Ayckbourn, in Watson, op. cit., pp. 85–6.

23. Ibid., p. 86.

24. Michael Billington, 'Controlling Our Shapes', review of *Body Language* at the Stephen Joseph Theatre, *Country Life*, 7 June 1990.

25. Brandreth, Gyles, 'A Knight at the Theatre', *Daily Telegraph*, 18 April 2002.

26. This was the last of Ayckbourn's plays to be directed by Joseph, who died prematurely from cancer in 1967, aged forty-six.

27. All play quotations from Ayckbourn, *Relatively Speaking* (London: Samuel French, 1968).

28. *Relatively Speaking* undoubtedly helped Briers's career to take off. He had had a degree of success earlier in the 1960s with the television sitcom *Marriage Lines* (opposite Prunella Scales), but his was not yet a household name. Hordern and Johnson were established actors both with distinguished records in theatre and film; Hordern had accepted the part after being persuaded to read the script by his wife, who had admired Ayckbourn's earlier *Mr Whatnot*. Hilary, by some way the youngest in the cast, had begun her acting career at the Liverpool Playhouse and achieved critical success in 1964 as Milly Theale in the West End production of Henry James's *The Wings of the Dove*.

29. 'Tea for Two', with Alan Ayckbourn and Richard Derrington, Stephen Joseph Theatre, 24 July 2008, http://relativelyspeaking.alanayckbourn.net, accessed 10 June 2011.

30. Anon., review of *Present Laughter*, *The Times*, 22 April 1965.

31. Allen, op. cit., p. 113.

32. Billington, *Alan Ayckbourn* (London: Macmillan, 1983), p. 19. Billington himself suggested that the comparison of Ayckbourn with Coward was 'misleading'.
33. Brian Connell, 'Playing for Laughs to a Lady Typist: A *Times* Profile', *The Times*, 5 January 1976.
34. Michael Billington, *State of the Nation: British Theatre Since 1945* (London: Faber and Faber, 2007), p. 201.
35. Laura Barnett, 'Portrait of the Artist: Alan Ayckbourn, Playwright', *Guardian*, 5 October 2010.
36. Oscar Wilde, *The Importance of Being Earnest* (London: Leonard Smithers, 1898), pp. 17–18.
37. For a fuller impression of the Watermill's production see www.thestage.co.uk/reviews/review.php/31366/relatively-speaking, accessed 14 June 2011. Alan Strachan's 2008 production for Bath Theatre Royal took a similar approach, with designer Paul Farnsworth making Ginny's flat redolent of 'swinging' London, with the setting for 'The Willows' the more blandly suburban by contrast. See www.britishtheatreguide.info/reviews/relspeak-rev.htm, accessed 14 June 2011.
38. Holly Berry, review of *Relatively Speaking* at the Watermill, *Marlborough People*, 22 February 2011.
39. Simon Murgatroyd, *Relatively Speaking* (Alan Ayckbourn Guides), 2007, www.alanayckbourn.net, accessed 14 June 2011.
40. The year also saw the passing of the Abortion Act in the UK, legislation that came into force in April 1968. Like the introduction and then increased availability of the Pill, the Act has been represented as an achievement of women's liberation; while it can be viewed in this context, the new legislation was at least as much a response to fundamental concerns over the public health risks attached to backstreet abortion practices.
41. *Honey*, August 1969, p. 96. *Honey* was launched in 1960 and continued until September 1986.
42. Ibid., p. 3.
43. Ayckbourn, 'Writing *Relatively Speaking*', www.alanayckbourn.net, accessed 16 June 2011.
44. Ayckbourn, programme note for *How the Other Half Loves* at the Library Theatre, Scarborough, 1969.
45. Ayckbourn, *How the Other Half Loves* (London and New York: Samuel French, 1972), p. 1 (all quotations from this edition).
46. Ayckbourn, 'Little Boxes', programme note for *How the Other Half Loves* at the Phoenix Theatre, Leicester, 1974.
47. Billington, *State of the Nation*, op. cit., p. 196.
48. Allen, 'How the Other Half Fights', programme note for the 1988 revival at the Greenwich Theatre, London.
49. See for example Allen, *Alan Ayckbourn*, pp. 123–5; Watson, op. cit., pp. 58–9.
50. Anonymous review of *How the Other Half Loves* at the Derngate Theatre, Northampton, www.bbc.co.uk/northamptonshire/stage/how_the_other_review.shtm 12003, accessed 21 June 2011.

51. Allison Vale, review of *How the Other Half Loves* at Bath Theatre Royal, 2007, www.britishtheatreguide.info/reviews/otherhalfPH-rev.htm, accessed 20 June 2011.

52. Ayckbourn, *The Sentinel*, 4 September 2009.

53. Anon., 'The Unbearable Lightness of Ayckbourn', *The Economist*, 7 March 1998.

54. Ayckbourn, *Family Circles* (London and New York: Samuel French, 1997), p. 6. All quotes from this edition.

55. Ayckbourn, programme note for the opening of *The Story So Far* . . . at the Library Theatre, Scarborough, 1970.

56. *Family Circle* folded in 2006. Attempts were made to update its image, but it seemed that the magazine failed to keep pace with contemporary women's roles and the changing character of families. Julia Day, 'Declining Sales Force *Family Circle* to Close', *Guardian*, 9 August 2006.

57. This was *Honey*'s tagline by 1962, replacing the somewhat blander 'for the teens and twenties', employed when launched two years previously.

58. *Family Circle*, vol. 23, no. 1, April 1969, p. 113.

59. *Woman's Weekly*, 12 December 1970.

60. *Woman*, 1 November 1969, p. 68.

4 Documents

John Arden

1. A radio play which revisited the themes of *Vandaleur's Folly* and was broadcast in June 1984.
2. The play Olivier was in would have been *Semi-Detached* by David Turner.
3. Sir David Lyndsay.

Harold Pinter

1. The AHRC-funded Theatre Archive Project, established by the British Library in partnership with the University of Sheffield and subsequently De Montfort University, explores British theatre history from 1945 to 1968, from the perspectives of both the theatregoer and the practitioner. It constitutes a unique oral history with over 200 interviews whose recordings and written transcripts can be freely accessed on the British Library website (sounds.bl.uk).
2. The material presented here was edited by Célia Charpentier, an independent researcher.

Afterword

John Arden

1. Tish Dace, 'Who Wrote John Arden's Plays?', in Jonathan Wike (ed.), *John Arden and Margaretta D'Arcy: A Casebook* (London: Garland, 1994), pp. 199–221.
2. John Arden, *To Present the Pretence* (London: Eyre Methuen, 1977), pp. 106, 110. Subsequent quotation from *Vandaleur's Folly: Plays One* (London: Methuen Drama, 1991).
3. John Arden and Margaretta D'Arcy, *Non-Stop Connolly Show* (London, Pluto Press, 1977–78), five vols, vol. 2, pp. 44–7.
4. *To Present the Pretence*, pp. 11–12.
5. Michael Anderson, 'Edinburgh 72', *Plays and Players*, November 1972, p. 51.
6. *To Present the Pretence*, pp. 155–6.
7. Michael Billington, 'Serjeant Musgrave Rides Again', *Guardian*, 23 September 2003.
8. D. A. N. Jones, 'Reviews', *The Listener*, 18 February 1982.
9. John Arden, 'Plays in the Theatre of the Mind', *Sunday Times*, 22 August 1982.

Edward Bond

1. Edward Bond, 'Four Little Essays on Drama' (2010/2011). See www.edwardbond.org/Theory/theory.html.
2. Edward Bond, *Letters Volume III* (London: Routledge, 1996), p. 10.
3. Edward Bond, 'On the State of British Theatre', unpublished letter to Tom Erhardt, 23 March 2011. See www.edwardbond.org/Letters/230311.doc.
4. Michael Mangan, *Edward Bond* (Plymouth: Northcote House Publishers Ltd, 1998), p. 44.
5. Bond, *Letters Volume III*, p. 57.
6. Edward Bond, unpublished letter to Peggy Ramsay.
7. 'I still get letters written in blood', BBC interview with Edward Bond, 20 October 2010. See www.bbc.co.uk/news/entertainment-arts-11534846.
8. Bond, 'On the State of British Theatre'.
9. 'Playwright Blasts Royal Court', *Standard*, 22 March 2006. See Royal Court Archive.
10. Bond, *Letters Volume III*, p. 85.
11. Ibid., p. 8.
12. Bond, unpublished letter to Peggy Ramsay.
13. Edward Bond, unpublished letter to Peter Hall.
14. Bond, unpublished letter to Peggy Ramsay.
15. Bond, unpublished letter to Peter Hall.
16. Bond, unpublished letter to Peggy Ramsay.
17. Edward Bond, unpublished letter to the author, February 2005.
18. Edward Bond, interview with John Tusa. See www.bbc.co.uk/radi03/johntusainterview/bond_transcript.shtml.

19. Bond, *Letters Volume III*, p. 84.
20. Ibid., p. 55.
21. Letter to the author.
22. Bond, unpublished letter to Peggy Ramsay.

Harold Pinter

1. Michael Billington, quoted in Esther Addley, 'Theatrical World Applauds Life and Art of Our Greatest Modern Playwright', *Guardian*, 27 December 2008.
2. Michael Billington, 'Obituary: Harold Pinter', *Guardian*, 27 December 2008.
3. Joe Penhall, quoted in Addley, op. cit.
4. Ibid.
5. Ibid. (David Hare).
6. Ibid. (Michael Gambon).
7. 'Old Times: Actors Remember Harold Pinter', *Guardian*, 8 January 2009.
8. Ibid. (Douglas Hodge).
9. Ibid. (Thomas Baptiste).
10. Mel Gussow, *Conversations with Pinter* (London: Nick Hern Books, 1994), p. 20.
11. Ibid., pp. 42–3.
12. Ibid., p. 149.
13. Ibid., p. 115.
14. www.bl.uk/projects/theatrearchive/goldengenconf.html.
15. Harold Pinter: Nobel Lecture, 7 December 2005: 'Art, Truth and Politics'. See www.nobelprize.org/nobel_prizes/literature/laureates/2005/pinter-lecture-e.pdf.
16. Gussow, op. cit., p. 53.
17. Ibid., p. 16.
18. See www.haroldpinter.org/films/films_theproust.shtml.
19. Gussow, op. cit., p. 73.
20. See Harold Pinter archive.
21. *Edward Bond: Letters Volume III* (London: Routledge, 1996), p. 1.
22. Pinter: Nobel Lecture.
23. Harold Pinter, 'Radical Departures', *The Listener*, 27 October 1988; quoted in Malcolm Page, *File on Pinter* (London: Methuen, 1993), p. 88.
24. Gussow, op. cit., p. 102.
25. Michael Billington, 'Obituary: Harold Pinter'.
26. Alastair Macaulay, *Financial Times*, 29 June 2001.
27. Pinter: Nobel Lecture.
28. See www.haroldpinter.org/home/index.shtml.
29. Harold Pinter: Nobel Lecture.

Alan Ayckbourn

1. http://biography.alanayckbourn.net/BiographyFAQPopularity.htm.
2. See, for example, Paul Allen, *Alan Ayckbourn: Grinning at the Edge* (London: Methuen,

2002), pp. 25, 43; and Michael Billington, *Alan Ayckbourn* (London: Macmillan Education, 1983/1990), pp. 151, 211.

3. Allen, op. cit., p. lx.
4. Michael Gambon, interviewed for 'Alan Ayckbourn – Greetings from Scarborough', a BBC television arts documentary in the series *Imagine*, first broadcast 16 November 2011.
5. Billington, op. cit. p. 1.
6. Alan Ayckbourn, *The Crafty Art of Playmaking* (London: Faber and Faber, 2004), p. ix.
7. Ian Watson, *Conversations with Ayckbourn* (London: Faber and Faber, 1981), p. 84.
8. Ibid., p. 72.
9. Ayckbourn, op. cit., pp. 3–4.
10. Allen, op. cit., p. 240.
11. Ibid., p. 250.
12. Billington, op. cit., p. 210.
13. 'Greetings from Scarborough', op. cit.
14. Albert-Reiner Glaap and Nicholas Quaintmere (eds), *A Guided Tour Through Ayckbourn Country* (Trier: Wissenschaftlicher Verlag Trier, 1999), p. 5.
15. Ibid., p. 12.
16. Allen, op. cit., p. 191.
17. Watson, op. cit., p. 90.
18. Allen, op. cit., p. 223.
19. Watson, op. cit., p. 90.
20. 'Greetings from Scarborough', op. cit.

SELECT BIBLIOGRAPHY

Books on the 1960s

Caute, David, *Sixty-eight: The Year of the Barricades* (London: Paladin, 1988).

Cooper, R., S. Fielding and N. Tiratsoo, *The Wilson Governments 1964–1970* (London: Pinter Publishers, 1993).

Green, Jonathon, *All Dressed Up: The Sixties and the Counterculture* (London: Pimlico, 1999).

Hewison, Robert, *Too Much: Art and Society in the Sixties 1960–1975* (London: Methuen, 1986).

Marr, Andrew, *A History of Modern Britain* (London: Macmillan, 2007).

Marwick, Arthur, *The Sixties* (Oxford: Oxford University Press, 1998).

Moorhouse, Geoffrey, *Britain in the Sixties: The Other England* (Harmondsworth: Penguin, 1964).

Morgan, Kenneth O., *The People's Peace: British History 1945–1990* (Oxford: Oxford University Press, 1990).

Sampson, Anthony, *Anatomy of Britain Today* (London: Hodder & Stoughton, 1965).

Sandbrook, Dominic, *Never Had It So Good: A History of Britain from Suez to the Beatles* (London: Abacus, 2006)

——, *White Heat: A History of Britain in the Swinging Sixties: 1964–1970* (London: Abacus, 2007).

Sinfield, Alan, *Society and Literature 1945–1970* (London: Methuen, 1983).

——, *Literature, Culture and Politics in Post-War Britain* (Oxford: Blackwell, 1989).

Recommended books on British theatre in the 1960s

The focus of many of these books extends beyond a single decade, but they all contain substantial and valuable material which is directly relevant to the 1960s.

Acheson, James (ed.), *British and Irish Drama Since 1960* (Basingstoke: Macmillan, 1993).

Ansorge, Peter, *Disrupting the Spectacle* (London: Pitman, 1975).

Artaud, Antonin, *The Theatre and Its Double* (London: Calder and Boyars, 1970).

Aston, Elaine and Janelle Reinelt (eds), *The Cambridge Companion to Modern British Women Playwrights* (Cambridge: Cambridge University Press, 2000).

Bigsby, Christopher W. E. (ed.), *Contemporary English Drama* (London: Edward Arnold, 1981).

Billington, Michael, *State of the Nation: British Theatre Since 1945* (London: Faber and Faber, 2007).

Bradby, David, Louis James and Bernard Sharratt (eds), *Performance and Politics in Popular Drama: Aspects of Popular Entertainment in Theatre, Film and Television 1800–1976* (Cambridge: Cambridge University Press, 1980).

Brook, Peter, *The Empty Space* (London: MacGibbon & Kee, 1969).

Browne, Terry W., *Playwrights' Theatre: The English Stage Company at the Royal Court Theatre* (London: Pitman, 1975).

Davies, Andrew, *Other Theatres: The Development of Alternative and Experimental Theatre in Britain* (London: Macmillan, 1987).

Devine, Harriet (ed.), *Looking Back: Playwrights at the Royal Court 1956–2006* (London: Faber and Faber, 2006).

Doty, Gresdna A. and Billy J. Harbin (eds), *Inside the Royal Court Theatre 1956–1981: Artists Talk* (Baton Rouge and London: Louisiana State University Press, 1990).

Esslin, Martin, *Theatre of the Absurd* (London: Eyre & Spottiswoode, 1962).

Eyre, Richard and Nicholas Wright, *Changing Stages: A View of British Theatre in the Twentieth Century* (London: Bloomsbury, 2000).

Findlater, Richard (ed.), *At the Royal Court: 25 Years of the English Stage Company* (Ambergate: Amber Lane Press, 1981).

Fowler, Jim, *Unleashing Britain: Theatre Gets Real 1955–1964* (London: V&A Publications, 2005).

Gaskill, William, *A Sense of Direction: Life at the Royal Court* (London: Faber and Faber, 1988).

Goorney, Howard, *The Theatre Workshop Story* (London: Eyre Methuen, 1981).

Griffiths, Trevor R. and Margaret Llewellyn-Jones (eds), *British and Irish Women Dramatists Since 1958 – A Critical Handbook* (Buckingham: Open University Press, 1993).

Hall, Peter, *Peter Hall's Diaries: The Story of a Dramatic Battle*, ed. John Goodwin (London: Oberon, 2000).

Hallifax, Michael, *Let Me Set the Scene: Twenty Years at the Heart of British Theatre 1956 to 1976* (Hanover: Smith & Kraus, 2004).

Hayman, Ronald, *British Theatre Since 1955: A Reassessment* (Oxford: Oxford University Press, 1979).

Holdsworth, Nadine, *Joan Littlewood* (London: Routledge, 2006).

——, *Joan Littlewood's Theatre* (Cambridge: Cambridge University Press, 2011).

Hunt, Albert, *Hopes for Great Happenings: Alternatives in Education and Theatre* (London: Eyre Methuen, 1976).

Innes, Christopher, *Modern British Drama 1890–1990* (Cambridge: Cambridge University Press, 1992).

Itzin, Catherine, *Stages in the Revolution* (London: Eyre Methuen, 1980).

Kitchin, Laurence, *Drama in the Sixties: Form and Interpretations* (London: Faber and Faber, 1966).

Lacey, Stephen, *British Realist Theatre: The New Wave in Its Context 1956–1995* (London: Routledge, 1995.

Leach, Robert, *Theatre Workshop: Joan Littlewood and the Making of Modern British Theatre* (Exeter: Exeter University Press, 2006).

Little, Ruth and Emily McLaughlin, *The Royal Court Theatre Inside Out* (London: Oberon Books, 2007).

Littlewood, Joan, *Joan's Book: Joan Littlewood's Peculiar History as She Tells it* (London: Methuen, 1994)

Marowitz, Charles and Simon Trussler, *Theatre at Work: Playwrights and Productions in the Modern British Theatre* (London: Methuen, 1967).

Marowitz, Charles, Tom Milne and Owen Hale, *The Encore Reader: A Chronicle of the New Drama* (London: Methuen, 1965).

——, *New Theatre Voices of the Fifties and Sixties: Selections from Encore Magazine 1956–1963* (London: Eyre Methuen, 1981).

Patterson, Michael, *Strategies of Political Theatre: Post-War British Playwrights* (Cambridge: Cambridge University Press, 2003).

Peacock, Keith D., *Radical Stages: Alternative History in Modern British Drama* (London: Greenwood Press, 1991).

Rabey, David Ian, *British and Irish Political Drama in the Twentieth Century: Implicating the Audience* (Basingstoke: Macmillan, 1986).

——, *English Drama Since 1940* (London: Longman, 2003).

Rees, Roland, *Pioneers of Fringe Theatre on Record* (London: Oberon Books, 1992).

Roberts, Philip, *The Royal Court Theatre and the Modern Stage* (Cambridge: Cambridge University Press, 1999).

Shellard, Dominic, *British Theatre Since the War* (New Haven, CT and London: Yale University Press, 1999).

Shellard, Dominic, Steve Nicholson and Miriam Handley, *The Lord Chamberlain Regrets: A History of British Theatre Censorship* (London: British Library, 2004).

Sinfield, Alan, *Out on Stage: Lesbian and Gay Theatre in the Twentieth Century* (New Haven, CT, and London: Yale University Press, 1999).

Taylor, John Russell, *Anger and After: A Guide to the New British Drama* (London: Eyre Methuen, 1977).

——, *The Second Wave: British Drama of the Sixties* (London: Eyre Methuen, 1978).

Tynan, Ken, *A View of the English Stage 1944–1965* (London: Methuen, 1984).

Tytell, John, *The Living Theatre: Art, Exile and Outrage* (London: Methuen, 1997).

Wandor, Michelene, *Look Back in Gender: Sexuality and the Family in Post-War British Drama* (London: Methuen, 1987).

Wardle, Irving, *The Theatres of George Devine* (London: Jonathan Cape, 1978).

Williams, David (ed.), *Peter Brook: A Theatrical Casebook* (London: Methuen, 1988).

Worth, Katharine J., *Revolutions in Modern English Drama* (London: G. Bell, 1972).

Forthcoming:

Nicholson, Steve, *The Censorship of British Drama 1900–1968: Volume Four – The Sixties* (Exeter: Exeter University Press, 2013).

The playwrights

John Arden

Plays

Arden, John, *Plays One* (London: Methuen, 1977).
——, *Plays Two* (London: Methuen, 2002).

Recommended books

Arden, John, *To Present the Pretence: Essays on the Theatre and Its Public* (London: Eyre Methuen, 1977).

D'Arcy, Margaretta, *Loose Theatre: In and Out of My Memory* (Manchester: Trafford Publishing, 2006).

Gray, Frances, *John Arden* (London: Macmillan, 1982).

Hayman, Ronald, *John Arden* (London: Heinemann, 1968).

Hunt, Albert, *Arden: A Study of His Plays* (London: Methuen, 1974).

Leach, Robert, *Partners of the Imagination: The Lives, Art and Struggles of John Arden and Margaretta D'Arcy* (Stoney Stanton, Leicestershire: Indigo Dreams Publishing, 2012).

Leeming, Glenda, *John Arden* (London: Longman, 1974).

Page, Malcolm, *John Arden* (Boston: G. K. Hall, 1984).

—— (ed.), *Arden on File* (London: Methuen, 1985).

Trussler, Simon, *John Arden* (New York: Columbia University Press, 1973).

Wike, Jonathan (ed.),. *John Arden and Margaretta D'Arcy: A Casebook* (London: Garland, 1994).

Edward Bond

Plays

Bond, Edward, *Plays: One* (London: Methuen, 1977).
——, *Plays: Two* (London: Methuen, 1978).

Recommended books

Bond, Edward, *The Hidden Plot: Notes on Theatre and the State* (London: Methuen, 1999).

Coult, Tony, *The Plays of Edward Bond: A Study* (London: Eyre Methuen, 1978).

Hay, Malcolm and Philip Roberts, *Bond: A Study of His Plays* (London: Methuen, 1980).

Hirst, David L., *Edward Bond* (London: Macmillan, 1985).

Mangan, Michael, *Edward Bond* (Plymouth: Northcote House, 1998).

Roberts, Philip, *Bond on File* (London: Methuen, 1985).

Stuart, Ian (ed.), *Selections from the Notebooks of Edward Bond: Volume One: 1959 to 1980* (London: Methuen, 2000).

—— (ed.), *Edward Bond: Letters Volume IV* (Amsterdam: Harwood Academic Publishers, 1998).

Recommended website
www.edwardbond.org.

Harold Pinter
Plays
Pinter, Harold, *Plays 1* (London: Faber and Faber, 1996).
——, *Plays 2* (London: Faber and Faber, 1996).
——, *Plays 3* (London: Faber and Faber, 1997).
——, *Various Voices: Prose, Poetry, Politics 1948–2005* (London: Faber, 2005).

Recommended books
Batty, Mark, *About Pinter: The Playwright and the Work* (London: Faber and Faber, 2005).
Billington, Michael, *Harold Pinter* (2nd edn, London: Faber, 2007).
Fraser, Antonia, *Must You Go? My Life with Harold Pinter* (London: Weidenfeld, 2010).
Gussow, Mel, *Conversations with Pinter* (London: Nick Hern, 1994).
Naismith, Bill, *Harold Pinter: Faber Critical Guides – The Caretaker, The Birthday Party and The Homecoming* (London: Faber and Faber, 2000).
Page, Malcolm, *File on Pinter* (London: Methuen, 1993).
Raby, Peter (ed.), *The Cambridge Companion to Harold Pinter* (Cambridge: Cambridge University Press), 2009.
Smith, Ian, *Pinter in the Theatre* (London: Nick Hern Books, 2005).

Recommended journal
The Pinter Review (Vol. 1 1987–date).

Recommended website
www.haroldpinter.org.

Alan Ayckbourn
Plays
Alan Ayckbourn, *Relatively Speaking* (London: Evans Plays, 1968).
——, *How the Other Half Loves* (London: French, 1972).
——, *Mr Whatnot* (London: French, 1992).
——, *Family Circles* (London: French, 1997).
Some (though by no means all) of Ayckbourn's other plays are published in several collections by Faber.

Recommended books
Allen, Paul, *Alan Ayckbourn: Grinning at the Edge* (London: Methuen, 2001).
——, *A Pocket Guide to Alan Ayckbourn's Plays* (London: Faber and Faber, 2004).

Ayckbourn, Alan, *The Crafty Art of Playmaking* (London: Faber and Faber, 2002).

Billington, Michael, *Alan Ayckbourn* (London: Macmillan, 1983).

Glaap, Albert-Reiner and Nicholas Quaintmere (eds), *A Guided Tour Through Ayckbourn Country* (Trier: Wissenschaftlicher Verlag Trier, 1999).

Holt, Michael, *Alan Ayckbourn* (Plymouth: Northcote House, 1999).

Page, Malcolm (ed.), *File on Ayckbourn* (London: Methuen, 1989).

Watson, Ian, *Conversations with Ayckbourn* (London and Boston: Faber and Faber, 1988).

Recommended website
www.alanayckbourn.net.

Web resources

'TheatreVoice': www.theatrevoice.com.

INDEX

Note: Play titles are entered in the index under authors' names, if known. Page references in **bold type** denote main references to topics.

abortion 3, 25
Action Theatre 51–3, 83
Africa 21, 22, 23
    Belgian Congo 20, 126, 131
    in drama 68–9
    Nigeria 25, 28, 70
    South Africa 13–14, 20, 24, 96
Aldwych Theatre 54, 57, 171
Allen, Paul 105, 208
Allen, Roland *see* Ayckbourn, Alan
Anderson, Lindsay 17, 37
    and Arden 111, 118, 216–17, 220–1
architecture 18
Arden, John 29, 51, 59, **85–91**, **108–36**, **243–9**
    All Fall Down 87
    Armstrong's Last Good Night **126–34**, 218, 221, 222, 223
    The Ballygombeen Request 136, 218, 245
    Books of Bale 222–3, 248
    Cogs Tyrannic 248
    Gallows and Other Tales 248
    Garland for a Hoar Head 247–8
    The Happy Haven 120, 134, 222
    Harold Muggins is a Martyr 135
    The Hero Rises Up 135
    interviewed **216–24**
    Island of the Mighty 135
    The Life of Man 87
    Live Like Pigs 89–90, 120, 134, 220
    The Non-Stop Connolly Show 136, 218, 220, 244, 245
    novels 222–3, 248
    Pearl 247
    radio plays 87, 247–8
    The Royal Pardon 135

Serjeant Musgrave's Dance 30, 35, 86, 108, 109, **110–19**, 126, 132, 216–18, 245–7
    and Anderson 111, 118, 216–17, 220–1
    on TV 217
Silence Among the Weapons 248
Soldier, Soldier 88
The True History of Squire Jonathan 134
Vandaleur's Folly 109, 136, 218, 244, 245
The Waters of Babylon 87–9
Wet Fish 88
When is a Door Not a Door? 89
The Workhouse Donkey 50, 86, 88, **119–26**, 134, 220, 221, 223–4
Arout, Gabriel
    Cet Animal étrange 176
art 17–18
Artaud, Antonin 35, 36, 50, 51, 77
    Spurt of Blood 54
Arts Council 34, 61, 84, 119, 252, 260
Arts Theatre 161, 162, 163, 179, 239
avant-garde 72–4, 83
Ayckbourn, Alan **102–7**, **190–215**, **260–5**
    Absurd Person Singular 190–1, 204, 263–4
    awards 260
    Christmas V Mastermind 106, 193
    The Crafty Art of Playmaking 192
    Dad's Tale 193
    Family Circles (The Story So Far/Me Times Me Times Me) 210
    The Forest 261
    Henceforward 215
    House and Garden 261

How the Other Half Loves **205–10**
Intimate Exchanges 261
Jeeves 261–2
Just Between Ourselves 204
Life of Riley 214–15
Love After All 104–5, 192
Mr A's Amazing Maze Plays 261
Mr Whatnot 106, **193–6**
The Norman Conquests 260–1
Relatively Speaking 106, 190, **198–204**, 205, 215
Sisterly Feelings 261
A Small Family Business 264
The Sparrow 106, 205
The Square Cat 104, 192
Standing Room Only 105, 193
A Trip to Scarborough 261
Way Upstream 261, 264
Woman in Mind 204, 261, 264

Baldwin, James
  Blues for Mr Charlie 69
Bannen, Ian 30, 111
Barnes, Peter
  The Ruling Class 75
Barnsley 86, 90, 111, 120, 223–4
Baron, David *see* Pinter, Harold
Barton, John 223
Bates, Alan 177
BBC radio 16, 87
  comedy 19
  see also radio plays
BBC TV 15–16, 46
  The Black and White Minstrels 56, 67
  comedy 19
Beatles, the 9, 11
Beaton, Norman
  Jack of Spades 69
  Sit Down Banna 69
Beaumarchais, Pierre
  The Barber of Seville 104
Beckett, Samuel 37, 87, 175–6, 179, 257
  Endgame 155
  Happy Days 184
  Krapp's Last Tape 254
  Play 50–1, 177, 184
  Waiting for Godot 38, 52
Belgian Congo 20, 126, 131
Belgrade Theatre (Coventry) 61–2
Berlin Wall 20, 26, 155

Berliner Ensemble 60
Berman, Ed 79–80
Beyond the Fringe 41–3
Big Brum youth theatre 253
Billington, Michael 71, 74, 80, 82, 108, 123, 134, 140–1, 165, 173, 174–5, 184, 197, 208, 247, 262, 263, 264
Bird, John 153
Black and White Minstrels, The 56, 67–8
Blakemore, Michael 71
Blin, Roger 176
Blow-Up (film) 17, 95
Bond, Edward 70, **91–7**, 136–61, **249–54**
  Bingo 250
  Black Mass 96
  The Bundle: New Narrow Road to the Deep North 250
  A Chaste Maid in Cheapside 94
  Derek 251
  Early Morning 95, **147–54**, 226–7, 231
  films 17, 95, 229–30
  The Fool 250
  Human Cannon 251
  In the Company of Men 253
  interviewed **224–33**
  Lear 96, **154–9**, 226, 230, 231, 250
  Narrow Road to the Deep North 250
  Passion 96–7
  and Pinter 257–8
  The Pope's Wedding 92–4, 139, 227, 231
  Restoration 250–1
  Saved 94, 137, **138–47**
    Bond speaks of 141, 160, 161, 225–6, 231
    censorship 139, 144, 180–1
    Teach-In 142–3, 228
    title 227–8
  The Sea 250
  Summer 251
  The Three Sisters 92, 95
  Walkabout 95, 229, 230
  The War Plays 251
  The Woman 250
  The Worlds 250
books 11–12
  Lady Chatterley's Lover 4, 12
Boorne, Bill 55–6
Boys, Barry 105

Bradford 67
Bramley, Philip 240
Brearley, Joseph 97, 164, 188–9
Brecht, Bertolt 60, 83, 88, 134, 222, 233
   Antigone 81
   Coriolanus 60
   The Days of the Commune 60
   Galileo 60
   Mother Courage 117, 134
Brenton, Howard 74
Bridge, Peter 199
Briers, Richard 199
Bristol University 98, 177, 222, 233–4
British Empire 23
Britten, Benjamin
   War Requiem 10–11
Brook, Dorien 241
Brook, Peter 34–5, 37, 39, 51, 54, 57, 61,
   64, 66, 77, 155–6
Brown, Kenneth H.
   The Brig 46–7
Bruce, Lenny 4
Burge, Stuart 119, 217, 220–1
Bury, John 182

Cadbury, Peter 56, 57
Campaign for Nuclear Disarmament 20,
   96
Carry On films 193–4
cars 8
Carson, Rachel
   Silent Spring 7
CAST 135
Cathy Come Home 5
censorship (Lord Chamberlain's Office)
   4–5, 48, 50, 54, 55, 63, 83,
   178–82
  on Arden 89
  Ayckbourn 103
  Bond 94, 95, 137, 147, 153, 227
    Saved 139, 144, 180–1
  end 5, 79–80, 84, 179, 180
  Pinter 100, 178–80
  racism 68, 69
Centre 42 33–4
Cheeseman, Peter 62, 105, 106, 194
   The Knotty 62
Chekhov, Anton
   The Three Sisters 92, 95
   Uncle Vanya 261

Chichester Festival Theatre 57, 119, 132,
   221
children
  Ayckbourn's plays for 106, 193, 261
  Bond on 253–4
  pantomimes 58
  see also Theatre-in-Education
Christie, Agatha
   The Mousetrap 30, 56, 68
Churchill, Sir Winston 24
  in drama 48
cinemas 17
  see also films
Clare, John 250
Clark, John Pepper
   The Masquerade 70
   Song of a Goat 70
Codron, Michael 236, 239
Cold War 26, 97
'Come Out' (loop composition) 10
comedy
  Ayckbourn's 201, 263–4
  Loot 59–60
  radio and TV 19, 43
  satire 19, 41–3, 57
Commonwealth Arts Festival 70
computers 9
contraception 3, 21, 201–2
Covent Garden 66
Coward, Noël 199–200, 262
Criterion Theatre 41
Crucible Theatre (Sheffield) 230
Cuba 20, 21, 26
Curse of the Daleks, The 58
Cyprus 20, 110–11, 119

Dace, Tish 136, 243
Daily Mail 19, 38, 39, 40, 44, 46, 50, 54,
   60, 72, 73, 83, 94, 140, 152
Daily Mirror 19
Daily Telegraph 19, 55, 70, 94, 102, 152
D'Arcy, Margaretta 87, 89, 90, 108, 109,
   120, 134–5, 218, 220, 221, 224,
   243–5
Davies, David 235, 241
Davion, Alexander 177
de Gaulle, General 22, 24, 25, 27
  in drama 76
de Jongh, Nicholas 82
Dench, Judi 37

'Destruction in Art' (symposium) 66
Detmer, Sarah 240–1
Devine, George 87, 89, 92, 219–20, 221,
Dexter, John 132, 220, 221
Diamond, Gillian 239
documentary theatre (Theatre of Fact)
    62–7, 84, 106
D'Oliveira, Basil 13–14
Drama Review, The 78–9
drugs 6, 22
    The Connection 38–41
Drury Lane Arts Lab 79
Duke of York's Theatre 199
Duncan, Ronald 90
Dylan, Bob 10, 83

Edinburgh 14, 60, 131, 132, 223
    Arden in 86–7
    Festival 41
        Fringe 246
    International Drama Conference, 1963
        51–3
education 5
    see also Theatre-in-Education
Eichmann, Adolf 20, 21, 36
Encore (magazine) 29–30, 31–2, 58
Engel, Susan 233–4
English Stage Company 30, 119, 180
Enoch Show, The 95–6
environment 6–7
Equal Pay Act 3, 7
Esslin, Martin 35, 41, 53, 164, 175, 178
European Common Market 21
European Economic Community 22, 25
Evans, Graham 88
Evening News 55, 119
Evening Standard 50
Everyman Theatre (Liverpool) 69, 237

Farmer, Sir George 181
Farnsworth, Paul 209
Fascism 13, 36, 97, 141, 257–8
films 17
    Bond's scripts 17, 95, 229–30
        Walkabout 95, 229, 230
    Carry On 193–4
    Pinter's scripts 17, 100, 182
Finlay, Frank 119
Finney, Albert 132
'first nighters' 40–1

Foster, Paul
    Tom Paine 73–4
Foster, Richard 238
Frankfurt 74, 162
Fraser, Antonia 257
Frayn, Michael 43

Gaia Hypothesis 7
Gambon, Michael 255, 262
Garrick Theatre 84
Garson, Barbara
    Macbird 72
Gaskill, William
    and Arden 108, 127, 132, 133, 219,
        220, 223
    and Bond 91–2
        Early Morning 153–4
        Saved 139, 140, 141, 143, 145,
            146
Gelber, Jack 53
    The Connection 38–41
Gielgud, John 256
Gielgud, Val 57
Grotowski, Jerzy 80
    Towards a Poor Theatre 80
Guardian 19, 33, 54, 68, 106, 196
Guthrie, Tyrone 223

Hair 80, 83
Hall, Sir Peter 29, 49, 57
    and Ayckbourn 191, 193, 209, 264
    and Bond 251, 253
    and Pinter 167–8, 171, 173, 180, 181,
        240
Hallifax, Michael 180
Hampstead Theatre Club 63, 161, 234–5
Hang Down Your Head and Die 62–3
happenings (Action Theatre) 51–3, 83
Hare, David 228, 229, 255
Hartley, L. P.
    The Go-Between 100, 182
Hawthorne, Nigel 68–9
Haynes, Jim 79
Hendrix, Jimi 10
Herbert, Jocelyn 111
Hilary, Jennifer 199, 201
Hobson, Harold 58–9, 60, 66, 99, 118,
        119, 132, 153, 173, 184–5, 236
Hochhuth, Rolf
    The Representative 50, 63

Holmes, Sean 142
Honey (magazine) 202, 212
Hordern, Michael 199
housing 5–6
Hughes, Ted 162–3
    Oedipus 77

ICA 80, 135
If.... (film) 17
Ingrams, Richard
    Mrs Wilson's Diary 75–6
Inter-Action 80
International Drama Conference, 1963
    51–2
Ionesco, Eugene 37, 52, 83
    Rhinoceros 41, 162
IRA 24, 243
Iraq 131, 218, 245, 246–7, 259
Ireland 24, 28, 132, 136, 218, 245–6
Israel 20, 21, 24, 36
ITV 15, 16

Jackson, Glenda 65
Jellicoe, Ann 70
    The Knack 49–50
Johnson, Celia 199
Johnson, Lyndon 22, 26
    in drama 72, 76
Johnstone, Keith 92
Jonson, Ben 248, 260
Joseph, Stephen 103, 104, 105, 107, 194,
    261
Joyce, James 185, 255–6
    Exiles 185, 187
    A Portrait of the Artist as a Young Man
        184, 185, 186
    Stephen Hero 186

Kahane, Eric 172
Kane, Sarah 231
    Blasted 138
Kellerman, Julia 235
Kennedy, J. F. 20, 21
    in drama 72
Kesselaar, Anna 52, 53
King, Martin Luther 21, 24, 25
Kipphardt, Heinar
    In the Matter of J. Robert Oppenheimer
        63–4
Kirbymoorside, Yorkshire 120, 220

Kitchin, Laurence 36, 37
Kott, Jan 37
Kubrick, Stanley 17
Kustow, Michael 80

La MaMa company 73, 80
Lady Chatterley's Lover (D. H. Lawrence)
    4, 12
Lamble, Anthony 201
LAMDA Theatre Club 54
Larkin, Philip 3, 12
Lawson, Wilfred 89
Lee, Jennie 34, 61
Leeds Civic Theatre 195
Leigh, Mike 196
Levin, Bernard 54–5, 94
Lewis, Peter 73–4
Library Theatre (Scarborough) 103, 104,
    105–6, 107, 193, 198, 260
    see also Stephen Joseph Theatre
Littler, Emile 57
Littlewood, Joan 29, 31–2, 33, 44, 45, 51,
    53, 72
Living Theater (New York) 38, 46, 54,
    80–2
Lloyd Webber, Andrew 261
Lord Chamberlain's Office *see* censorship
Losey, Joseph 17, 100
Lyndsay, David
    Three Estates 223

Macmillan, Harold 20, 21, 22, 41
Magic Roundabout, The (TV) 16
Manchester Guardian 30–1
Mandela, Nelson 22
Marcus, Frank
    The Killing of Sister George 59
Marlowe Society 223
Marowitz, Charles 36, 51–2, 54, 74, 80
Martin, Jean 176
McDonnell, Bill 216–24, 294
McDowell, Malcolm 17
McGrath, John 218, 245, 246
    Events While Guarding the Bofors Gun
        77
Melville, Pauline 220
Mercer, David 186–7
Merchant, Vivien 98, 165, 183
Mexico Olympics 14, 15
middle class 42–3, 264–5

Middleton, Thomas
  A Chaste Maid in Cheapside 94
Miller, Arthur 84, 258
  The Crucible 127
  A View from the Bridge 262
Miller, Jonathan 41–2
Milligan, Spike 50
  The Bed-Sitting Room 50
Milne, Tom 132
  'The Hidden Face of Violence' 35–6
Mississippi 21, 22, 69
Mitchell, Adrian 64
moon landings 24, 27
Morley, Robert 208–9
Morris, Desmond
  The Naked Ape 11
Mortimer, John 51
Muller, Robert 40
music 9–10
musicals 10, 30, 56, 58, 82
  Hair 80, 83
  Jeeves 261–2
  My Fair Lady 30, 56
Oliver! 30, 56
'My Generation' (the Who) 84

National Anthem 15, 31
  US 10
National Service 20, 86–7, 91, 97, 105
National Theatre 29, 48, 50, 71–2, 77
  and Arden 132
  and Ayckbourn 260, 261, 262, 264
  and Bond 230–1, 250, 251, 252–3
National Union of Students
  Drama Festival 84
National Youth Theatre 77
New York
  Arden in 134
  La MaMa 73, 80
  Living Theatre 38, 46, 54, 80–2
  Pinter's plays in 175, 177, 178
newspapers 19
Nichols, Peter
  A Day in the Death of Joe Egg 74–5
  Forget-Me-Not Lane 174
  The National Health 71–2
Nicholson, Steve 224–33
Nigeria (Biafra) 25, 28, 70
Nitsch, Hermann 66
Nobel Prize for Literature 259

Nottingham Playhouse 49
nuclear power 6–7, 21
Nunn, Trevor 67
Nymphs and Satires 68

Obscene Publications Act 4
Observer 29, 70, 73, 141, 153, 184
Oh, What a Lovely War! 43–5, 50, 62
O'Horgan, Tom 80
Old Vic Theatre 36, 37, 60
Olivier, Sir Laurence 38, 48, 140, 146,
    162, 221
  as *Othello* 71
O'Loughlin, Orla 201
O'Neill, Eugene 73
Orange Tree Theatre (Richmond) 210
Orton, Joe 57, 74
  Entertaining Mr Sloane 50, 55
  Loot 59
Osborne, John 59, 264
  Inadmissible Evidence 50
  Look Back in Anger 83
  Plays for England 50
Out of the Ashes 61
Owens, Rochelle
  Futz 73
Oxford Stage Company 247
Oxford University 262
  Experimental Theatre Club 62

Page, Anthony 89, 219
pantomimes 58
Paradise Now 81–2
Paris 25, 175–7, 178
Paris Review
  Pinter interview 172, 182
Patrick, Nigel 199
Peaslee, Richard 64
Pinter, Harold 29, 51, 59, 73, **97–102,**
    161–89, 254–9
  Ashes to Ashes 188, 258
  awards 254
  Betrayal 185, 257
  The Birthday Party 35, 49, 99, 100–1,
    102, 103, 161, 162, 164, 165,
    188–9, 236–7, 238
  censorship 179–82
  in Paris 175
  on TV 161, 169, 170
  in US 177

and Bond 257–8
The Caretaker 41, 100, 161, 162, **163–8**, 169, 170, 172, 237–9
in Paris 175–6
in US 177
Celebration 187–8
The Collection 168, 176–7
Dialogue for Three 186
The Dumb Waiter 99–100, 161, 162
The Dwarfs 168, 169
films 17, 100, 182
The Homecoming 58, 59, 100, **171–5**, 239–40
censorship 180
in US 178
interviewed **233–42**
Paris Review 172, 182
Landscape 178–9, **181–7**
The Lover 100, 168, 176, 177
memory plays 182–8
Mountain Language 188, 258
Night 182, 184, 189
A Night Out 71, 162, 169, 170
No Man's Land 256, 257
Nobel Prize for Literature 259
Old Times 185, 257
One for the Road 188, 258
Party Time 258
radio plays 162, 169, 170, 178, 186
The Room 36, 98–9, 100, 161, 164, 233–6
Silence **182–7**
A Slight Ache 169
Pip Simmons Theatre Group 79
Piper, Ann 219, 241
Plays and Players 54, 62, 84, 246
Pleasance, Donald 177
poetry 12
Powell, Enoch 26, 27, 28, 95–6
Private Eye (magazine) 21, 43, 76
Proust, Marcel
À la recherche du temps perdu 182, 257

Race Relations Act 24, 27
race riots 21, 24
racism 14, 20, 26, 27
in theatre 68–72
The Black and White Minstrels 56, 67
16, 169

radio
BBC 16, 87
comedy 19
plays
Arden 87, 247–8
Pinter 162, 169, 170, 178, 186
stations 16
Radio Leeds 106
Raid, The (film) 111
railways 8, 22
Rattigan, Terence 57, 199, 262
Ravenhill, Mark 264
Reckord, Barry
Skyvers 50, 69
You in Your Small Corner 69
Red Ladder company 79
Reeves, Geoffrey 77–8, 133
Régy, Claude 176
Resnais, Alain 176
Revenger's Tragedy, The 66–7
Rhodesia 22, 23–4
Richardson, Ralph 219, 256
Richardson, Tony 90, 219–20
Rigby, Terence 239–40, 241–2
Rix, Brian 56
Robeson, Paul 71
Rochefort, Jean 176
Roland, Christine 104, 212
Roundhouse, Camden 77–9
Royal Court Theatre 29, 31, 32, 37, 41, 49–50, 58, 60, 83, 162
and Arden 30, 87–8, 89, 90, 111, 119–20, 218–20, 222
avant-garde 72
and Bond 91–4, 95, 137, 139–40, 146, 152, 153, 156, 157, 228, 229, 231, 251, 252
Teach-In 142–3, 228
and censorship 139–40, 180–1, 201
and Pinter 161, 168
racial drama 69, 70
Writers' Group 70, 91, 139
Royal Shakespeare Company (RSC) 29, 35, 46, 49, 50, 54–5, 57, 58, 78, 154
and Arden 135
and Bond 230–1, 250, 251, 252, 253
and censorship 180, 181
documentary dramas 63, 64, 66–7
and Pinter 168, 180, 182, 239–40

Rudkin, David
  Afore Night Come 35, 49, 54, 180
Russia
  Revolution 67
  see also Soviet Union

Sanders, Peter 56
Sartre, Jean-Paul
  Huis Clos 100, 166
satire 19, 41–3, 57
Schnitzler, Arthur
  La Ronde 211
science 8–9
7:84 company 218, 245–6
sexuality 3, 4, 83
  The Killing of Sister George 59
  legislation 25
  Spring Awakening 60
Seyrig, Delphine 176
Shaffer, Peter
  The Royal Hunt of the Sun 50, 62
Shakespeare, William 35, 36–8, 97–8,
      154, 223
  in Bond's *Bingo* 259
  Coriolanus 60
  Henry V 37–8
  Julius Caesar 37, 223
  King Lear 37, 154, 155–6, 230
  Macbeth 72, 91, 183
  Othello 71
  Richard II 75
  Romeo and Juliet 37
  The Tempest 77–9
Shaw, Robert 89
Sheffield Playhouse 238
Shelley, Mary
  Frankenstein 81
Sheridan, Richard 261
Shield Productions 186
Simpson, N.F.
  One Way Pendulum 41
Smith, Auriol 234–5
Smith, T. Dan 124, 224
Sound of Music, The 10, 30
South Africa 13–14, 20, 24, 96
Soviet Union (USSR) 20, 22, 23, 25, 26,
      157
Soyinka, Wole
  The Lion and the Jewel 70–1
  The Road 59, 70

Speight, Johnny 27
sport 12–15
  and politics 13–14
Stein, Peter 153–4
Stephen Joseph Theatre, Scarborough 107,
      214, 260, 265
  see also Library Theatre
Stephens, Robert 50, 88, 132
Stewart, Ellen 73
Stoke 84, 105–6
Stoney, Heather 212
Stoppard, Tom
  Rosencrantz and Guildenstern Are Dead
      76
student risings 25
Sun 19, 140
Sunday Times 35, 82, 94, 99, 140, 153,
      168
  article by Arden 248
Sylvestre, Cleo 71
Synge, J. M. 70

Tati, Jacques 106, 194
Taylor, A. J. P. 45
technology 8–9
television 15–16, 46
  The Black and White Minstrels 56, 67
  comedy 19, 43
  plays
    Arden 217
    Pinter 161, 162, 169
Terson, Peter
  Zigger Zagger 76–7
That Was the Week That Was 19, 43
Theatre Archive Project 233
theatre clubs (private) 94, 139, 180
Theatre of the Absurd 41, 57, 162
Theatre of Cruelty 35, 36, 37, 54, 57,
      155, 180
Theatre of Fact (documentary theatre)
      62–7, 84, 106
Theatre Royal, Bath 209
Theatre Royal Stratford East 31, 44, 70,
      72
    Theatre Workshop 29, 30, 31, 43–4,
      45, 62, 76
Theatre-in-Education (TIE) 61–2, 83
  Big Brum youth theatre 253
Theatres Act 5, 79, 84, 179, 182
Till Death Us Do Part (TV) 19, 27

Times, The 19, 36, 41, 42, 45, 49, 54, 56, 57, 58, 59, 60, 66, 68, 70, 73, 75, 76, 80, 110, 153, 199
    on *The Black and White Minstrels* 56, 67–8
Town Hall Theatre (Galway) 217–18
Trades Union Congress 32–3
travel 8, 18
Turkey 258
Tynan, Kenneth 4, 29, 50, 51, 53, 88, 90, 167

Unity Theatre 135
US 64–6

Vallins, Gordon 61
van Itallie, Jean-Claude
    America Hurrah 72
Victoria Palace 67
Victoria Theatre (Stoke) 62, 194
Vietnam 14, 20, 22. 23, 24, 25, 26, 27, 64–6, 76, 177
    in staged productions 64–6, 76
Vietnam Action Group 66, 67
violence
    crimes 3–4
    'The Hidden Face of Violence' 35–6
    staged 35–7, 46–8, 49, 50, 57–8, 83, 89–90, 213, 247
        in Arden 114–18, 129–32, 136
        in Ayckbourn 207–8
        in Bond 94, 96–7, 137–8, 142–7, 154–9
        in Pinter 164, 168, 173, 257
    Theatre of Cruelty 35, 36, 37, 54, 57, 155, 180
Vitrac, Roger
    Victor 55

Walkabout (film) 95, 229, 230
Wardle, Irving 73, 153
Warhol, Andy 17

Wars of the Roses, The 46
Watermill Theatre (Newbury) 201
Wax, Jimmy 236
Wedekind, Frank
    Spring Awakening 60
Weiss, Peter
    The Investigation 59, 63
    Marat/Sade 54–5
Welfare State company 79
Welles, Orson 162
Wells, John
    Mrs Wilson's Diary 75–6
Wesker, Arnold 29, 32–4, 51, 220, 221
    The Kitchen 36, 62
    Roots 32
West, Timothy 236–7, 238
Whitehouse, Mary 22, 157–8
Whiting, John
    The Devils 49
    Saint's Day 35
Wilde, Oscar
    The Importance of Being Earnest 200
Williams, Tudor 237
Wilson, Harold 8, 22, 23, 24, 25
    in drama 76
Wolfit, Sir Donald 91, 98, 103
women
    in Ayckbourn's plays 197–8, 201–4, 210–11
women's liberation 7, 197–8, 202
women's magazines 212–13
Wood, Charles
    Dingo 47–8
Woodstock Festival 9–10, 11
Woolf, Henry 97, 98, 102, 233–4, 235
working class 11, 17, 29, 32–3, 77, 86
    Ayckbourn and 197
    in Bond's plays 140–1, 149, 225, 251
Wyndham's Theatre 44, 58

Zeffirelli, Franco 37

NOTES ON CONTRIBUTORS

Jamie Andrews is Head of English and Drama at the British Library. He is a member of the Working Group on UK Literary Heritage, a Governor of De Montfort University and a Trustee of Sheffield Theatres Trust. Recent publications include: 'A Cornelian Cold War?', in Andrew Hammond (ed.), *Cold War Literatures: Western, Eastern and Postcolonial Perspectives* (Routledge, 2011); John Osborne, *Before Anger: The Devil Inside Him and Personal Enemy*, edited and with an Introduction by Jamie Andrews (Oberon, 2009); '"The Bourgeoisie is Puking up Pinter": Digesting Pinter in Paris', in *Talking Drama*, ed. Judith Roof (Cambridge: Cambridge Scholars Publishing, 2009).

Frances Babbage is Reader in Theatre and Performance at the University of Sheffield. She has published on modern and contemporary theatre, practices of stage adaptation and rewriting, and theatre for development. She has published two monographs, *Re-visioning Myth: Modern and Contemporary Drama by Women* (Manchester University Press, 2011) and *Augusto Boal* (Routledge Performance Practitioners, 2005).

Bill McDonnell is a Senior Lecturer in Theatre and Performance at the University of Sheffield. Between 1975 and 2002 he worked in alternative and community theatres as a performer, writer and facilitator. He has published on British political and activist theatres of the twentieth-century, and is the author of *Theatres of the Troubles: Theatre, Resistance and Liberation in Ireland* (University of Exeter Press, 2008), shortlisted for the 2008 Theatre Book of the Year; and *Social Impact in UK Theatre* (Arts Council England, 2005).